CURRENTS IN THE
THEORY OF COMPUTING

Prentice-Hall
Series in Automatic Computation

George Forsythe, editor

AHO, editor, *Currents in the Theory of Computing*
AHO AND ULLMAN, *The Theory of Parsing, Translation, and Compiling,*
  Volume I: *Parsing;* Volume II: *Compiling*
(ANDREE),[3] *Computer Programming: Techniques, Analysis, and Mathematics*
ANSELONE, *Collectively Compact Operator Approximation Theory*
  and Applications to Integral Equations
ARBIB, *Theories of Abstract Automata*
BATES AND DOUGLAS, *Programming Language/One,* 2nd ed.
BLUMENTHAL, *Management Information Systems*
BRENT, *Algorithms for Minimization without Derivatives*
COFFMAN AND DENNING, *Operating-Systems Theory*
CRESS, et al., *FORTRAN IV with WATFOR and WATFIV*
DANIEL, *The Approximate Minimization of Functionals*
DESMONDE, *Computers and Their Uses,* 2nd ed.
DESMONDE, *Real-Time Data Processing Systems*
DRUMMOND, *Evaluation and Measurement Techniques for Digital Computer Systems*
EVANS, et al., *Simulation Using Digital Computers*
FIKE, *Computer Evaluation of Mathematical Functions*
FIKE, *PL/1 for Scientific Programers*
FORSYTHE AND MOLER, *Computer Solution of Linear Algebraic Systems*
GAUTHIER AND PONTO, *Designing Systems Programs*
GEAR, *Numerical Inital Value Problems in Ordinary Differentizl Equations*
GOLDEN, *FORTRAN IV Programming and Computing*
GOLDEN AND LEICHUS, *IBM/360 Programming and Computing*
GORDON, *System Simulation*
HARTMANIS AND STEARNS, *Algebraic Structure Theory of Sequential Machines*
HULL, *Introduction to Computing*
JACOBY, et al., *Iterative Methods for Nonlinear Optimization Problems*
JOHNSON, *System Structure in Data, Programs, and Computers*
KANTER, *The Computer and the Executive*
KIVIAT, et al., *The SIMSCRIPT II Programming Language*
LORIN, *Parallelism in Hardware and Software: Real and Apparent Concurrency*
LOUDEN AND LEDIN, *Programming the IBM 1130,* 2nd ed.
MARTIN, *Design of Man-Computer Dialogues*
MARTIN, *Design of Real-Time Computer Systems*
MARTIN, *Future Developments in Telecommunications*
MARTIN, *Programming Real-Time Computing Systems*
MARTIN, *Systems Analysis for Data Transmission*
MARTIN, *Telecommunications and the Computer*
MARTIN, *Teleprocessing Network Organization*
MARTIN AND NORMAN, *The Computerized Society*

MATHISON AND WALKER, *Computers and Telecommunications: Issues in Public Policy*
MCKEEMAN, et al., *A Compiler Generator*
MEYERS, *Time-Sharing Computation in the Social Sciences*
MINSKY, *Computation: Finite and Infinite Machines*
NIEVERGELT et al., *Computer Approaches to Mathematical Problems*
PLANE AND MCMILLAN, *Discrete Optimization: Integer Programming and Network Analysis for Management Decisions*
PRITSKER AND KIVIAT, *Simulation with GASP II: a FORTRAN-Based Simulation Language*
PYLYSHYN, editor, *Perspectives on the Computer Revolution*
RICH, *Internal Sorting Methods: Illustrated with PL/1 Program*
RUSTIN, editor, *Algorithm Specification*
RUSTIN, editor, *Computer Networks*
RUSTIN, editor, *Data Base Systems*
RUSTIN, editor, *Debugging Techniques in Large Systems*
RUSTIN, editor, *Design and Optimization of Compilers*
RUSTIN, editor, *Formal Semantics of Programming Languages*
SACKMAN AND CITRENBAUM, editors, *On-line Planning: Towards Creative Problem-Solving*
SALTON, editor, *The SMART Retrieval System: Experiments in Automatic Document Processing*
SAMMET, *Programming Languages: History and Fundamentals*
SCHAEFER, *A Mathematical Theory of Global Program Optimization*
SCHULTZ, *Spline Analysis*
SCHWARZ, et al., *Numerical Analysis of Symmetric Matrices*
SHERMAN, *Techniques in Computer Programming*
SIMON AND SIKLOSSY, *Representation and Meaning: Experiments with Information Processing Systems*
STERBENZ, *Floating-Point Computation*
STERLING AND POLLACK, *Introduction to Statistical Data Processing*
STOUTEMYER, *PL/1 Programming for Engineering and Science*
STRANG AND FIX, *An Analysis of the Finite Element Method*
STROUD, *Approximate Calculation of Multiple Integrals*
TAVISS, editor, *The Computer Impact*
TRAUB, *Iterative Methods for the Solution of Polynomial Equations*
UHR, *Pattern Recognition, Learning, and Thought*
VAN TASSEL, *Computer Security Management*
VARGA, *Matrix Iterative Analysis*
WAITE, *Implementing Software for Non-Numeric Application*
WILKINSON, *Rounding Errors in Algebraic Processes*
WIRTH, *Systematic Programming: An Introduction*

CURRENTS IN THE
THEORY OF COMPUTING

Edited by

ALFRED V. AHO

Bell Telephone Laboratories
Murray Hill, N.J.

Contributing Authors:

RONALD V. BOOK
ALLAN BORODIN
ZOHAR MANNA
JAMES W. THATCHER
JEFFREY D. ULLMAN

PRENTICE-HALL, INC.

ENGLEWOOD CLIFFS, N.J.

Library of Congress Cataloging in Publication Data

AHO, ALFRED V.
  Currents in the theory of computing.

  (Prentice-Hall series in automatic computation)
  Bibliography: p.
  1. Sequential machine theory. 2. Formal languages.
I. Book, Ronald V. II. Title.
QA267.5.S4A33   001.6′4   72-12477
ISBN 0-13-195651-5

© 1973 by Prentice-Hall, Inc.,
Englewood Cliffs, N.J.

10 9 8 7 6 5 4 3 2 1

Printed in the United States of America

PRENTICE-HALL INTERNATIONAL, INC., *London*
PRENTICE-HALL OF AUSTRALIA, PTY. LTD., *Sydney*
PRENTICE-HALL OF CANADA, LTD., *Toronto*
PRENTICE-HALL OF INDIA PRIVATE LIMITED, *New Delhi*
PRENTICE-HALL OF JAPAN, INC., *Tokyo*

PREFACE

This book surveys five areas of current interest to computer scientists: formal language theory, the complexity of algorithms, program schemata, tree automata, and compiler design theory. These particular topics were selected on the basis of their general interest to computer scientists and also on the basis of their potential impact on computing.

Each article has been written by an active contributor to his field. The articles are tutorial in nature, and are intended to be a guide to the current research being conducted in these areas. Much of the material covered in this book is at present available only in scattered papers published in many different research journals.

Early versions of several of the papers in this monograph were given at a session entitled "An Overview of Theoretical Computer Science" that I was asked to organize for the Fourth Annual Princeton Conference on Information Sciences and Systems. The favorable response given that session led to this monograph.

The papers appear alphabetically by author, and the bibliography at the end serves the entire volume.

ALFRED V. AHO

CONTENTS

1 TOPICS IN FORMAL LANGUAGE THEORY†

Ronald V. Book
Center for Research in Computing Technology
Division of Engineering and Applied Physics
Harvard University

1-1. INTRODUCTION

Formal language theory is concerned with the specification, recognition, and manipulation of sets of strings of symbols (i.e., languages). The theory has evolved from problems in automata theory, theory of programming languages, and linguistics, and along with automata theory plays an important role in theoretical computer science. In this chapter some of the important motivating questions and themes are pointed out, and it is shown how the theory has (and has not) developed from these questions.

What is a "language"? From the standpoint of formal language theory, a "language" is a set of strings over a finite alphabet. Formally, for any finite set Σ of symbols (Σ is an "alphabet"), let $\Sigma^* = \{\sigma_1 \ldots \sigma_n \mid n \geq 1,$ each $\sigma_i \in \Sigma\} \cup \{e\}$, where e is the "empty string," i.e., the string of zero length.‡ A set L is a *language* if and only if there is a finite alphabet Σ_L such that $L \subseteq \Sigma_L^*$. Thus, a language is a set of strings (of finite length) expressible in a linear manner by concatenating a finite number of symbols. This definition of language is broad enough to encompass natural languages and programming languages, as well as the recursive and recursively enumerable sets

---

†It is a pleasure to thank Brenda Baker, T. E. Cheatham, Jr., Peter Downey, Miriam Lucian, Gerald Popek, and Judy Townley for their comments on drafts of this paper.

‡Thus Σ^* is a free semigroup with identity e generated by Σ under the (associative binary) operation of concatenation.

1

studied in automata theory.† [However, it is not clear how this definition can be generalized to include as languages sets of multidimensional objects (e.g., graphs, trees) without losing their geometric "power of representation."]

One of the principal goals of formal language theory is to provide mathematical models for properties of natural languages, of programming languages, and of sets of strings manipulated by automata. A great deal of research has been performed and many diverse questions pursued. The results obtained have been very useful in providing formal tools for the specification of programming languages and their compilers, in showing the limitations of algorithmic manipulation of programs and programming languages, and in providing a better understanding of such problems as parsing. Applications of the theory are found in new areas of theoretical computer science such as the study of tree automata and tree manipulating systems and the study of semantics of programs and programming languages. Thus the elements of formal language theory must play a vital role in any theory of computation.

Regardless of the source of one's interest in formal languages, several questions must be investigated. First, it is necessary to "finitely specify" each language, even though the language may be an infinite set. Second, it is necessary to determine whether a language is recursive (i.e., does there exist an algorithm such that for any string w one can determine whether $w \in L$ or $w \notin L$), and if it is recursive, to find an efficient method of recognizing all and only strings in the language (i.e., an efficient method of deciding its membership problem). Given methods of specification and/or recognition of languages, one may define families of languages by relating all languages specified by a given method or recognized by a given method. By studying operations on families of languages or on individual languages, the method of specification or recognition can be more sharply characterized. And finally, one wishes to know whether certain questions about languages can be answered algorithmically: Is $L = \varnothing$? Is $L_1 \cap L_2$ infinite? Can the complement of L be specified by the same method which specifies L?

In Section 1-2, examples are given to explain the notion of finite specification of languages and the Chomsky hierarchy is defined. In Sections 1–3 through 1–5, several sets of questions are discussed with answers phrased in terms of the Chomsky hierarchy. Some of the results on context-free

---

†Indeed, this definition may be too broad. The study of all possible languages over a given alphabet is of little interest, and attention is limited to those languages (or families of languages) which may be described in some "reasonable" way and possess properties which accurately reflect the behavior of the phenomenon under investigation. The intuitive meaning of "reasonable" may be broader in one area than in another. For example, an automata theorist may be quite happy to study arbitrary recursively enumerable sets, while a software engineer might prefer never to consider a set that is not real-time recognizable. Indeed, finding a "reasonable" notion of "reasonable"—in the sense of finding properties common to all classes—is one of the goals of the theory.

languages are stated in Section 1–6, and extensions of context-free languages are sketched in Section 1–7. In Section 1–8, some questions on context-sensitive grammars are discussed, and in Section 1–9, complexity classes of formal languages are studied. Section 1–10 contains a description of the metatheory and Section 1–11 highlights work still to be done.

If the topics discussed in this paper are of interest to the reader, he may find more extensive treatment in four books on the subject: Hopcroft and Ullman (1969), and Gross and Lentin (1970), which cover the general field, Ginsburg (1966), which is restricted to context-free languages, and Aho and Ullman (1972e), which emphasizes applications to compiler design. There are also several survey papers which give many more details than are presented here: Aho and Ullman (1968), Fischer (1965), and Harrison (1972) are concerned with automata theory, Ullman's chapter in this book and Feldman and Gries (1968) with compiler theory, Borodin's chapter with computational complexity, Manna's chapter with semantics, Kuno (1967) with computer analysis of natural languages, and Thatcher's chapter with trees and tree manipulating systems. Current research is reported in the *Proceedings* of the annual IEEE Symposium on Switching and Automata Theory and the annual ACM Symposium on the Theory of Computing as well as in the following journals: *Journal of Computer and System Sciences, Information and Control, Mathematical Systems Theory, SIAM Journal of Computing*, and *Journal of the Association for Computing Machinery*.

1-2. BASIC CONCEPTS

There are two methods of finitely specifying languages which have received a great deal of attention—generation by means of grammars or rewriting systems and recognition by automata.

To generate a language one must specify a mechanism which will produce a string in the language when activated. This process corresponds to proving a theorem in a formal system—one starts with axioms and deduces theorems by means of rules of inference. We first define a general notion of rewriting system and then restrict this notion to obtain the Chomsky hierarchy.

A *rewriting system* is a quadruple $G = (N, \Sigma, P, S)$, where N is a finite set of *nonterminal* symbols; Σ is the set of *terminal* symbols, $\Sigma \cap N = \varnothing$; $S \in N$ is the *initial* symbol; and $P \subset (N \cup \Sigma)^* \times (N \cup \Sigma)^*$ is a finite set of ordered pairs. Each pair in P is thought of as a "production" or "rewriting rule" and $(\rho, \gamma) \in P$ is usually written $\rho \rightarrow \gamma$ to denote the fact that ρ may be "rewritten" (i.e., replaced) by γ upon application of $\rho \rightarrow \gamma$. This is formalized by defining a binary relation $\underset{G}{\Rightarrow}$ on $(N \cup \Sigma)^*$ as follows: For any α, $\beta \in (N \cup \Sigma)^*$ and any $\rho \rightarrow \gamma \in P$, define $\alpha\rho\beta \underset{G}{\Rightarrow} \alpha\gamma\beta$. A *derivation* in G is any finite sequence of strings $\theta_0, \theta_1, \ldots, \theta_n \in (N \cup \Sigma)^*$ such that for

$i = 1, \ldots, n$, $\theta_{i-1} \underset{G}{\Rightarrow} \theta_i$, and in this case we write $\theta_0 \underset{G}{\overset{*}{\Rightarrow}} \theta_n$. The *language generated* by G is

$$L(G) = \{w \in \Sigma^* \,|\, \text{there is a derivation } S \underset{G}{\Rightarrow} \ldots \underset{G}{\Rightarrow} w \text{ in } G\}.\dagger$$

If $G = (N, \Sigma, P, S)$ is a rewriting system, then the strings in $L(G)$ can be effectively enumerated so that $L(G)$ is a recursively enumerable set.‡ Conversely, it can be shown that for every finite alphabet Σ and every recursively enumerable set $L \subseteq \Sigma^*$ there is a rewriting system G such that $L(G) = L$. Hence studying arbitrary rewriting systems does not aid in studying many interesting properties of languages.

[In practice it is appropriate to limit the rewriting power to nonterminal symbols, that is, the elements of Σ are considered as symbols which cannot be rewritten. Thus the rules are of the form

$$w_1 \rho_1 \ldots w_n \rho_n w_{n+1} \longrightarrow w_1 \gamma_1 \ldots w_n \gamma_n w_{n+1},$$

where each $w_i \in \Sigma^*$, each $\rho_i \in N^*$, and each $\gamma_i \in (N \cup \Sigma)^*$. By doing this we do not restrict the weak generative capacity (i.e., the class of languages obtained by such grammars).]

A grammar is a finite structure, the question of whether or not a sequence of strings is a derivation in a given grammar is a decidable question, and the notion of "language generated by grammar G" is a well-defined notion. Hence to specify a language L, it is enough to specify a grammar to generate L.

To restrict the weak generative power of rewriting systems, we place restrictions on the form of the rewriting rules. The most widely used restriction in formal language theory forces the rules to be "context-free."

A *context-free grammar* is a rewriting system $G = (N, \Sigma, P, S)$ such that each rule in P is of the form $Z \longrightarrow \gamma$, where $Z \in N$ and $\gamma \in (N \cup \Sigma)^*$. In a derivation of G, any symbol of N already generated may be rewritten at any step. A "derivation tree" which represents this derivation is easily constructed. The root is labeled with the initial symbol S, and each node with branches is labeled with a symbol from N (the symbol on the left-hand side of the appropriate rule), and the nodes at the end of the branches are labeled with symbols from $N \cup \Sigma$ (the symbols on the right-hand side of the appropriate rule). Thus any node with a label in Σ is a "leaf"—no branch can start there. Every

---

†In describing grammars we follow the convention of using letters such as $A, B, C, \ldots$ for nonterminal symbols; $a, b, c, \ldots$ for terminal symbols; $u, v, w, \ldots$ for strings of terminal symbols; and $\alpha, \beta, \gamma, \theta, \psi, \ldots$ for strings of terminal and/or nonterminal symbols. The empty string is always denoted by e.

‡For if $w \in L(G)$, then there is a least n such that there is a derivation of w from S with n steps. Hence by listing all strings in Σ^* obtained from S in derivations of length 1, then derivations of length 2, and so on, one obtains $L(G)$.

derivation of a string $w \in L(G)$ has "yield" or "frontier" w; that is, the labels on the leaves read from left to right form the string w.

For example, consider the grammar $G = (N, \Sigma, P, S)$, where $\Sigma = \{a, b\}$, $N = \{S\}$, and $P = \{S \longrightarrow SS, \ S \longrightarrow aSb, \ S \longrightarrow ab\}$. A sample derivation is

$$S \Rightarrow SS \Rightarrow aSbS \Rightarrow aabbS \Rightarrow aabbab,$$

and the corresponding derivation tree appears in Figure 1.

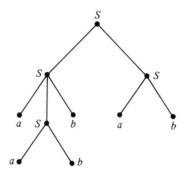

Figure 1

Placing a further restriction on the form of the rules of a context-free grammar yields a "finite-state" grammar. A *finite-state grammar* is a rewriting system $G = (N, \Sigma, P, S)$ such that each rule in R is in one of the forms $A \longrightarrow aB$, $A \longrightarrow a$, or $A \longrightarrow e$, where $A, B \in N$, $a \in \Sigma$.†

One method of relaxing the restrictions on the form of the rules of a context-free grammar is to allow the use of "context." A *context-sensitive grammar* is a rewriting system $G = (N, \Sigma, P, S)$ such that each rule is of the form $\alpha C \beta \longrightarrow \alpha \gamma \beta$, where $\alpha, \beta, \gamma \in (N \cup \Sigma)^*$, $C \in N$, and $\gamma \neq e$. Thus a symbol C may be rewritten as γ if the context surrounding C is α on the left and β on the right.

A language L is a *finite-state (context-free, context-sensitive) language* if there is a finite-state (context-free, context-sensitive) grammar G such that $L(G) = L$.

These four classes of grammars—rewriting systems, finite-state, context-free, and context-sensitive grammars—and the corresponding classes of languages constitute the basic classes of the Chomsky hierarchy.‡ If we allow special rules to be added to a context-sensitive grammar so that the empty word can be generated but no other "erasing" may be performed, then one can show that every context-free language is context-sensitive. From the

---

†The name "finite state" for grammars stems from the connection with "finite-state acceptors" ("finite automata").

‡These grammars are the "phrase-structure" grammars of Chomsky. See Chomsky (1957, 1963) and Chomsky and Miller (1963).

definition it is clear that every finite-state language is context-free and every context-sensitive language is a recursively enumerable set.

Let us turn to the specification of languages by means of recognition by automata. By an automaton we mean a device which obtains input and produces output, has a finite-state control mechanism, and may or may not have auxiliary storage. Both as examples of specification of languages and as counterparts to the classes of grammars described above, we define four specific classes of automata.

A *finite-state acceptor* $M = (Q, \Sigma, \delta, q_0, F)$ has a finite set Q of *states* (or "internal configurations"); a finite input *alphabet* Σ; a *transition* (or "next-state") function, $\delta: Q \times \Sigma \to Q$; an *initial* state $q_0 \in Q$; and a set $F \subseteq Q$ of *accepting* states. The transition function can be extended to $Q \times \Sigma^* \to Q$ by defining for every $q \in K$, $a \in \Sigma$, and $w \in \Sigma^*$, $\delta(q, e) = q$ and $\delta(q, wa) = \delta(\delta(q, w), a)$. The *language accepted by M* is

$$L(M) = \{w \in \Sigma^* \mid \delta(q_0, w) \in F\}$$

A set L is a *regular set* if there is a finite-state acceptor M such that $L(M) = L$.

Intuitively, a finite-state acceptor has an input tape which initially contains some string of symbols. The tape is read (by a read-only "tape head") in one direction, say from left to right, the machine changes states depending on the current state and the currently scanned input symbol, and the input string is accepted if the machine is in an accepting state when the entire string has been processed. Otherwise, the string is rejected.

In the above definition of finite-state acceptor, the transition function δ assigns precisely one state to each state–symbol pair. Thus the machine is *deterministic*—at each step in a computation there is exactly one transition defined by δ and this depends on the current state and the currently scanned input symbol. In automata theory it has been useful to consider *nondeterministic* machines, that is, machines with a finite number (including 0) of possible transitions at each step. For nondeterministic finite-state acceptors, the transition function assigns a finite set of states to each state–symbol pair. A "computation" of a nondeterministic machine on a given input is any sequence of transitions such that each step follows from the preceding step by making a choice of "next state" from the possibilities given by δ. Thus there is a finite number (including 0) of possible computations on a given input, and there may be more than one accepting computation.† An input string is accepted by a nondeterministic machine if there exists at least one accepting computation of the machine on that string, and is rejected if there is no such accepting computation.

---

†An accepting computation is a computation which ends in an accepting state.

In the case of finite-state acceptors, the class of nondeterministic machines is no more powerful that the class of deterministic machines, that is, the same family of languages is specified (Rabin and Scott, 1959). However, this is not the case for some other classes of machines. Although nondeterministic machines are not "realistic" in the sense that they model actual computing devices, they are very useful in specifying various families of languages and in representing various situations where "choice" is involved.[†]

A *pushdown store acceptor* $M = (Q, \Sigma, \Gamma, \delta, q_0, F)$ has a finite set Q of states, a finite input alphabet Σ, a finite *pushdown* alphabet Γ, a transition function δ from $Q \times (\Sigma \cup \{e\}) \times (\Gamma \cup \{e\})$ to the class of finite subsets of $Q \times \Gamma^*$, an initial state $q_0 \in Q$, and a set $F \subseteq Q$ of accepting states.

Intuitively, a pushdown store acceptor has an input tape which initially contains some string of symbols. The finite-state control mechanism is similar to that of a finite-state acceptor. However, there is an auxiliary storage facility, a pushdown store—that is, a last-in, first-out data structure. Thus transitions depend on the current state, the currently scanned input symbol, and the symbol read on the "top" of the pushdown store. In one step the acceptor may or may not read a new input symbol, change state, and alter its storage (by either "popping" the currently scanned symbol on the "top" of the pushdown store or writing a string on the pushdown store and "pushing" it into the store). The action is nondeterministic since $\delta(q, a, Z)$ is a finite subset of $Q \times \Gamma^*$—each element of $\delta(q, a, Z)$ is a possible transition.

Formally, an *instantaneous description* of a pushdown store acceptor $M = (Q, \Sigma, \Gamma, \delta, q_0, F)$ is an element of $Q \times \Sigma^* \times \Gamma^*$. For any $p, q \in Q$, $a \in \Sigma \cup \{e\}$, $Z \in \Gamma \cup \{e\}$, $u, v \in \Gamma^*$, if $(p, u) \in \delta(q, a, Z)$, then define $(q, aw, Zv) \vdash (p, w, uv)$. Let $\vdash^{\underline{*}}$ be the transitive reflexive closure of $\vdash$. The relation $\vdash$ can be interpreted as "computes in one step" and $\vdash^{\underline{*}}$ "computes (in zero or more steps)." The language accepted by M is

$$L(M) = \{w \in \Sigma^* \mid \text{for some } p \in F, (q_0, w, e) \vdash^{\underline{*}} (p, e, e)\}.$$

A more powerful device is a *Turing acceptor* $M = (Q, \Sigma, \Gamma, \delta, q_0, F)$, where Q is a finite set of states, Σ is a finite input alphabet, Γ is a finite set of *tape* symbols $(\Sigma \subset \Gamma)$,

$$\delta : Q \times (\Gamma \cup \{\beta\}) \to Q \times (\Gamma \cup \{\beta\}) \times \{L, N, R\}$$

is the transition function (where β stands for "blank" and L, N, and R stand for "move left," "do not move," and "move right," respectively), $q_0 \in Q$ is the initial state, and $F \subseteq Q$ is the set of accepting states.

[†]One should note that nondeterministic machines as described here are not probabilistic or stochastic. See Paz (1971) for a study of probabilistic machines. The fact that nondeterminism involves "guessing" and is related to the generation process is exemplified (for Turing machines) by results in Book and Greibach (1970).

Intuitively, M has a single tape on which the input initially appears. There is a single tapehead which can both read and write on the tape. The transitions depend on the current state and currently scanned symbol, and in one step the machine can change state, rewrite the contents of a single tape square, and move one square to the left (L) or one square to the right (R) or not move at all (N). It can write on a blank tape square or "erase" a symbol by replacing it with the symbol β (for "blank"). If M halts in an accepting state, then M accepts the input—otherwise, M rejects the input. We omit formal details.

If a Turing acceptor cannot write on blank tape squares or create new blanks, then it is a *linear bounded automaton*. If a Turing acceptor has a transition function δ from $K \times (\Gamma \cup \{\beta\})$ to the finite subsets of $K \times (\Gamma \cup \{\beta\} \times \{L, N, R\})$, then it is nondeterministic.

In each case an acceptor has been defined as a finite structure, and its behavior is well defined. Hence, in each case it provides a finite specification of a language, the set of strings it accepts.

These particular devices have been described here because they specify the classes of the Chomsky hierarchy:

1. A set is regular if it is accepted by a finite-state acceptor. But a set is accepted by a finite-state acceptor if and only if it is generated by a finite-state grammar. Hence we have two different specifications of the regular sets (or finite-state languages).

2. A language is context-free if it is generated by a context-free grammar. But a language is generated by a context-free grammar if and only if it is accepted by a nondeterministic pushdown store acceptor. (It is known that one cannot specify all context-free languages by deterministic pushdown store acceptors.) Hence we have two different specifications of the context-free languages.

3. A language is context-sensitive if it is generated by a context-sensitive grammar. But a language is generated by a context-sensitive grammar if and only if it is accepted by a nondeterministic linear bounded automaton. (It is an open question whether or not every context-sensitive language can be accepted by a deterministic linear bounded automaton.) Hence we have two different specifications of the context-sensitive languages.

4. A set is recursively enumerable if it is generated by a rewriting system. But a set is generated by a rewriting system if and only if it is accepted by a Turing acceptor. Hence we have two different specifications of the recursively enumerable sets.

Each of the families described in 1–4 has been studied in detail. Positive and negative closure properties have been studied to sharpen our knowledge of the generative capacity of the method of specification. Various questions have been classified as "decidable" or "undecidable" depending on the method of specification which yields the most information (see Section 1-5).†

Each of the families described in 1–4 has been studied in one or more contexts. The regular sets (or finite-state languages) and their specification by means of finite-state machines have arisen in switching theory, and in combinational complexity, as well as in various aspects of abstract automata theory (Arbib, 1969). The context-free languages and their specifications both by means of pushdown store acceptors and context-free grammars play a role in models for natural languages, models of programming languages and compiler theory, and in computability theory. The context-sensitive languages have been important in the study of subrecursive predicates as well as in formal language theory. And the recursively enumerable sets arise in various areas of logic as well as formal language theory, automata theory, and the study of natural languages.

One should note that the regular sets, the context-free languages, and the context-sensitive languages each form families of recursive sets since the membership (recognition) problem is decidable when these families are specified by the methods above.

Much effort has been spent in providing alternative specifications and characterizations for many families of languages studied in the literature. This has been done for several reasons. First it was a matter of discovering that two apparently different families were in fact the same; e.g., it was not immediately apparent that context-free grammars and nondeterministic pushdown store acceptors both specify the family of context-free languages. Also it has been demonstrated for certain families of languages that some properties are more easily established by one type of specification than by another. Another reason for alternative specifications is to better understand the "power" of a family in terms of what it does and does not contain, and to better compare different families. For a study of these families, see Hopcroft and Ullman (1969).

1-3. NATURAL LANGUAGES AND PROGRAMMING LANGUAGES

Before discussing the properties of formal languages that have been studied in the theory itself, let us briefly comment on some of the motivation for the theory which has come from the study of natural languages and the study of programming languages.

†Informally, a question is *decidable* or *recursively solvable* if there is an algorithm which gives the correct answer when presented with the appropriate input. For example, the *membership* or *recognition* problems for a language L is the problem of determining for any string w whether or not $w \in L$. (A set is *recursive* if its membership problem is decidable.)

In attempting to develop a theory of generative grammars for natural language, Chomsky considered finite-state, context-free, and context-sensitive grammars [see Chomsky (1957), Chomsky and Miller (1963), and Kuno (1967)]. In such a grammar nonterminal symbols represent "parts of speech" and the derivation tree (or "structural description") represents the relationship between the parts of speech which provide the "structure" of the sentence and the actual words of the sentence itself. The words of the sentence are the terminal symbols labeling the leaves of the derivation tree. (See Figure 2.) Thus a grammar may provide a syntactic description of a language.

Context-free grammars have been of use to linguists interested in the formal structure of natural language and in the computer analysis of natural language, since they provide a simple method of representing the syntax of a language. Since context-free languages are recursive sets, these grammars provide a model which agrees with the linguist's belief that the question of whether or not a string is a sentence should be a decidable question in any theory of natural language. Also, the fact that the set of derivation trees of a context-free grammar is a recursive set (in fact, a "regular" set of trees—see Thatcher's chapter) adds to the usefulness of context-free grammars in analysis of syntax.

In transformational theory a grammar has a "deep" structure or "base" component determining the semantic interpretation and often this is provided by a phrase structure grammar. There is a set of rules which maps phrase markers (i.e., trees) to phrase markers. This "transformational" component produces the phrase markers which represent the "phonetic"

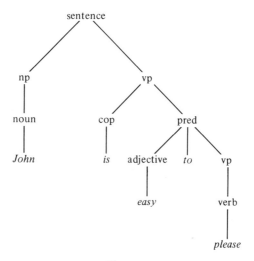

Figure 2

component. Thus the sentences "John is easy to please" and "It is easy to please John" have the same semantic interpretation but different syntactic representation, while "John is eager to please" has the same syntactic representation as but different semantic interpretation from "John is easy to please." No mechanism to model this process mathematically has been widely accepted, although several models have been proposed and analyzed.

Another aspect of linguistics of interest to computer science is the study of mechanical translation of natural language. In many attempts to cope with problems of computational linguistics, context-free grammars have been used to specify parts of the language studied and the pushdown store has had extensive use as a data structure. (This is especially true in "predictive analysis.") However, results on context-free grammars show that some of the problems faced in mechanical translation cannot be solved algorithmically. For example, there can be no algorithm which can be applied to large classes of context-free grammars in order to test whether or not a grammar is ambiguous—i.e. to determine whether or not there exists $w \in L(G)$ with two different derivation trees. Although the chances of success of mechanical translation are no longer thought to be high, the work in this area has uncovered many important problems of natural language.

For a survey and excellent discussion of the issues involved in computer analysis of natural language and the relationship of notions in formal language theory to natural language, see the paper by Kuno (1967). For examples of mathematical models for transformational grammars and analysis of these models, see Peters and Ritchie (1969), Kimball (1967), Ginsburg and Partee (1969), Salomaa (1971), and Rounds (1970). For a discussion of many issues in linguistics and how mathematical models can and cannot help, see Bar-Hillel (1964).

One of the important goals in the development of automata theory has been the need for an accurate (and adequate) mathematical model for computers or (more reasonably) for various aspects of the computing process. From one viewpoint the theory of automata developed from the invention of Turing machines as a representation for algorithms (or the computation of algorithms or partial recursive functions), and from another viewpoint automata theory generalizes the theory of sequential machines used to model switching circuits. [See the papers in Shannon and McCarthy (1956).] However, much of the work in automata theory in the last 10 to 15 years has come from attempts to characterize aspects of the computing process. This has been particularly true in that part of automata theory which is related to formal language theory.

In attempting to describe aspects of the computing process, parts of formal language theory have been developed in order to model and to provide mathematical tools for the syntactic description of programming languages and for syntactic analysis within the compiling process. Indeed a large part of formal language theory centers around attempts to describe syntactic properties common to many programming languages and to describe the syntax itself. Many devices have been studied in an effort to develop an adequate model for the translation performed by a compiler. Thus context-free grammars provide simple specifications of much of the syntax of languages such as ALGOL, and the use of a pushdown store is common in the syntax-directed translation of such languages. Further, formal language theory has provided a useful formalism for expressing many of the properties of programming languages, as well as indicating the algorithmic limitations of many processes used in programming languages. This is described in the tutorial paper of Feldman and Gries (1968), and is spelled out in detail in Aho and Ullman (1972e).

The families of the Chomsky hierarchy, particularly the family of context-free languages, are not adequate for the characterization of many properties of programming languages. Although many programming languages are context-sensitive, the use of context-sensitive grammars (or linear bounded automata) to specify programming languages is unacceptable, mainly because of the algorithmic and syntactic complexity involved—the weak generative power of context-sensitive grammars is much more than is needed to describe most features of programming languages. On the other hand, context-free grammars are inadequate in that all the syntactic features cannot be specified by context-free rules alone. For example, multiple occurrences of identical substrings cannot be recognized. More specifically, there is no way to coordinate the declaration of an identifier with the several uses of that particular identifier. (In terms of formal language theory, this is equivalent to noting that a language such as $\{wcw \mid w \in \{a, b\}^*\}$ is not context-free.) Also if a programming language (such as ALGOL) allows declaration statements where different data types must be specified, then the validity of the application of certain operations is in question until these data types are interpreted. For example, concatenation of strings or lists may be meaningful while concatenation of integers or trees may not. The amount of "memory" available in a context-free grammar is not sufficient for retention of the appropriate restrictions and restoration of previous conditions following the application of a prohibited operation.

Another inadequacy of these grammars (particularly context-free grammars) for the specification of programming languages is the desire to produce some representation of program "meaning." The representation and meaning of various identifiers, their scope, data type, and allocation, plus some representation of the sequence of operations in a computation, cannot be carried out by context-free grammars. However, extensions of context-free grammars have been employed in attacking the problem.

Both grammars and automata have been used in the description of restricted classes of programs and program schema. Here the undecidability of questions about context-free grammars [e.g., for G_1 and G_2, is $L(G_1) =$

$L(G_2)$?] has shown that these classes do not have some of the properties one needs in order to optimize programs and compilers algorithmically.

See Aho and Ullman (1973), Cheatham (1967), and Cocke and Schwartz (1970) for a discussion of these problems and the papers in Engeler (1971) for a discussion of recent work on semantics.

1-4. PARSING

Regardless of the method of specifying a language or the motivation for studying languages, one of the important problems is to find a method of "parsing" strings purported to be in the language. This is easily illustrated by considering context-free grammars.

Let $G = (N, \Sigma, P, S)$ be a context-free grammar and let w be an arbitrary string. We wish to determine whether or not $w \in L(G)$—this is the "membership" or "recognition" problem: Given G, construct a deterministic device which upon input w eventually will give output "yes" if $w \in L(G)$ and "no" if $w \notin L(G)$. However, if $w \in L(G)$, we wish to obtain some (possibly every) "syntactic description" of w with respect to G. Since G is context-free, this means a representation of some derivation tree in G which has S as root and w as "yield" or "frontier." Each such syntactic description is a "parse" of w, and any given grammar may have more than one parse for any or all strings it generates. [Further, there exist "inherently ambiguous" context-free languages L: For any context-free grammar G such that $L(G) = L$, there exists $w \in L(G)$ with at least two parses in G.]

A "parsing device" is either an automata-theoretic structure or an algorithm which can be implemented on a "real" computer and which will give two types of output: "yes" and some parses if $w \in L(G)$, or "no" if $w \notin L(G)$.† An important problem in formal language theory is to find an upper bound on the "size" of a parsing device or the "amount of resource" (e.g., time) a parsing device must use if it is to accomplish its task. When possible, given a method of specification of a family of languages, one wishes to find a type of parsing device which will perform the parsing task for any given language. For example, one wishes to find a method of parsing based on context-free grammars so that given a context-free grammar, some (efficient) parsing device is produced.

This problem is of interest both in "practical" and "theoretical" situations. Clearly, obtaining the syntactic description of a source program is an essential prerequisite for translating it into machine code by many modern compilers. If there is to be any type of automatic translation of (natural or artificial) languages, then this translation must rest on correspondences between syntactic descriptions. To obtain these syntactic descriptions is

---

†In many cases one is interested only in some restricted type of parse. However, one could require that all possible parses be produced as output.

the problem of parsing. (A similar problem arises in parts of mathematics: One wishes to determine the different possible "factorizations" of a well-formed expression in some algebraic structure.)

In automata theory the principal focus is on the recognition problem and not the parsing problem. Indeed one method of specification of languages is recognition by automata. If the device is deterministic, then a parsing algorithm usually follows easily from the description of the recognition automaton. However, in the case of specification by nondeterministic automata, a parsing algorithm must involve more than simply enumerating all possible computations of the recognition automaton if it is to be efficient (since a nondeterministic automaton may have nonaccepting computations as well as accepting computations on an accepted input).

Let us briefly review the known results on parsing languages in the Chomsky hierarchy. As a measure on efficiency, we count the number of "steps" in the parsing process as a function of the length of the input string. The definition of "step" is not precise until a model is specified, but one may think of the steps in Turing machine's computation as being representative, and we shall describe results in these terms.

A regular set can be specified by a finite-state acceptor. That is, for any regular set L there is a finite-state acceptor M such that $L(M) = L$. Now a finite-state acceptor M scans a new input symbol at each step of its computation so that for input w, M accepts or rejects w in $|w|$ steps.† (Any device which accepts or rejects within this bound is said to operate in *real time*.) Since M is deterministic, for any input string w there is a unique computation of M on w and hence a unique specification.

A context-free language can be specified by a pushdown store acceptor. But in general the pushdown store acceptor is nondeterministic, so that one must consider all computations on a given input if one wishes to find all parses. If the language is specified by a grammar $G = (N, \Sigma, P, S)$ in Greibach normal form (so that each rule in P is of the form $A \rightarrow a$, $A \rightarrow aB$, or $A \rightarrow aBC$, where $A, B, C \in N$, $a \in \Sigma$), then a pushdown store acceptor M can be constructed from G such that M is nondeterministic but operates in real time.‡ But since M is nondeterministic, there may be $k^{|w|}$ computations of M on input w (where k depends on M). Thus one wishes to obtain a more efficient parsing algorithm than can be obtained from simply enumerating the computations of a nondeterministic pushdown store acceptor.

Several parsing algorithms for context-free languages are available.

---

†For any string w, $|w|$ is the length of w, i.e., $|e| = 0$; for $a \in \Sigma$, $|a| = 1$; for $w \in \Sigma^*$, $a \in \Sigma$, $|wa| = |w| + 1$.

‡Every context-free language can be specified by a grammar in Greibach normal form (Greibach, 1965). A pushdown store acceptor M constructed from a Greibach normal form grammar G has the property that for any input string w, if $w \in L(M)$, then every accepting computation of M on w has exactly $|w|$ steps. This is what is meant by saying that a nondeterministic machine operates in real time.

Younger has shown that for every context-free grammar G one can construct a deterministic multitape Turing machine which parses $L(G)$ and which operates within time bound $|w|^3$ on any input string w. Earley has a similar result in which the parsing algorithm is implemented on a random-access machine and has the same upper bound ($|w|^3$) for the general case but much lower bounds for specific subfamilies of context-free languages. The parsing algorithm of Earley is widely discussed in the literature on programming languages and compilers [see Earley (1968), Ullman's chapter, Younger (1967), or Aho and Ullman (1972e)].

It is not known if the time bound n^3 is necessary (where n is the length of the input) for recognition. In fact, there is no known example of a context-free language whose recognition has been shown to require more than kn (k a constant) steps by means of some parsing algorithm implemented on a random-access machine. It should be pointed out that a bound for recognition may not be a bound for parsing—there may be many nonequivalent parses in some grammar with unbounded degree of ambiguity—and it is not clear that this is simply a matter of time necessary to output the parses already obtained. If one restricts attention to certain Turing machine models, it is known that some languages need at least $n^2/\log n$ steps for recognition (Gallaire, 1969).

An important subfamily of the context-free languages is the family of "deterministic" context-free languages. A language is a *deterministic* context-free language if it is accepted by a deterministic pushdown store acceptor (Ginsburg and Greibach, 1966b). An alternative specification of these languages important in compiler theory is given by $LR(k)$ grammars (Knuth, 1965). For any deterministic pushdown store acceptor M_1, one can construct a deterministic pushdown store acceptor M_2 such that $L(M_2) = L(M_1)$ and such that M_2 operates within time bound $2n$. Since M_2 is deterministic, each string in $L(M_2)$ has a unique parse with respect to the definition of M_2. The problem of efficiently constructing a deterministic pushdown store acceptor from an $LR(k)$ grammar is of much interest for compiler theorists (DeRemer, 1971) and this problem has motivated related research in software engineering. For a thorough discussion of the problems in parsing context-free languages, see Aho and Ullman (1972e).

The results on the parsing of context-free languages point to the fact that the characterization of families of languages by means of resource bounds for parsing or recognition will not necessarily yield known families specified by other means. For example, many non-context-free languages can be recognized by deterministic multitape Turing machines which operate in real time.

Little is known about parsing context-sensitive languages. It is known that a deterministic Turing machine can recognize a context-sensitive language within time bound k^n for $k > 1$ (Cook, 1971), and that a deterministic Turing machine can recognize a context-sensitive language while visiting at most n^2 tape squares on its tape (Savitch, 1970). It is an open question whether the tape bound can be brought below n^2, and whether the time bound k^n can be realized while at the same time using less than n^2 tape squares. One parsing algorithm has been given without specifying resource bounds (Woods, 1970).

Of course there can be no algorithmic parsing of recursively enumerable sets since there is no algorithm to decide the membership problem.

In all approaches to parsing, one must keep in mind the fact that a parsing algorithm depends on the method of specification of the language. In programming languages and compiler theory the specification is usually by grammars, and hence the problem of building an efficient parser from a given grammar is of great importance.

In order to compare the relative efficiencies of parsing algorithms, it is necessary to define the notion of "step" in the parsing process in a way which is independent of implementation and/or machine and which is more "realistic" than time bounds on Turing machine computations. [See Cobham (1964) for a discussion of this problem in the computation of functions.] If the software engineer expects to gather meaningful data on the efficiencies of various algorithms for specific (common) classes of languages, then the design of the experiment must include some measure of difficulty of parsing based on a definition of "step" which accurately reflects the specific hypothesis of syntactic complexity of the class of languages (or grammars) put forth by the experimentor. Although there is no universally accepted notion of "step" in the parsing process, it is generally accepted that a "step" must be carried out by some bounded number of operations performed by a computer. [See Earley (1968) and Woods (1969) for examples of this type of "step."] The most appropriate relationship between "syntactic complexity," basic linguistic operations, and "step" in the parsing process is still to be publicized.

1-5. DECIDABILITY AND UNDECIDABILITY

Regardless of the motivation for studying formal languages, there are certain questions one wishes to classify as decidable or undecidable. Specific questions asked about context-free grammars will illustrate what may be asked of languages in general, and we state the following important results for the purpose of example.

1. The following questions are decidable for a context-free grammar $G = (N, \Sigma, P, S)$:
   a. Is $L(G) = \varnothing$?
   b. Is $L(G)$ finite?
   c. Is the symbol $A \in N$ ever used in a derivation; i.e., do there exist w_1, $w_2, w_3 \in \Sigma^*$ such that $S \xRightarrow{*} w_1 A w_3 \xRightarrow{*} w_1 w_2 w_3$?
2. The following questions are undecidable for a context-free grammar $G = (N, \Sigma, P, S)$:

    a. Is $L(G)$ regular?
    b. Is $L(G) = \Sigma^*$?
    c. Is $L(G) = L_0$ for some specific regular set L_0?
    d. Is G ambiguous; i.e., does there exist $w \in L(G)$ with two different derivation trees?
    e. Is $L(G)$ inherently ambiguous; i.e., does there exist a context-free grammar G' such that $L(G') = L(G)$ and G' is unambiguous?
    f. Is $\Sigma^* - L(G)$ context-free?
    g. Is $\Sigma^* - L(G)$ regular?
    h. Is $\Sigma^* - L(G)$ finite?
    3. The following questions are undecidable for context-free grammars G_i, $i = 1, 2$:
    a. Is $L(G_1) = L(G_2)$?
    b. Is $L(G_1) \subseteq L(G_2)$?
    c. Is $L(G_1) \cap L(G_2) = \varnothing$?
    d. Is $L(G_1) \cap L(G_2)$ finite?
    e. Is $L(G_1) \cap L(G_2)$ context-free?
    f. Is $L(G_1) \cap L(G_2)$ regular?

Recall that even to consider such questions it is necessary to assume a recursive enumeration or presentation of the context-free grammars and that decidability or undecidability always depends on this enumeration. Of course, there is no difficulty when considering specification by context-free grammars.

There are other questions which arise in specific contexts. See Ginsburg (1966) and Hopcroft and Ullman (1969) for discussions and proofs of these results.

It should be pointed out that some questions that are undecidable for arbitrary context-free languages are decidable for deterministic context-free languages when these languages are specified by deterministic pushdown store acceptors [or $LR(k)$ grammars]. For example, if M is a deterministic pushdown store acceptor with input alphabet Σ, then it is decidable whether $L(M)$ is regular, and whether $L(M) = L_0$ for a given regular set L_0. One question which is important both for compiler theory and for the study of programming language semantics, and which is still an open question, is the decidability of the weak equivalence of deterministic pushdown store acceptors, i.e., whether $L(M_1) = L(M_2)$ for deterministic pushdown store acceptors M_1 and M_2.

Nearly any question one asks about regular sets specified by deterministic finite-state acceptors is decidable, while the opposite is true for context-sensitive languages. Thus the questions asked about context-free languages must be carefully considered when restricting attention to subfamilies of context-free languages (particularly, deterministic context-free languages) or when extending the context-free languages to subfamilies of the context-sensitive languages.

Most proofs of the undecidability of certain questions in formal language theory hinge on the ability to encode accepting or rejecting Turing machine computations within a system for specifying languages or to encode Post correspondence problems within such a system. The degree of unsolvability of many of these questions has been studied, and attempts have been made to find "minimal bases" for questions to be undecidable. See Hartmanis and Hopcroft (1970), Cudia (1970), and Baker and Book (1972) for discussions of these problems.

A different approach to such problems has focused on certain reducibilities among questions. For example, to show that the question "is $L(G)$ deterministic context-free?" is undecidable for context-free G, it is enough to be able to show that the question "is $L(G) = \Sigma^*$?" is undecidable. The basis for such work is to note that certain effective closure operators are powerful enough to carry out the appropriate encoding and that certain questions can be shown to be undecidable if the corresponding properties dichotomize the family of languages under study. See Greibach (1968) and Hopcroft and Ullman (1968a).

1-6. CONTEXT-FREE LANGUAGES

In applications to programming languages as well as in automata theory, the context-free languages arise so frequently that their study is fundamental to the theory. Some of the results on context-free languages are sketched in this section. The reader should refer to Ginsburg (1966) for a detailed development and to Aho and Ullman (1972e) for applications to programming languages and compilers.

The context-free languages are specified by the class of context-free grammars. From these grammars the notion of derivation tree naturally arises (as indicated in Section 1-2), and from the study of derivation trees, certain results about context-free grammars are suggested. We consider several such results.

1. Admissibility: If G_1 is a context-free grammar, then one can construct a context-free grammar $G_2 = (N, \Sigma, P, S)$ such that either $\Sigma = P = \varnothing$, $N = \{S\}$, and $L(G_2) = L(G_1) = \varnothing$, or $L(G_2) = L(G_1) \neq \varnothing$ and G_2 has the following properties:

   a. If $A \in N$ and $A \neq S$, then $A \rightarrow e \notin P$ but there exist $\alpha, \beta \in \Sigma^*$ such that $\alpha\beta \neq e$ and $S \overset{*}{\underset{G_2}{\Rightarrow}} \alpha A \beta$.

   b. If $A \in N$, then there exists $w_A \in \Sigma^*$ such that $A \overset{*}{\underset{G_2}{\Rightarrow}} w_A$, and if $A \neq S$, then $w_A \neq e$.

   c. If $L(G_2)$ is infinite, then for each $A \in N$, $\{w \in \Sigma^* \mid A \overset{*}{\underset{G_2}{\Rightarrow}} w\}$ is infinite.

2. Chomsky normal form: If G_1 is a context-free grammar, then one can construct a context-free grammar $G_2 = (N, \Sigma, P, S)$ such that $L(G_2) = L(G_1)$

and such that each rewriting rule in R is of the form $S \longrightarrow e$ or $A \longrightarrow BC$ or $A \longrightarrow a$, where $A \in N$, $a \in \Sigma$, and $B, C \in N - \{S\}$.

3. Intercalation: If $G = (N, \Sigma, P, S)$ is a context-free grammar, then there exist integers p and q such that if $z \in L(G)$ and $|z| \geq p$, then there exist $u, v, w, x, y \in \Sigma^*$, where $z = uvwxy$, $vx \neq e$, $|vwx| \leq q$; and for every $n \geq 0$, $uv^nwx^ny \in L(G)$.†

The result on admissibility comes from noting that we can "prune" a tree to eliminate branches that will not lead to leaves with a label in Σ, the Chomsky normal form theorem from noting that we can add new symbols and change the rewriting rules so that every derivation tree has only binary branching except when it produces a leaf, and the intercalation theorem from noting that if one has a finite set of labels but arbitrarily long paths in the set of derivation trees, then some nodes in a sufficiently long path from the root to a leaf must have the same label.

Another result stemming from the study of derivation trees is a characterization of the family of context-free languages as the smallest family containing a set consisting of a single letter and closed under union with sets of this type, intersection with regular sets, and a type of substitution called "nested iterated substitution." This has been pointed out in various forms by Greibach (1970), Kral (1970), Gruska (1971), and McWhirter (1971). This characterization leads to "substitution expressions" for context-free languages similar to "regular expressions" for regular sets. Indeed, just as the representation of regular sets by regular expressions is based on the Kleene–Myhill theorem (Rabin and Scott, 1959), the representation of context-free languages by substitution expressions can be based on the "generalized" Kleene–Myhill theorem for "regular" sets of trees, those sets of trees corresponding to the set of derivation trees of context-free grammars (Thatcher and Wright, 1968).

The study of derivation trees also yields the following result. For a finite set $\Sigma = \{a_1, \ldots, a_n\}$ and a string $w \in \Sigma^*$, let $S(w) = \langle i_1, \ldots, i_n \rangle$, where for each $j = 1, \ldots, n$, i_j is the number of occurrences of a_j in w. For any n, an n-vector is an n-tuple of nonnegative integers. If $c \geq 0$ is an integer and $v = \langle i_1, \ldots, i_n \rangle$ an n-vector, then $cv = \langle ci_1, \ldots, ci_n \rangle$, and if $v = \langle i_1, \ldots, i_n \rangle$ and $u = \langle j_1 \ldots, j_n \rangle$ then $v + u = \langle i_1 + j_1, \ldots, i_n + j_n \rangle$. A set N of n-vectors is *linear* if there are n-vectors $c, p_1, \ldots, p_k$ such that

$$N = \left\{ c + \sum_{i=1}^{k} a_i p_i \,\middle|\, \text{each } a_i \geq 0 \text{ an integer} \right\},$$

and a *semilinear* set is a finite union of linear sets. The result can be stated

---

†For a string w, $w^0 = e$ and $w^{n+1} = ww^n$ for $n \geq 0$. We write w^* in place of $\{w\}^* = \{w^n \mid n \geq 0\}$.

as follows: If $L \subseteq \Sigma^*$ is context-free, then $S(L)$ is a semilinear set (Parikh, 1961).

Closure properties of the family of context-free languages are also of interest. Knowledge of positive and negative closure properties has helped to sharpen the specification and further understand the power of this family. The family of context-free languages is closed under union, concatenation, Kleene $*$, reversal, intersection with regular sets, and substitution, but not under intersection or complementation.† This family is also closed under certain types of mapping operations which can be realized by finite-state devices, in particular arbitrary homomorphic mappings and inverse homomorphism.‡ To obtain these results (as well as many others) it is often easier to use one specification rather than another; for example, proof of closure under homomorphic mappings is easier by constructing grammars than by constructing pushdown store acceptors, and the converse is true when proving closure under inverse homomorphism. This is an important reason to study alternative specifications for this or any other family of languages.

The study of closure properties yields another characterization of the family of context-free languages. For any $n > 0$, let Δ_n be a set of $2n$ symbols representing n pairs of parentheses (of different types). For example, $\{(,), [,]\}$ could be Δ_2. Let $D_n \subseteq \Delta_n^*$ be the set of all well-formed strings of matched parentheses, so that $D_n^* = D_n$ and D_n is closed under "nesting" of pairs of parentheses in Δ_n. The result, which is commonly called the Chomsky–Schutzenberger theorem, asserts that a language L is context-free if and only if for some regular set R, homomorphism h, and integer $n > 0$, $L = h(D_n \cap R)$. A stronger version asserts that L is context-free if and only if for some regular set R and homomorphisms h_1 and h_2, $L = h_1[h_2^{-1}(D_2) \cap R]$. [See Chomsky and Schutzenberger (1963) for one version of this result.]

There are two principal ways of restricting the power of context-free grammars. One is to restrict the form of the rules and the other is to restrict the way that the rules are applied. If every rewriting rule of a context-free grammar has at most one nonterminal symbol on the right-hand side, then the grammar is a *linear* grammar. Note that every finite-state grammar is linear context-free. The family of linear context-free languages is a proper subfamily of the family of all context-free languages and has many (but not all) of the same properties (in particular, is not closed under concatenation and Kleene $*$). These languages are very useful in showing certain questions

---

†For languages L_1 and L_2, the concatenation of L_1 and L_2 is $L_1 L_2 = \{w_1 w_2 \mid w_i \in L_i, i = 1, 2\}$. If $L^0 = \{e\}$ and $L^{n+1} = L L^n$ for $n \geq 0$, then the Kleene $*$ of L is $L^* = \bigcup_{i=0}^{\infty} L^i$. The reversal of a string $a_1 \cdots a_n$ is $(a_1 \cdots a_n)^R = a_n \cdots a_1$; the reversal of a language L is $L^R = \{w^R \mid w \in L\}$.

‡Thus, if $h: \Sigma_1^* \longrightarrow \Sigma_2^*$ is a (semigroup) homomorphism, and $L_1 \subseteq \Sigma_1^*$ and $L_2 \subseteq \Sigma_2^*$ are both context-free, then $h[L_1] = \{h(w) \mid w \in L_1\}$ and $h^{-1}[L_2] = \{w \in \Sigma_1^* \mid h(w) \in L_2\}$ are both context-free.

to be undecidable since they are powerful enough to represent encodings of correspondence problems and yet weak enough to be embeddable in many classes of languages defined in various ways [see Greibach (1963)].

Restrictions on the way that the rules of a grammar may be applied have been studied. In particular one may specify a language whose strings represent the sequence of rules to be applied. Thus one has a "control set" which specifies derivations. Subfamilies of the context-free languages have been obtained in this way. These results are summarized in Ginsburg and Spanier (1968a, 1968b).

Nondeterministic pushdown store acceptors provide a useful specification for context-free languages since sometimes one can see that a language can be accepted by a pushdown store acceptor more easily than one can see how to generate it with a grammar, and there are two types of restrictions on pushdown store acceptors which yield interesting subfamilies of the family of context-free languages. If one considers only deterministic pushdown store acceptors, then one obtains a proper subfamily of the family of context-free languages which is very useful in syntax-directed compiling. This subfamily is closed under complementation (since one can "force" a pushdown store acceptor to halt on every input string and a deterministic automaton has only one computation on any input string), inverse homomorphism, and intersection with regular sets but is not closed under concatenation, Kleene $*$, or homomorphic mappings (Ginsburg and Greibach, 1966b). An alternative specification is provided by the class of $LR(k)$ grammars (Knuth, 1965). See Aho and Ullman (1972e) for a study of the use of deterministic context-free languages in compiling.

Restricting the behavior of the pushdown store of a pushdown store acceptor shows some of the rich "algebraic" structure of the family of context-free languages. A pushdown store has *dimension n* if there exist n distinct words $w_1, \ldots, w_n$ such that the contents of the store is always an element of $w_1^* \ldots w_n^*$, and has k *turns* if in every computation there are at most k changes from "pushing" to "popping" between times when the store is empty. For each pair, $n \geq 0$, $k \geq 0$, the class of nondeterministic pushdown store acceptors with dimension n and k turns specifies a proper subfamily of the family of context-free languages with many of the same properties as the entire family (Greibach, 1969). For example, the family of languages specified by one turn nondeterministic pushdown store acceptors with no bound on the dimension and which cannot "restart" with the store empty is the family of linear context-free languages. The family of languages specified by nondeterministic pushdown store acceptors with dimension one (and unrestricted turns) is the family of the "one-counter" languages, since dimension one implies that the contents of the pushdown store represent an integer in unary notation (so the pushdown store can only "add" and "subtract" in unary).

One may ask if there are any proof techniques which are predominant in the study of context-free languages. On the one hand, the answer is yes: As indicated above, many results can be obtained by studying the properties of derivation trees. On the other hand, the answer is no: The only known proofs of some results depend on complicated constructions of grammars of pushdown store acceptors. Recent research in the "metatheory" suggests that there may be unifying principles on which new proofs for these results can be based, and it is hoped that these will simplify the theory (see Section 1-10). This is particularly important if the results are to find application in other aspects of computer science.

1-7. EXTENSIONS OF CONTEXT-FREE LANGUAGES

As pointed out in Section 1-3, the generative power of context-free grammars is not strong enough to represent certain sets which model some important properties of powerful programming languages. Thus there have been several efforts to specify families of languages which extend the context-free languages but do not contain all the context-sensitive languages. There are two "natural" approaches to extending the context-free languages: by means of machines and by means of grammars. We first sketch the possibilities for extending the power of pushdown store acceptors and then consider extending the power of context-free grammars.

Recall that a pushdown store acceptor (as defined in Section 1-2) has an input tape which is read from left to right (i.e., a "one-way" input tape), finite-state control, and a last-in, first-out auxiliary storage tape. There are two obvious ways of extending this notion. One can allow the input tape to be read in both directions during a computation and/or one can alter the tape of the auxiliary storage. If the input is read in both directions during a computation, then one says that the device has a "two-way" input tape. Clearly, the class of two-way pushdown store acceptors specifies a family of languages which contains all the context-free languages and is closed under intersection. (It is an open question whether every context-free language can be accepted by a deterministic two-way pushdown store acceptor.) However, the family of languages specified by two-way pushdown store acceptors has not been precisely characterized in terms of other devices. See Gray, Harrison, and Ibarra (1967), Aho, Hopcroft, and Ullman (1968), and Cook (1971a) for results on two-way pushdown store acceptors.

There are several ways of altering the type of auxiliary storage of a pushdown store acceptor. If the storage tape has the power of a Turing machine tape, then the resulting automaton is equivalent to a Turing machine. Thus one wishes to extend the power of the pushdown store while at the same time restricting the resulting storage tape to something less than a Turing tape. One way to do this is to allow the machine to read "below" the "top" of the pushdown store while allowing it to write and erase only at the "top" of the store just as with a pushdown store acceptor. Such a device is called a *stack automaton*. One-way nondeterministic stack automata specify a family of languages which properly contains the family of context-free languages (e.g., $\{ww \mid w \in \{a, b\}^*\}$ can be accepted by such a device) and which is a subfamily of the family of context-sensitive languages. Two-way nondeterministic stack automata specify a family of recursive languages which properly contains the context-sensitive languages.

Stack automata have been studied extensively and many variations have been proposed. One can choose between one-way or two-way input and between deterministic or nondeterministic control. Further, one can restrict the stack so that no part of it is ever erased (a "nonerasing" stack). In some cases the corresponding families of languages have been shown to be the same as those specified by Turing machines with restrictions on the amount of time or tape used in a computation. Stack automata were defined first by Ginsburg, Greibach, and Harrison (1967a, 1967b). Many of the results on the various types of stack automata were established in a series of papers by Hopcroft and Ullman; these are presented in a uniform manner in Chapter 13 of Hopcroft and Ullman (1969). Alternative specification by means of grammars is given in Harrison and Schkolnick (1971).

Another method of altering the auxiliary storage of a pushdown store acceptor is to allow more than one storage tape. Since a Turing machine tape can be simulated by two pushdown stores, this is not an appropriate alternative unless one places a bound on some aspect of the computing process, for example by bounding the number of steps in the computation as a function of the length of the input. Various classes are defined by allowing two or more storage tapes and by bounding the amount of time allowed for the computation. See Book and Greibach (1970) and Book, Greibach, and Wegbreit (1970) for a summary of the results on these classes.

To extend the family of context-free languages by extending the power of context-free grammars, there are two possible approaches. One is to allow the use of context and thus obtain all context-sensitive languages. Some properties of context-sensitive grammars are discussed in Section 1-8 and we do not consider these grammars here. The other approach is to place restrictions on how rules can be applied. This has been done in several different ways in the form of matrix grammars (Abraham, 1965), indexed grammars (Aho, 1968, 1969), macro grammars (Fischer, 1968), programmed grammars (Rosenkrantz, 1969), scattered-context grammars (Greibach and Hopcroft, 1969), and property grammars (Stearns and Lewis, 1969).

In each of these cases either the rules are a variation of context-free or context-sensitive rules or there are restrictions on how the rules can be applied. For example, a scattered-context grammar $G = (N, \Sigma, P, S)$ has context-free rules and "scattered context rules," rules of the form

$$(Z_1, \ldots, Z_n) \longrightarrow (\gamma_1, \ldots, \gamma_n)$$

where each $Z_i \in N$ and $\gamma_i \neq e$. If $\theta = \delta_1 Z_1 \delta_2 Z_2 \ldots \delta_n Z_n \delta_{n+1}$, each $\delta_i \in$ $(N \cup \Sigma)^*$, then $(Z_1, \ldots, Z_n) \rightarrow (\gamma_1, \ldots, \gamma_n)$ can be applied to θ to obtain $\psi = \delta_1 \gamma_1 \delta_2 \gamma_2 \ldots \delta_n \gamma_n \delta_{n+1}$. Thus the context can be "scattered" through the strings to which the rule is applied. In a matrix grammar, $G = (N, \Sigma, P, S, M)$, (N, Σ, P, S) is a context-free grammar and M is a finite set of finite sequences of rules in P. To apply $(r_1, \ldots, r_t) \in M$ to a string $\theta \in (N \cup \Sigma)^*$, one must match each $r_1, \ldots, r_t$ to $\theta_1, \ldots, \theta_t$ where $\theta_1 = \theta$, and θ_{i+1} is the result of applying r_i to the string θ_i at the left-most possible place. The matrix rule $(r_1, \ldots, r_t)$ can be applied if and only if each r_i can be applied to the appropriate θ_i.

Some of these grammars have been compared and placed in an overall framework (Salomaa, 1969, 1970), and variations are possible. Possibly the most important classes are the indexed grammars and the macro grammars, since they generalize certain "duplicate" and "substitute" operations on trees and show that the study of "functionals" on both derivation trees and sentential forms yields many results on the generative process. From one viewpoint the indexed languages are the natural "first extension" of the context-free languages (Greibach, 1970). See Rounds (1970) for a treatment of these languages by means of trees.

Finally, let us note that it is possible to specify context-free languages by means of formal power series. This leads to a formal algebraic view of languages which again depends on derivation trees. For an explanation of the specification of context-free languages by formal power series, see Chomsky and Schutzenberger (1963) and Gross and Lentin (1970). An algebraic approach to certain aspects of language theory is presented in Eilenberg and Wright (1967) and Mezei and Wright (1967). See Thatcher's article in this book for an overview.

1-8. CONTEXT-SENSITIVE GRAMMARS AND LANGUAGES

We have sketched some of the important results on the family of context-free languages and its extensions (Sections 5 and 6), but have not considered the family of context-sensitive languages. From the viewpoint of phrase-structure grammars, this family is the first generalization of the context-free languages, but the specification of languages by means of context-sensitive grammars is not well understood. In this section we sketch some of the results and questions on context-sensitive grammars and languages.

How does the use of context allow a context-sensitive grammar to generate a non-context-free language; i.e., what does context do for you? If one is constructing a context-sensitive grammar to generate some given non-context-free language, often one proceeds as if context can be used to "store and transmit information." Thus one builds rules so that in derivations "messages" are transmitted along a string. Sometimes this effect is achieved by building a grammar which imitates the action of a linear bounded automaton. Although these notions have not been formalized, they do provide an intuitive "handle" for studying some questions and for gaining perspective on some results concerning context-sensitive grammars and languages. Here we consider two types of results: the various restrictions on context-sensitive rules which do not force the language generated to be context-free and those that do.

If $G = (N, \Sigma, P, S)$ is a rewriting system such that $\rho \rightarrow \theta \in R$ implies $|\rho| \leq |\theta|$, then $L(G)$ is context-sensitive. Thus one may consider possibilities for "normal forms" for context-sensitive grammars (just as we have Chomsky normal form and Greibach normal form for context-free grammars). The best known normal form was introduced by Kuroda (1964): For every context-sensitive grammar G_1, one can construct a grammar $G_2 = (N, \Sigma, P, S)$ such that $L(G_2) = L(G_1)$ and every rule in P is of one of the forms:

$$\left.\begin{array}{l} A \rightarrow BC \\ AB \rightarrow CB \\ AB \rightarrow AC \\ A \rightarrow B \\ A \rightarrow a \end{array}\right\} A, B, C \in N, \quad a \in \Sigma.$$

The restriction on the form of the rules of a context-sensitive grammar prevents the empty word from being generated, although this restriction is usually altered so that the empty word can be generated but no other "erasing" can take place in a derivation. An amount of erasing which is "linear" with respect to the length of the terminal string generated preserves context sensitivity (Ginsburg and Greibach, 1966a), but a "polynomial" amount of erasing may not (Book and Wegbreit, 1971). The least upper bound for such "limited use" of erasing is not known.

If one considers those context-sensitive grammars which allow only context-free rules to be applied first and then only length-preserving non-context-free rules, one still can generate all the context-sensitive languages. However, if one considers those context-sensitive grammars such that each rule is either length-increasing or generates a terminal symbol, then the family $\mathfrak{L}$ of languages generated has the following properties (Book, 1971):

1. If L is a context-free language such that $e \notin L$, then $L \in \mathfrak{L}$.

2. For every recursively enumerable set L_1, there exists $L_2 \in \mathfrak{L}$ and a homomorphism h such that $h(L_2) = L_1$. Hence, $\mathfrak{L}$ contains some non-context-free languages.

3. $\mathcal{L}$ is a proper subfamily of the context-sensitive languages, in particular $\{wcw^Rcw \mid w \in \{a, b\}^*\} \notin \mathcal{L}$.

Condition 2 implies that a grammar of this form must have some "message-sending capacity," but the proof of 2 depends on the grammar also generating some "padding," which is eventually erased by the homomorphism. On the other hand, condition 3 shows that the power to "send messages" is quite restricted.

One effect of context is the ability to achieve a permutation of symbols; that is, using context-sensitive rules one can obtain $AB \overset{*}{\Rightarrow} BA$. It is natural to ask if, in fact, context-sensitive rules do more than this (Chomsky, 1963). It has been shown that if G is a context-sensitive grammar having only context-free rules and rules of the form $AB \rightarrow BA$, then $L(G)$ is infinite if and only if $L(G)$ has an infinite context-free subset (Sillars, 1968). For example, $\{a^n b^n c^n \mid n \geq 1\}$ is a context-sensitive but non-context-free language which cannot be generated by such a grammar. Thus, to obtain all the context-sensitive languages, one must have more than just the power to perform permutations.

Any grammar has two specific context-free languages associated with it, languages which come from considering the structure of derivations. In an arbitrary grammar or rewriting system $G = (N, \Sigma, P, S)$, a derivation $\psi_0 \Rightarrow \psi_1 \Rightarrow \cdots \Rightarrow \psi_n$ is a *left-to-right* derivation if for each $i = 1, \ldots, n$, there are strings $\alpha \in \Sigma^*$, $\beta \in (N \cup \Sigma)^*$, and a rule $\rho \rightarrow \theta \in P$ such that $\psi_{i-1} = \alpha\rho\beta$ and $\psi_i = \alpha\theta\beta$—that is, at each step the rewriting rule is applied at the leftmost possible position in the string. The set of terminal strings obtained from the initial symbol by left-to-right derivations is a context-free subset of $L(G)$ (Evey, 1963; Matthews, 1964). A derivation $\psi_0 \Rightarrow \psi_1 \Rightarrow \cdots \Rightarrow \psi_n$ is a *two-way* derivation if for each $i = 1, \ldots, n$, there are strings α, β and a rule $\rho \rightarrow \theta \in P$ such that $\psi_{i-1} = \alpha\rho\beta$, $\psi_i = \alpha\theta\beta$, and either $\alpha \in \Sigma^*$ or $\beta \in \Sigma^*$—that is, at each step the rewriting rule is applied at either the leftmost or the rightmost possible position in the string. The set of terminal strings obtained from the initial symbol by two-way derivations is a context-free subset of $L(G)$ (Matthews, 1967).

If one places constraints on the form of the rules of a context-sensitive grammar such that the language generated can be obtained by left-to-right derivations or two-way derivations (possibly with bounded "lookahead"), then the language is context-free. This is the technique used to show that if $G = (N, \Sigma, P, S)$ is a grammar such that every non-context-free rule is of the form $\alpha A\beta \rightarrow \alpha\gamma\beta$, where $\alpha \in \Sigma^*$, $\beta \in (N \cup \Sigma)^*$, and $|\alpha| \geq |\beta|$, then $L(G)$ is context-free (Book, 1972a). In this case the fact that one can restrict attention to left-to-right derivations comes from noting that the restriction on context allows "messages" to be "transmitted" by the context only a bounded distance.

"Barriers" erected in order to prevent "messages" from being "transmitted" often force a grammar to generate only a context-free language. In particular, if one considers a grammar $G = (N, \Sigma, P, S)$ such that each rule in P is of the form $\rho \rightarrow \theta$, where $\rho \in N^*$ and $\theta \in (N \cup \Sigma)^*\Sigma(N \cup \Sigma)^*$, then $L(G)$ is context-free (Ginsburg and Greibach, 1966a). Here the fact that terminal symbols cannot be used as part of context (since $\rho \in N^*$) and a new terminal symbol is generated at each step (since θ has at least one terminal) forces the erection of a new "barrier" at each step so that the "message-sending" capacity is very limited.

If one studies the proofs of the results cited above, one concludes that a context-sensitive grammar generates a non-context-free language only if an infinite number of strings in the language are generated by derivations which transform symbols arbitrarily far from either the leftmost or rightmost nonterminal symbol and which have arbitrarily many steps which "interact" in some way. What is needed is a formalization of the notion of "message sending" and of "barrier" in order to prove the appropriate results. It is hoped that such results would lead to a better understanding of the use of context.

The structure of derivations in grammars has been studied from several viewpoints; in particular, see Gladkii (1964), Griffiths (1968), and Book (1971, 1973). Simple proofs of the results on conditions forcing a context-sensitive grammar to generate only a context-free language are given in Baker (1973).

1-9. COMPLEXITY CLASSES OF FORMAL LANGUAGES

As suggested in previous sections, there are many types of automata that appear in the literature. The input tape may be one-way or two-way, there may be one or more auxiliary storage tapes of the same or of different types, and the operation may be deterministic or nondeterministic. The types of auxiliary storage range from pushdown stores of dimension 1 (i.e., counters) to full-fledged Turing tapes with "instant erase" or "tab" operations. Some classes of automata are studied in order to model certain data structures or aspects of the computing process, others are studied to extend or restrict classes already studied, and still others are studied in order to complete certain schemes which classify power of computation (i.e., to answer the mathematically "natural" questions). For example, a stack is an extension and a counter is a restriction of a pushdown store. It is then "natural" to investigate a "stack counter" (i.e., a stack of dimension 1).

Another parameter used in classifying automata is the restriction of some resource in the computation process. The most familiar examples are bounds on the running time (i.e., number of steps in a computation) and on the size of the storage (i.e., number of auxiliary tape squares visited in a computation). Thus one may consider any class of devices and partition this class according to bounds on running time or storage. Doing this leads to an interesting and important set of questions which are natural for the computer scientist (or applied mathematician) to ask since they concern questions of efficiency of resource allocation in the computation process and of complexity of representation and specification.

We phrase these questions in terms of multitape Turing acceptors: automata with an input tape and some finite number of auxiliary storage tapes each having the power of a Turing tape. This model was presented formally by Hartmanis and Stearns (1965). For any "nice" function f, a multitape Turing acceptor M *operates within time-bound f (tape-bound f)* if for any input string w accepted by M, any accepting computation of M on w has at most $f(|w|)$ steps [respectively, visits at most $f(|w|)$ tape squares on any one of its tapes].

1. For any function f, is it the case that for every n there is a language accepted by a machine with $n + 1$ tapes which operates within time bound f but is not accepted by any machine with n tapes which operates within time bound f? That is, with a given time bound, do you gain power by adding tapes? For the case of deterministic machines, there are only a few results. It is known that for the case of real time $[f(x) = x]$, two tapes are "better" than one (Rabin, 1963). Also, the power gained cannot be too great since all such languages can be accepted by one tape machine which operates within time bound $g(x) = (f(x))^2$ (Hartmanis and Stearns, 1965). However, for nondeterministic machines it is known that two tapes will always be enough, but it is not known whether two storage tapes (as opposed to one) are ever needed (Book and Greibach, 1970).

2. For any function f, if L is accepted by a nondeterministic Turing machine which operates within time bound f, how much time is needed for a deterministic machine to accept L? It is easy to see that for any given nondeterministic machine one can find a deterministic machine and a constant k such that the new machine accepts the same language and operates within time bound $g(x) = k^{f(x)}$. There are special cases which yield tighter bounds [e.g., every context-free language can be accepted by a nondeterministic pushdown store acceptor in real time and by a deterministic multitape Turing machine within time bound $f(x) = x^3$], but no better results are known for the general case.

3. Question 2 can be altered by considering tape bounds. In this case it is known that if $f(x) \geq \log x$ is a "nice" function, then a language accepted by a nondeterministic Turing machine which operates within tape bound f is accepted by a deterministic Turing machine which operates within tape bound $g(x) = (f(x))^2$ (Savitch, 1970). One of the best known open problems con-

cerns the case $f(x) = x$. In this case the Turing machines are equivalent to linear bounded automata, and the family of languages accepted by non-deterministic linear bounded automata is the family of context-sensitive languages. The question of whether every context-sensitive language can be accepted by a deterministic linear bounded automata is known as "the LBA problem."

4. A machine which operates within time bound f certainly operates within tape bound f. But can one say anything stronger? In general nothing is known about this, although there are some results for special cases (Hopcroft and Ullman, 1968b). The converse relation is also of interest. It is known that a language accepted by a nondeterministic machine operating within tape bound $f(x) \geq \log x$ can be accepted by a deterministic machine operating within time bound $g(x) = k^{f(x)}$ for some $k > 1$, but it is not known if these classes are the same (Cook, 1971b). A particularly interesting open question is whether a machine operating in polynomial time accepts only a context-sensitive language (Book, 1972b).

In general, questions such as those in 2 and 3 are referred to as questions of "deterministic simulation of nondeterministic machines" and those in 4 as questions of "time–space tradeoffs." Such questions can be asked for arbitrary measures of "complexity" and for arbitrary bounding functions. However, the interest for formal language theory seems to center around the measures discussed above and on bounding functions which are "small." This stems from the fact that many of the automata theoretic devices studied specify families of languages which can be characterized by means of these measures and "small" functions.

Several techniques are commonly used in investigating time–space trade-offs and deterministic simulation of nondeterministic machines. The ability to simulate involves both being able to determine whether an instantaneous description could either succeed or precede another in some computation, and also being able to determine whether the contents of auxiliary storage could be altered at a later step of the computation. Also, to show that two classes are different, the ability to enumerate and diagonalize is needed. These techniques are nicely illustrated in the work of Hopcroft and Ullman on stack automata. See Hopcroft and Ullman (1969), particularly Chapter 13, for a unified treatment of results on stack automata using these techniques.

Other specifications of languages have been studied in terms of measures on "complexity." For example, one may consider the "size" of a grammar needed to generate a language (Snively, 1970) or the "time" needed for a grammar to generate a language (Book, 1971). The notion of "syntactic" complexity has not been formally defined in such a way as to determine the appropriate measure, and it is not clear whether syntactic complexity and computational complexity are related.

Many other questions involving measures of computational complexity are of interest for formal language theorists. It is not known how to classify languages as sets of numbers, although there are some results which assert that certain sets cannot be regular (Minsky and Papert, 1966). Also, it is not known how to classify families of languages in terms of sets of subrecursive predicates, although there are some results which show that certain families are contained in certain classes of predicates (Jones, 1969; Ritchie, 1963).

In considering questions of computational complexity of formal languages, one may be inclined to dismiss the case of nondeterministic machines since any "real" computational process must be deterministic. However, doing this necessarily limits the scope of one's results, since there are some important families of languages for which the only known specifications are essentially nondeterministic. For example, if one sees that derivations in phrase-structure grammars are essentially nondeterministic, since choice of rules to be applied is involved, and that constructions used in proofs of closure under homomorphic mappings for one-way devices often require nondeterminism, one notes that all the specifications for the context-free languages given in Sections 1-2 and 1-6 imply a nondeterministic mechanism. Thus not only does nondeterminism offer a simplicity of representation but it also appears to be necessary. This point is developed by Cook (1971c), Karp (1972), and Book (1972b).

For a survey of automata-based complexity see Hartmanis and Stearns (1969). The overview by Borodin in this book shows that many of the questions considered here are only special cases of much more general questions of computational complexity, and Borodin discusses many of the techniques used to compare different classes.

1-10. METATHEORY

In the study of automata and formal languages, many types of acceptors have been defined. Usually there are three components: an input tape, which may be one-way or two-way; a finite-state control; and some type of auxiliary storage. Further, the operation may be deterministic or nondeterministic, and some bound may be placed on the amount of time or storage (or other measure) used in a computation. Thus one may define an arbitrarily large number of classes of acceptors and hence an arbitrarily large number of families of languages. To understand any of the resulting collection of results, one must find a general framework and develop a metatheory.

To a limited extent a metatheory has been developed. Simultaneously, and independently, Hopcroft and Ullman (1967) developed the theory of "balloon automata" and "closed classes of balloon automata" and Ginsburg and Greibach (1969) developed the theory of "abstract families of languages" and "abstract families of acceptors." Both approaches consider an abstract notion of machine with three components: input, finite-state control, and auxiliary storage (the "balloon"). An acceptor uses that information from the auxiliary storage given to it by a "storage information" function and transforms storage in each step in a computation by means of a "storage transformation" function. By classifying the set of "storage symbols," the set of "instructions," the storage information function, and the storage transformation function, a "storage schema" is determined. Based on a given storage schema, one may then specify the class of acceptors by choosing between one-way or two-way input and by choosing between deterministic and nondeterministic operations. The transitions of each acceptor depend on the input, the state of the control, and the information obtained from the storage. While certain restrictions are placed on the definitions of storage information function, storage transformation function, and the transition function of an acceptor, many classes of acceptors studied in the literature can be represented in this way. Properties of the abstract classes of acceptors can be used to establish some of the properties of the families of languages specified by realizations of these classes, and in so doing abstract classes of languages are studied.

There have been only a few papers investigating balloon automata, but there are many papers on abstract families of acceptors (AFA) and the corresponding classes of languages. The definition of AFA involves storage schema but restricts attention to acceptors which read their input only one way and operate nondeterministically. For example, the class of one-way pushdown store acceptors is an AFA and the class of two-way pushdown store acceptors is not an AFA.

The formal definition of AFA is cumbersome, but AFA have a simple algebraic structure which often is obscured by the notation used to define the concept. On the other hand, the class of languages corresponding to AFA can be defined simply. An *abstract family of languages* (AFL) is a nonempty family containing a nonempty language and closed under union, concatenation, Kleene $*$, intersection with regular sets, homomorphic mappings such that $h(w) = e$ implies $w = e$, and inverse homomorphism. Each family of the Chomsky hierarchy is an AFL, as are the family of recursive sets, each family associated with bounded turn and dimension pushdown store acceptors (see Section 1-6), the family of languages accepted by one-way (or two-way) nondeterministic stack automata, and many families defined by time- or tape-bounded multitape Turing machines. Many families of languages are AFLs even though we know of no "natural" AFA corresponding to these families [e.g., the families of languages generated in linear time by context-sensitive grammars (Book, 1971)]. However, for every AFL there is an AFA whose acceptors specify precisely the languages in that AFL. Also, for any AFA the acceptors specify a class of languages which form an AFL.

By studying AFLs and AFA one obtains certain results about the power of AFLs and AFA—hence certain results about any family of languages which is an AFL and any family of acceptors which is an AFA. For example, every AFL contains every regular set. A particularly important class of AFLs are those which have a single language as "generator." Thus an AFL is *principal with generator L* if it is the smallest AFL containing L, so that (in some sense) L is "universal" for this AFL (Ginsburg and Greibach, 1970). Each family in the Chomsky hierarchy is a principal AFL, but the family of recursive sets is not. (Notice that the Chomsky–Schutzenberger theorem noted in Section 1-6 shows that D_2 is a generator of the family of context-free languages, since every context-free language is obtained from D_2 by use of AFL operations.)

Although the original goal of developing a metatheory was to give structure to the theory and to provide a basis for order and comparison, much of the research has been focused on the metatheory itself. To some extent this is natural since the metatheory needs body—and this is provided by examples and counterexamples which are necessary to delineate and sharpen comparisons. However, only a few papers focus on specific families of languages and use the theory of AFA and AFL to obtain new information about these families. One such paper by Greibach (1970) generalizes results on substitution for subfamilies of the family of context-free languages and shows that these results are simply a special case of properties of a very general type of substitution. This result is very important in developing an "algebraic theory of languages."

Another example is of a different type. In Book and Greibach (1970) it is shown that a nondeterministic multitape Turing acceptor which operates in real time need have only two auxiliary storage tapes, and that a language is accepted by a nondeterministic multitape Turing operating in real time if and only if it is of the form $h(L_1 \cap L_2 \cap L_3)$, where each L_i is context-free and h is a homomorphism with the property that $h(w) = e$ implies that $w = e$. These are not results of AFL theory but were not established until a method of representation used in AFL theory was discovered.

Knowledge of interrelations between closure properties and the closure properties of specific families of languages may aid in comparing these families. An example of this is found in Book (1972b).

In the definition of AFA, the class of acceptors have one-way input and are nondeterministic. These two restrictions limit the usefulness of this model since many devices studied in the literature either have two-way input or are deterministic (or both). In order to classify languages accepted by deterministic devices, "abstract families of deterministic acceptors" and "abstract families of deterministic languages" have been introduced (Chandler, 1969), and the families of languages corresponding to closed classes of two-way deterministic balloon automata have been characterized in terms of closure operations (Aho and Ullman, 1970).

Just as the value of a formal theory depends to some extent on how well it reflects the "real-world" objects it models, the value of a metatheory depends on how well it structures the theory it models. There will be much work in metatheory in the future (in particular, developing an algebraic approach), and it is hoped that some researchers will focus on the use of the metatheory to order the many classes of automata and formal languages already in the literature.

1-11. FUTURE RESEARCH

As indicated in the preceding sections, there are various flavors to the specific questions studied in formal language theory. On the one hand, the models studied should accurately reflect the properties of the "real" languages under consideration (e.g., programming languages). The results of the theory should yield insight into specific problems such as parsing and translating. On the other hand, the models should describe the structural properties which underlie the properties of the real languages; i.e., a formal theory should evolve. Thus one wishes the theory to speak to specific questions concerning the languages studied while having a richness of structure which goes beyond an ad hoc collection of "tricks."† In taking an overview of the subject or in pursuing specific lines of development, it is necessary to consider not only the motivating questions from the "real world" but also the attempt to develop a mathematical theory. (In doing this it is necessary to keep in mind one's own goals: Do you want to solve "real-world" problems, or do you want to do the "pure mathematics" of the subject? It may not be possible to do both simultaneously.)

In the preceding sections some of the central results and motivating questions of formal language theory have been sketched (and many topics have been omitted). Future research will continue in this area, many of the results sketched here will be refined, and some of the open questions will be resolved. However, it is not clear which topics will dominate the theory in the next 10 years. Let us conclude by mentioning three areas which will receive a good deal of attention.

One area not covered in this paper is the study of two-dimensional languages. Part of the motivation for studying such languages is the desire for mechanical recognition of types of patterns, such as handwritten characters and spark film patterns. Similarly, one wishes to generate two-dimensional

---

†In most areas of the mathematical sciences, there comes a time when so much mathematical machinery has been developed that one can view the subject as part of mathematics and ignore the original motivation. Thus one may study the "pure mathematics" of structures which were developed in order to model phenomena in the "real world." This has been an important factor in the development of automata and formal language theory. In Arbib (1969), automata theory is described as the "pure mathematics of computer science."

patterns for graphical display. Some aspects of the work accomplished so far are of an engineering nature; others suggest methods for developing a formal theory of such languages [see Miller and Shaw (1968) and Montanari (1970)]. There are elements of a theory of two-dimensional languages in recent work on trees and tree-manipulating systems and in work on mechanical transformations on graphs. It is hoped that the development of an "automata and formal language theory" of objects with data more "structured" than strings will provide a basis for two-dimensional languages as well as to aid in studying questions of trees and graphs. For a discussion of this work on two-dimensional languages, see Rosenfeld (1969a, 1969b).

A promising area for research in formal languages is that relating to the study of trees and tree-manipulating systems. In order to represent linguistic algorithms that manipulate structural descriptions and to model devices which transform languages and their structural descriptions, various aspects of tree transducers have been studied. On the one hand, tree transducers and tree automata provide a simple model for processes such as the assignment of code by a compiler; on the other hand, they have a rich algebraic structure which allows one to develop a mathematical theory of a quite general nature. Thus the study of trees and tree-manipulating systems may provide both usable models for the solution of practical problems and a rich mathematical theory which accurately reflects many aspects of translation and which is more adequate than models which consider only strings. See Thatcher's article for a survey of this field and Rosen (1971) for a specific proposal on the development of a theory of translation.

Another important topic in theoretical computer science is the study of the semantics of programs and programming languages. In dealing with problems of equivalence of programs and of translating from one program schema to another, many techniques common to automata and formal language theory are useful. Results from formal language theory have been used in attempts to characterize the power of a class of schemata. It is hoped that more applications of results from formal language theory will be made in this area since in many cases it is only a matter of rephrasing such results in new terms. For a survey of this field, see Manna's article, and for examples of how formal language theory can be used in this area, see Garland and Luckham (1971), Constable and Gries (1971), and Rosen (1972).

Finally, note that there are many questions on languages and their specifications which remain to be answered, from finding the best possible parsing algorithms to resolving the many open questions involving automata-based complexity. At this time it appears that less emphasis will be given to these areas, but a new result could draw many researchers back to these questions. The decision as to whether formal language theory—or the parts of it one wishes to study—is part of computer science or part of mathematics will govern the emphasis of many researchers.

2 COMPUTATIONAL COMPLEXITY: THEORY AND PRACTICE

Allan Borodin
Department of Computer Science
University of Toronto

2-1. INTRODUCTION

Computational complexity—rarely has an area been blessed with such an appealing name. In fact, the name becomes something of a license, encouraging one to incorporate many diverse areas of research. The origins of computational complexity as an identifiable area of study can perhaps be traced to a few significant papers in the early 1960's. Indeed, Hartmanis and Hopcroft (1971) in their overview paper have identified three such papers (Rabin, 1960; Cobham, 1964; Hartmanis and Stearns, 1965).

However, the concern for efficient algorithms can hardly be considered a recent phenomenon. In this sense, the history of computational complexity is coincident with the concept of "algorithm." The remarkable work of Knuth (1968, 1969) in studying this history and development is well known to all computer scientists, and we shall not attempt a "poor man's version."

It seems fair to say that considerations of complexity play a significant role in almost all areas of computer science, especially in the more formal areas, such as formal languages, numerical analysis, graph theory, switching theory, and pattern recognition. Each of these areas has its own set of well-motivated issues and problems, and it would be presumptuous and hopeless to attempt a survey of these issues. To be sure, we will rely on examples from these areas (especially formal languages), but our main goal is to present a more restricted study of "the nature of complexity."

Rather than attempt an exact definition of our interests, consider the following classification of computational complexity into subareas.

1. Development of a theory of complexity in order to make precise and to understand better the implications of concepts such as the "difficulty" of computing a function.

2. Study of models of computation with respect to specific measures and complexity-related properties, hierarchies, tradeoffs, and simulations.

3. Analysis of the complexity of specific problems, or classes of problems, with respect to specific models of computation. More precisely, our interest in this subarea is motivated by the desire to know why certain problems have or appear to have a certain "difficulty."

The above categories are, of course, somewhat arbitrary, and no doubt many results do not lend themselves readily to this classification. Indeed, one of our main purposes is to show just how related are the many seemingly diverse aspects of computational complexity. For historical reasons (and for reasons of personal preference), most remarks will be phrased in terms of function computation or set (language) recognition. With regard to Sections 2-2 and 2-3, the remarks are usually equally appropriate to other types of computation (e.g., sequence generation and translation). This should not be too surprising since these sections mostly concern models of computation and measures of complexity, rather than what is being computed. The major sections that follow correspond to the subareas that have been introduced. For the most part, the sections may be read independently, although this seems to defeat the intended unifying objective of the chapter. We shall omit formal proofs but will sketch the arguments for some of the results. Finally, notation will be introduced sparingly and only as it becomes necessary.

2-2. THEORY OF COMPLEXITY

In the development of any theory, the main task is to define and make precise intuitive concepts, and then to explore the implications, relations, and limitations of those concepts. The theory of recursive functions and effective computability has provided a formal charcterization for concepts such as "algorithm" and "computable." Moreover, there is substantial evidence that these characterizations are "correct." One might argue, however, that such a theory relates only to ideal computation and not to "practical computation." And thus the question, "Is problem A algorithmically solvable?" is replaced by the question, "How difficult is it to solve problem A?".

A theory of complexity, then, must first define the concept of difficulty (efficiency, complexity). Suppose that we are able to define a notion of "complexity of an algorithm." One can then discuss the difficulty of a given problem (e.g., computing a function) by the existence or absence of an efficient (relative to the measure of complexity) algorithm for that problem. Two general types of measures of complexity may be distinguished.

Static or Definitional Measures

A standard example is the *size* of a program or algorithm. That is, if an algorithm is thought of syntactically as a string of symbols over a finite alphabet (which has semantic meaning perhaps in the form of statements), how many symbols are needed to specify the algorithm? According to this criterion, functions requiring large programs are considered difficult. Similarly, we can speak about the size of a generative grammar, and measure the difficulty of a language by the size of grammar required to generate the language.† But size is not the only static measure which relates to our intuitive feelings about definitional complexity. Algorithms and other "definitional constructs" also seem to exhibit a *structural* complexity. For example, we classify grammars according to the types of productions that appear and we consider programs without loops to be simpler than those with loops. In contrast to the size measure, it is not always clear which structures are to be considered simple and which more complex.

Dynamic Measures

A dynamic measure describes the behavior of the computations of an algorithm, a computation being the execution of an algorithm when applied to an input (or in considering grammars, when "applied" to generate a particular string). The most natural example is the number of instructions executed in a computation. For a given input, an algorithm either does not terminate, or it terminates having executed a certain number of instruction steps. Thus each algorithm induces a function (call it the *run-time function*) which describes, as a function of the input, the dynamic behavior of the algorithm. In the same way, the number of memory cells used in a computation is another dynamic measure that may be associated with an algorithm. With respect to grammars, we might consider the number of applications of production rules to produce a string of a specified length (if such a string exists) as a dynamic measure of the grammar. In all cases, we can again measure the difficulty of a function or language in terms of the (dynamic) complexity of the algorithm or grammar required.

In pursuing our theory, we should like to define such complexity measures more precisely, and then study properties associated with these measures. For definiteness, let us concentrate in this section on algorithms for computing functions with domain and range N, the nonnegative integers. From a

---

†The reader may wish to note our informal use of "algorithm" to include generative grammars and other "definitional constructs."

theoretical point of view, this is not too restrictive, since computational procedures over other countable domains and ranges can be "coded" so as to satisfy the restriction to $\mathbb{N}$.† We shall discuss first dynamic measures and then the size measure. Following that, we will call attention to the relation between certain structural and dynamic measures. The section will then conclude with a discussion of some of the inadequacies of the present theory.

Before beginning our study of complexity measures, let us recall a "programming language model of computation" (Shepherdson and Sturgis, 1963; Elgot and Robinson, 1964; Minsky, 1967).

DEFINITION 1

Let $X_1, X_2, \ldots$ represent a set of registers, each capable of containing an arbitrary nonnegative integer. A *program* is a sequence of labeled or unlabeled statements where each statement is one of the following:

(1) $X_j \leftarrow op_i(X_{j_1}, \ldots, X_{j_i})$

where $\{op_i\}$ is a set of recursive arithmetic operations $\{+, \dot{-}, \ldots\}$‡

(2) **if** $pred_k(X_{j_1}, \ldots, X_{j_k})$ **then** s_1 **else** s_2

where $\{pred_k\}$ is a set of recursive predicates $\{=, \neq, \ldots\}$ and s_1, s_2 are statements (or subprograms)

(3) **go to** $\langle$label$\rangle$

(4) DO X_i — END

(5) IN, OUT, HALT

The only construct which may need some explanation is the DO X_i — END loop, which specifies that the statements within the loop are to be executed x_i times where x_i is the contents of register X_i. In particular, if $x_i = 0$, the statements are bypassed.

The following two programs for the same function, $X_2 \leftarrow 2X_1$, should illustrate the semantics. (Assume that noninput registers are initialized to 0.)

```
                                 IN    X₁
        IN    X₁                 X₃ ← X₁
        DO    X₁          test:  if X₃ = 0 then go to
        X₂ ← X₂ + 1                 done else X₃ ← X₃ ∸ 1
        X₂ ← X₂ + 1              X₂ ← X₂ + 1
        END                      X₂ ← X₂ + 1
        OUT   X₂                 go to test
        HALT              done:  OUT   X₂
                                 HALT
```

---

†Here we are only considering interpreted programs; for the concept of uninterpreted programs, see Chapter 3 in this volume.

‡$x \dot{-} y$ denotes proper subtraction, i.e., $x \dot{-} y = \begin{cases} x - y & \text{if } x \geq y \\ 0 & \text{otherwise.} \end{cases}$

We shall refer to the permissible programs as a *programming language*. We will say that a language is GR (for general recursive) if every partial recursive function can be expressed as a program in that language. Shepherdson and Sturgis (1963) have shown that the three-statement language

$$G_3 = [X_i \leftarrow X_j + 1, X_i \leftarrow X_j \div 1, \text{if } X_i \neq 0 \text{ then go to } \langle \text{label} \rangle]$$

is a GR language. Thus, extending these languages to include more operations, dynamic access capabilities (e.g., $X_{X_i} \leftarrow X_{X_j} + X_{X_k}$), recursive procedures, or more convenient control structures (e.g., DO-WHILE) will not increase the number-theoretic computing power.[†]

For future reference, then, we can choose a specific set of arithmetics and predicates, or if not stated otherwise, (general recursive) *algorithm* can simply be taken to mean a program written in a GR language. We may refer to a particular algorithm as P_i, the ith algorithm, and denote by ϕ_i the partial recursive (computable) function computed by P_i.

As previously mentioned, computational complexity emerged as an active research area in the early 1960's. One of the important developments was the study of the specific dynamic measures of time (Hartmanis and Stearns, 1965) and tape or memory space (Stearns, Hartmanis, and Lewis, 1965) with respect to Turing machine computations. Relative to these resources or measures of complexity, classes of functions can be defined by bounding (by a function of the input) *the amount of resource used in a computation*.[‡] Several results were obtained concerning properties of this classification scheme, as well as properties of the measures (some of which will be mentioned in the next section).

The similarity of results for the various dynamic measures leads one to ask which properties of resource-bounded classification hold for all models of computation and all dynamic measures. Let $\{P_i\}$ represent any "reasonable" class of algorithms capable of computing all the partial recursive functions.

Motivated by the work of Rabin (1960), Blum (1967a) introduced two axioms which characterize any dynamic measure with respect to a general recursive model of computation.

DEFINITION 2

Associate with each partial recursive function ϕ_i or algorithm P_i the *resource function* Φ_i satisfying the axioms

a. $\phi_i(x)$ is defined if and only if $\Phi_i(x)$ is defined. That is, the amount of

[†]Again, we are not considering program schemata where such extensions can increase the computing power.

[‡]These original papers concerned sequence generation and language recognition, and complexity was taken as a function of input or output length rather than input value. We shall have more to say about this in Section 2-3.

"resource" $\Phi_i(x)$ used by the ith algorithm on input x is defined if and only if the ith algorithm on input x terminates.

b. There exists a recursive predicate M:

$$M(i, x, m) \text{ is true iff } \Phi_i(x) \leq m$$

That is, there is an effective way to decide if an algorithm has expended m units of a resource.

For those who do not like this axiomatic approach, it is best to interpret $\Phi_i(x)$ as $\text{TIME}_i(x) = $ the number of instruction steps (statements) executed by the ith algorithm on input x. It should be apparent that $\text{TIME}_i(x)$ does satisfy the two axioms. Another "natural" measure is $\text{MEMORY}_i(x) = $ "units of memory" used in computation. For Turing machines, this is usually the number of tape cells, and for our register machine model, it could be the product of (number of registers used) and the (largest number occurring in any register). It is easy to see that $\text{MEMORY}_i(x)$ does not satisfy axiom a, since a computation can loop using only a finite amount of memory. We can avoid this minor problem, however, if we define $\text{MEMORY}_i(x)$ to be undefined whenever the computation does not halt. $\text{MEMORY}_i(x)$ will satisfy both axioms, since we can decide (by observing a finite number of instruction steps) if a computation, using only m units of memory, is in a loop.†

In a sense, the above modification ensures that a bound on the MEMORY resource implies a bound on the TIME resource. Conversely, it is obvious that a bound on TIME imposes a bound on the amount of memory used. In fact, the axioms ensure that this type of relationship exists between any two dynamic measures.

FACT 1
(*Blum, 1967a*)

Let Φ and $\hat{\Phi}$ denote any dynamic resources; then there is a computable function h: (for all algorithms i) (for all inputs $x \geq i$) $\Phi_i(x) \leq h(x, \hat{\Phi}_i(x))$ and $\hat{\Phi}_i(x) \leq h(x, \Phi_i(x))$.

Proof. Using the axioms, define a computable function

$$p(i, x, m) = \begin{cases} \Phi_i(x) + \hat{\Phi}_i(x) & \text{if either } \Phi_i(x) \leq m \text{ or } \hat{\Phi}_i(x) \leq m \\ 0 & \text{otherwise} \end{cases}$$

Note that axiom 1 ensures that $\Phi_i(x)$ is defined iff $\hat{\Phi}_i(x)$ is defined. It follows that $h(x, m) = \max_{i \leq x} p(i, x, m)$ satisfies the theorem.

†See Ausiello (1971) for an axiomatic treatment of this problem.

The reader may be understandably disappointed in this result. For example, the theorem will not shed any light on the "exact nature" of time–space tradeoffs. However, the result is important, since it does guarantee the existence of some relationship. Moreover, for the purposes of our theory, it often allows us to study general properties of a specific measure, knowing that these properties will apply to any dynamic measure.

Let us now continue along the lines introduced by Hartmanis and Stearns (1965). That is, we want to classify functions according to their (dynamic) computational complexity.

DEFINITION 3

Let Φ be any dynamic measure or resource. For every computable function t, define the resource-bounded class $R_t^\Phi = \{$computable functions $f\,|\,$there exists an algorithm i for computing f such that $\Phi_i(x) \leq t(x)$ for all but a finite number of inputs $x\}$.

We should explain the use of the "for almost all x" rather than "for all x" condition in the definition of R_t^Φ.

From a theoretical point of view, "for almost all" is consistent with concepts such as majorization (e.g., Ackerman's function majorizes the primitive recursive functions). Also, for many measures (including TIME) there would be no one class (i.e., bound t) which would contain all the constant functions, which in a theoretical sense can be considered the simplest set of functions. Moreover, for much of the existing work in computational complexity, we are only interested in "asymptotic behavior." For example, later we shall discuss those sets which are recognizable in polynomial time (that is, the bound on TIME can be any polynomial). Finally, for a measure such as TIME on a register machine, with some sort of random access or computed go-to instruction, we can trade dynamic computational complexity at a finite number of inputs for size by the use of a finite table.

One would expect that a sufficiently fast-growing function would not be in a given class R_t^Φ. Moreover, a diagonalization technique (Rabin, 1960; Blum, 1967a) yields the following:

THEOREM 1

For any Φ and computable t, there is a 0–1-valued function f such that if $\phi_i = f$ (the ith algorithm computes f), then $\Phi_i(x) > t(x)$ for almost all x, and thus f is not in R_t^Φ. The 0–1 condition says that there are sets which cannot be recognized within the bound t.

Sketch of Proof. Say that an index i has been "canceled" if f has been defined so that $f(x) \neq \phi_i(x)$ for some x. Define f so that every algorithm i for which $\Phi_i(x) \leq t(x)$ for infinitely many x eventually gets canceled.

It is natural to ask just how difficult a function f must be to satisfy the above theorem. The next theorem is best expressed in terms of the concept of honesty (Robbin, 1965; Meyer and Ritchie, 1968). Basically, the honesty of a function measures the difficulty of a function relative to its values.

DEFINITION 4

Let g be a computable function of two variables. A function f is g *honest with respect to* Φ if f is in R_t^Φ, where $t(x) = g(x, f(x))$.

For notational convenience, let $h \circ t(x)$ denote $h(x, t(x))$ or $h(t(x))$ if $t(x)$ is "known to be" $\geq b(x)$ for some monotone increasing function b. The following "trilogy" applies to all measures.

THEOREM 2

a. *Compression Theorem* (*Blum, 1967a*). For every g there is an h such that if t is g honest, there are 0–1-valued functions f in $R_{h \circ t}^\Phi$, but not in R_t^Φ. That is, if we know something about the honesty of the bound t, then we know how much t must be increased to get something new.

b. *Gap Theorem* (*Trachtenbrot, 1967; Borodin, 1969*). For every computable function h there is an increasing t such that $R_t^\Phi = R_{h \circ t}^\Phi$. That is, the honesty condition is essential in the compression theorem.

c. *Honesty Theorem* (*McCreight and Meyer, 1969*). There is a function g (uniform for Φ) such that for every t there is a g honest t' with $R_t^\Phi = R_{t'}^\Phi$. That is, bounds can be restricted to a set of reasonably honest functions while still inducing the same set of classes.

Sketch of Compression Theorem. To simplify the proof, assume that t is increasing. A closer look at Theorem 2 shows that it is possible to estimate the TIME to compute $f(x)$ in terms of the TIME to compute $t(0), t(1), \ldots,$ $t(x)$, which is (approximately) $\leq [\text{TIME for } t(x)]^2 \leq [g \circ t(x)]^2$. This estimation then yields a bound of $h \circ t$ to compute f. A judicious application of Fact 1 can be used to show that the result applies to all measures rather than just the TIME measure.

The proof of the gap theorem is rather straightforward; the proof of the honesty theorem is relatively sophisticated and is based on the "priority technique" of recursive-function theory.

The compression theorem is a hierarchy theorem applicable to all measures. Hierarchy theorems were first derived for the specific measures of TIME and TAPE with respect to Turing machine models. Constable (1969a) discusses the essential difference between the "upward diagonalization" of the compression theorem (how much to increase the bound to get something new) and the "downward diagonalization" employed in Hartmanis and

Stearns (1965) (how much to decrease the bound to get something less). In contrast to the compression theorem, downward diagonalization (in the strict sense) is not applicable to all measures. On the other hand, we shall see in Section 2-3 that downward diagonalization does provide a convenient means for establishing how "refined" the hierarchy is for a specific measure (i.e., how big h is in the compression theorem). We will review some of the specific hierarchy results in the next section.

The importance of the compression theorem, diagonalization, and specific hierarchy theorems should be emphasized. Many "natural" problems are obviously solvable within an exponential time bound but appear not to be computable within polynomial time. The *fundamental inadequacy of computational complexity* is the lack of techniques for *proving* that "natural" recognition problems† are not polynomially (or even linearly) time-computable. On the other hand, diagonalization and hierarchy theorems at least guarantee that such problems do exist. Indeed, recent work by Meyer, Stockmeyer, and others demonstrates that diagonalization provides a basis for proving that truth or validity in various decidable logical theories is extremely difficult (exponential and sometimes non-elementary) to decide.

One of the more "controversial" results from the theory of complexity is the speedup theorem.

THEOREM 3
(*Blum, 1967a*)

For any measure Φ, and for any "speedup function" r, there is a 0–1-valued function f with the property that any algorithm i for f has an "r speedup;" that is, there is another algorithm j for f such that $r \cdot \Phi_j(x) \leq \Phi_i(x)$ for almost all x.

Sketch of Proof. The speedup theorem has attracted enough attention to cause new proofs to appear (Meyer and Fischer, 1968; Hartmanis and Hopcroft, 1971). The idea is to find a "complexity sequence" of functions $t_0, t_1, \ldots$ with the property $r \circ t_{i+1} \leq t_i$. Then the basic diagonalization of Theorem 1 is modified so that in defining f, if $\phi_i - f$, then $\Phi_i(x) > t_i(x)$ for almost all x, but for every k there is an algorithm j for f such that $\Phi_j(x) \leq t_k(x)$ for almost all x.

The speedup theorem thus warns (in the same sense that undecidability results are warnings) that the concept of a "best program" is not well defined in the context of dynamic measures and general models of computation. The

---

†The emphasis on recognition (YES–NO) problems is natural from our point of view, since neither the value nor the number of possible outcomes can dominate the complexity.

theorem does not preclude the possiblitity that "most functions encountered in actual computing" do have best (or "nearly best") programs. It is worth noting that if a function can be "significantly sped up," then it is basically dishonest.

FACT 2

It is not difficult to show that for every Φ there is a function s such that for every algorithm i, $\phi_i(x) \leq s(x, \Phi_i(x))$ for almost all x. That is, the value of a function cannot be much bigger (although it can be much smaller) than its complexity. If f is g honest, then there is an algorithm j for f such that $\Phi_j \leq g \circ \phi_j$. On the other hand, every algorithm j for f must satisfy $s^{-1} \circ \phi_j \leq \Phi_j$. Consequently, the amount of speedup is restricted.

Later in this section we shall discuss one more result (the union theorem) relating to the axiomatic study of dynamic measures. However, the few results discussed hardly do justice to the interest this area has attracted. We should at least mention the following significant works: Young (1968) in "introducing the priority argument to complexity theory," extensions of the gap (Constable, 1969b) and speedup (Meyer and Fischer, 1968) theorems to recursive operators, decision problems for complexity classes and index classes and enumeration of complexity classes (Landweber and Robertson, 1970; Lewis, 1970), building transfinite hierarchies of functions via the union and honesty theorems (Bass and Young, 1970), the use of complexity to study subrecursive degrees (Machtey, 1971), and efforts to axiomatize a theory of complexity for operators or program schema (Symes, 1971).

Size Measures

We will continue to use algorithms for computing functions as a basic framework for discussion. The concept of size, however, is very "stable" and applies to any "definitional scheme" (i.e., grammars, sequence generators, etc.). In fact, many of the theoretical considerations concerning size evolve from Kolmogorov's (1964) "size approach" for defining "random sequences."

It is beyond our purpose to review the various approaches concerning randomness, but suffice it to say that in Kolmogorov and related works (Chaitin, 1966; Loveland, 1969), a finite sequence is called random if its shortest description (in terms of a program for generating the sequence) is not much shorter than the sequence itself. An infinite sequence is called random if infinitely many of its initial segments are random. An infinite set is called random if its characteristic sequence is random. An easy but basic property is that "most" sequences (either finite or infinite) are random.

Blum (1967b) abstracts the important properties of any size measure as follows:

DEFINITION 5

A computable function s: {programs} $\rightarrow$ $\aleph$ is a *size measure* if there are only finitely many programs of a given size k and, moreover, all programs of size k can be effectively determined.

Following standard notation, let $|i|$ denote the size of program i. One example of size is the number of symbols used to express a program, and another is the number of statements in the program (if there is a bound on the size of any statement). These two measures are "related," and indeed, as a direct consequence of the definition, we can show that:

FACT 3

Given any two size measures $||_{s_1}$ and $||_{s_2}$, there is a computable function r such that for all i, $|i|_{s_1} \leq r|i|_{s_2}$ and $|i|_{s_2} \leq r|i|_{s_1}$.

Thus, as for dynamic measures, we can use properties concerning a specific size measure to deduce general properties. Let us illustrate the significance of the remarks concerning randomness with an example due to J. Malitz.

FACT 4

Let $|i|$ be the number of statements of program i. Let $f_n(x) = 2^{2^{\cdot^{\cdot^{\cdot 2^x}}}}$. Then there are infinitely many j such that the shortest program for f_j is bigger than the shortest program for f_{j+1}, and moreover there is an $n > j$ such that the shortest program for f_n is "much" smaller than the shortest program for f_j.

Sketch of Proof. The idea is that the use of the set of functions $\{f_n\}$ is somewhat immaterial. We observe that there is a constant c such that the shortest program for f_n is within c of the shortest program to compute the constant function $g_n \equiv n$, and conversely. Having made the observation (and ignoring some details), we need only establish the result for the set $\{g_n\}$. Suppose we assume that there are only binary operations and d statement types; then there can be at most k^{2kd} different programs of size $\leq k$ (and, therefore, at most that many constant functions of that size—that is, "most constants are random"). On the other hand, for any computable function r, $g_{r(k)}$ can have a program of size $\leq c + k$, (where c is the size of a program computing r). Then $g_{r(k)}$ has size $c + k$, while there are at most $(c + k)^{2(c+k)d}$ functions of size $\leq c + k$. Thus if we define $r(k) > (c + k)^{2(c+k)d}$ for almost all k, the result follows. (The "much smaller" is obtained by choosing r sufficiently big.)

In the context of general recursive programs, it should be apparent that we cannot effectively find the shortest program for a function. Moreover, the set of shortest programs is not recursive[†] and, in fact, is an "immune set" (i.e., it does not contain an infinite recursively enumerable subset). Blum (1967b) was the first to recognize and exploit this fact.

THEOREM 4

Let $g(0)$, $g(1)$, . . . be some (infinite, enumerable) set of programs and let r be any computable function. Then there exist programs i and $g(j)$ such that $\phi_i = \phi_{g(j)}$ and $r|i| < |g(j)|$. That is, some member of the enumerable set of programs must be very large (compared to some other program for computing the same function).

Sketch (Constable, 1970). Using Fact 3, we can take $|j| = j$. Then by the existence of a universal program, we can find a program for computing $\phi_{g(j)}$ whose size is approximately c_u (the size of the universal program) $+ c_g$ (the size of a program for computing g) $+ c_j$ (the size of a short program for computing $g_j \equiv j$). Recognizing that $s(j) =$ smallest program for g_j is the inverse of the Rado busy beaver function, it follows that for any computable r and infinite g, $r(c + s(j)) < g(j)$ for infinitely many j.

Unlike the axiomatization for dynamic measures, the size measure axioms are immediately appropriate for restricted classes of programs. Suppose we choose to restrict programs in such a way that the programs always terminate. Such a restricted class can obviously compute only a proper subset of the computable functions (since diagonalization is possible). But this subset may be the only functions we are "interested in" (e.g., the primitive recursive functions, the rational functions, etc.). Blum (1967b) observed that:

FACT 5

If we can decide that a program is of the restricted type, then the set of shortest restricted programs is recursively enumerable. That is, there is a computable g such that $g(0)$, $g(1)$, . . . is a list of the shortest programs of the restricted type. But then, by Theorem 4, there is a much shorter unrestricted program for one of the functions of interest.

We call this a size-shrinkage result, in that the larger, general recursive formalism (set of programs) affords "arbitrarily shorter" programs (as compared with the restricted formalism) for functions computable in the restricted formalism. Cook and, independently, Meyer and Bagchi (1972) have shown that this size shrinkage holds as long as the larger formalism is "universal" with respect to the smaller formalism (i.e., the larger formalism may itself be restricted). The set of constant functions, however, cannot be arbitrarily

---

[†]Precisely, the set is $\{i | j \geq i \text{ or } \phi_j \neq \phi_i\}$. Constable, Drumm, and Meyer have shown that membership in this set is (Turing) equivalent to decidability of program equivalence.

shrunk if the larger formalism is restricted. By looking at the Turing machine memory bounds needed for recognition, it is meaningful to say that the class of context-sensitive languages (CSL) is universal wrt the context-free language (CFL), and hence there are arbitrarily shorter descriptions for CFL when using context-sensitive grammars. Using different techniques, Meyer and Fischer (1971) have shown that context-free grammars permit arbitrary shrinkage for regular languages.

Structural Complexity

Restricting the types of programs allowed is one example of *structural complexity*. Specifically, suppose that we restrict programs to LOOP = $[X_i \leftarrow X_j, X_i \leftarrow X_j + 1, DO\ X_i - END]$. This language was introduced by Minsky (1967) and D. Ritchie (Meyer and Ritchie, 1967) and was shown to compute precisely the class of primitive recursive functions. (Denote this class of functions by R^1.) That is, a function f is in R^1 if there is a LOOP program which computes f.

In general, we can view much of the development of subrecursive (function) hierarchies and hierarchies in formal languages as examples of structural complexity. The Axt (1963) hierarchy of R^1 is based on the depth of nesting of the operation of primitive recursion in the (primitive recursive) definition of an R^1 function. The Grzegorczyk (1953) hierarchy of R^1 is induced by a class of initial functions which limit the growth of functions in each class of the hierarchy. The relationship between these hierarchies is exhibited elegantly by imposing a further structural restriction on LOOP programs. Let L_n be those loop programs with depth of DO loop nesting $\leq n$, and let $\mathcal{L}_n$ be the functions computed by such programs.

THEOREM 5
(Meyer and Ritchie, 1967)

For $n \geq 2$, $\mathcal{L}_n = (n + 1)$st Grzegorczyk class $= \mathcal{E}^{n+1}$
For $n \geq 4$, $\mathcal{L}_n = n$th Axt class $= \mathcal{K}_n$

The situation for the initial classes ($n \leq 3$) is surveyed in Tsichritzis (1971). In particular, Schwichtenberg (1969) has established the equivalence $\mathcal{L}_3 = \mathcal{K}_3$.

The proof of this theorem closely follows the arguments used to establish a relationship between the structural complexity and dynamic complexity of a function. This relationship, which holds for many classes of functions with respect to many computation models and dynamic measures, has become known as the Ritchie–Cobham property.[†]

[†]This relation was probably first observed by Kleene. Robert Ritchie (1963) made substantial use of the property, but it seems to have first been stated explicitly by Cobham (1964).

DEFINITION 6

A class of functions C is said to have the *Ritchie–Cobham property with respect to TIME* if f is in $C \leftrightarrow$ there is an algorithm i for f whose dynamic complexity $TIME_i$ is also in C.

Sketch of How to Establish Property for a Class C. One direction (f in $C \Rightarrow \ldots$) is a proof by induction on the (definitional) derivation of the function. The basis of the induction is to show that the initial functions are reasonably honest. This type of induction proof is also used to establish the inclusions $\mathcal{E}^{n+1} \subseteq \mathcal{L}_n$ or $\mathcal{K}_n \subseteq \mathcal{L}_n$ for Theorem 5.

The other direction evolves from the ability to define simulation functions $r_i(x, y)$ which determine the "state" of the ith algorithm after executing for y steps on input x. Those familiar with recursive-function theory will recognize the essential flavor of the Kleene T predicate. The crux of the argument is then to establish that the $\{r_i\}$ can be defined within the class C. Since we can extract the output from $r_i(x, TIME_i(x))$, then if $TIME_i(x)$ is in C and if C is closed under composition, it follows that $f = \phi_i$ is in C. The inclusions $\mathcal{L}_n \subseteq \mathcal{E}^{n+1}$ or $\mathcal{L}_n \subseteq \mathcal{K}_n$ can be obtained in this manner.

As corollaries of this line of reasoning, we have the following specific results of Cobham (1964) and Meyer and Ritchie (1967).

COROLLARY 1

a. A function f is in R^1 if there is an algorithm (and, in fact, a loop program) for f such that $TIME_i$ (or $MEMORY_i$) is in R^1.

b. (For $n \geq 2$) A function f is in $\mathcal{L}_n$ iff there is an algorithm (and, in fact, an $\mathcal{L}_n$ program) for f such that $TIME_i$ (or $MEMORY_i$) is in $\mathcal{L}_n$.

The Ritchie–Cobham property is quite general and applies to "natural" measures like TIME and MEMORY with respect to any model of computation whose computational process can be described and simulated in a relatively easy manner.

Expressing the corollary in terms of resource-bounded classes, we have

1. $R^1 = $ union of $\{R_t^\Phi \mid t$ in $R^1\}$ $\left.\right\}$ $\Phi = $ TIME, MEMORY
2. (For $n \geq 2$) $\mathcal{L}_n = $ union of $\{R_t^\Phi \mid t$ in $\mathcal{L}_n\}$

This formulation motivates our last result, the Union Theorem, due to McCreight and Meyer (1969), concerning axiomatic measures.

DEFINITION 7

Let C be a class of functions and $f_0 \leq f_1 \leq f_2 \ldots$ be an increasing sequence of functions in C. C is *self-bounded* (by $\{f_i\}$) if for every g in C there is an f_i such that $f_i(x) \geq g(x)$ for all x.

FACT 6

Let $f_0(x) = x + 1$, $f_{i+1}(x) = f_i^{(x)}(x)$, where $f_i^{(k)}(x) = \underbrace{f_i \circ f_i \ldots \circ f_i(x)}_{k \text{ times}}$.

Then

a. R^1 is self-bounded by $\{f_i \mid i = 1, \ldots\}$. The $\{f_i\}$ are analogous to the functions used to induce the Grzegorczyk hierarchy.

b. For all n, $\mathcal{L}_n$ is self-bounded by $\{f_n^{(p)} \mid p = 1, \ldots\}$.

THEOREM 6

Union Theorem

Let Φ be any dynamic measure. Let C be any set of computable functions, self-bounded by some enumerable set $\{f_i\}$. Then there is one fixed computable function t such that

$$\text{Union of } \{R_f^\Phi \mid f \text{ in } C\} = \text{union of } \{R_{f_i}^\Phi \mid i \geq 0\} = R_t^\Phi$$

COROLLARY 2

(McCreight and Meyer, 1969)

a. There is a function t such that $R^1 = R_t^\Phi$. $\left.\begin{array}{l}\end{array}\right\}$ $\Phi = $ TIME,

b. For all $n \geq 2$, there is a function $t_n: \mathcal{L}_n = R_{t_n}^\Phi$. $\left.\begin{array}{l}\end{array}\right\}$ MEMORY

Thus classes such as R^1 and $\{\mathcal{L}_n\}$ (self-bounded and possessing the Ritchie–Cobham property), which have been defined via structural complexity considerations, are precisely (dynamic) resource-bounded classes. That structural and dynamic properties can be strongly related should not be too surprising. For example, those familiar with formal languages (see Chapter 1 in this volume) are well aware of the study of time and space bounds for both context-free and context-sensitive languages.

We must apologize (again) for omitting much of the relevant material concerning subrecursive classes and hierarchies of functions. Particularly important is the R. Ritchie (1963)–Cleave (1963) type of hierarchy, where a larger class S' of functions is formed from a class S using functions from S as dynamic complexity bounds.

Inadequacies in the Present Theory

It is accepted that the Blum axioms for dynamic measures are so general that they include measures which must be considered pathological. One problem that has perhaps attracted more attention than it is worth is: How can we restrict the Blum axioms for dynamic measures so as to allow "only natural" measures?

A related question (Constable and Borodin, 1970) concerns axioms for dynamic measures in the context of subrecursive formalisms (restricted programs). For example, in the context of LOOP programs, it is possible to define $\Phi_i \equiv 0$ for every LOOP program i. While this definition would satisfy the axioms (LOOP programs always terminate), this measure would hardly describe the computational behavior of any loop program. Although it may be tempting to define such measures via a (primitive recursive) relation with the standard TIME and MEMORY, this approach is certainly not acceptable for a theory that aims at concepts which are as invariant and machine-independent as possible. It should be noted that (in contrast to general recursive formalisms) we do not know what constitutes an acceptable indexing for a subrecursive formalism. The questions of acceptable indexing and axiomatic dynamic measures for subrecursive formalism are perhaps different aspects of the same question.

In general, as we restrict further the classes of algorithms and functions, the problem of defining a dynamic measure becomes more difficult. In fact, for certain classes of algorithms, the distinction between dynamic and definitional measures becomes somewhat unclear. For example, using the straight-line program model (which we shall discuss in Section 2-4), we can compute rational functions of the inputs. The number of steps executed is, of course, the number of statements in the program. That is, the number of steps executed is independent of the input values. Going in the other direction, we also need to know how to define complexity measures for functions of higher or unrestricted type. [See Scott (1971) for one discussion on type-free procedures.] In particular, how should complexity be defined with respect to program schemata?

In spite of the fact that structural measures and classifications based on such measures are central to many areas of computer science, there has been no axiomatic study of "structure." In one sense, structural measures are certainly syntactic or definitional, although they differ significantly from size measures. (For a given structural constraint, there are usually an infinite number of algorithms satisfying the constraint, and an infinite number of functions, languages, etc., definable within the constraint. (Although Corollary 2b suggests just how closely dynamic and structural measures can be related, structural and dynamic considerations cannot always be "equated."

The successful development of complexity theory has been dependent, to a large extent, on the use of standard techniques from recursive function theory. In conjunction with these techniques, the motivation of complexity-oriented problems and the insight provided by specific models and measures is continuing to produce a substantial and distinct theory.

2-3. COMPLEXITY PROPERTIES FOR SPECIFIC MEASURES AND MODELS OF COMPUTATION

It is common to refer to many of the results in this section as machine-dependent complexity. Perhaps the most descriptive title would be "simulations, diagonalizations, tradeoffs, and equivalences." By any name, we wish to present a number of interesting results, with connections to both Section 2-2 and Section 2-4. Indeed, we hope that this section will provide a bridge, unifying what some would call the "extremes" of research interests (namely, theory and practice).

The emphasis in this section will be on dynamic measures. Moreover, following traditional lines, we shall often discuss dynamic complexity as a function of the input length (in contrast to the value of the input).

Certainly, with respect to problems concerning formal languages (as well as other "nonnumeric" problems), it is more natural to ask how difficult it is to recognize or parse a string of a given length, whereas the "value" of a string often does not have a natural interpretation. Even with respect to the computation of number-theoretic functions, the use of input length can be easily justified.

We shall also follow tradition in considering a number of results with respect to Turing machine (T.M.) models of computation. The reader should not feel that only tradition and sentiment bind us to Turing. To be sure, a number of "more realistic" models are now receiving the attention they deserve. However, our first few simulations will show that the Turing model is "not too inefficient."

Cobham's Class $\mathcal{L}$

In Section 2-1 we alluded to the notion of "practical computation." Although an analogue of Church's thesis has not yet emerged for practical computation, there are some classes of functions which do possess both some intuitive appeal and some mathematical invariance. Both the loop class $\mathcal{L}_2$ = Kalmar's class $\mathcal{E}$ of elementary functions (see Kleene, 1952 and Ritchie, 1963) and the class R^1 of primitive recursive functions satisfy these conditions. However, many people feel that these classes are still too inclusive. Perhaps the smallest class to have these important qualities (appeal and invariance) is Cobham's (1964) class $\mathcal{L}$ of functions computable within time bounded by a polynomial of the input length.

Definition 8

$\mathcal{L} = \{f \mid$ there is a T.M. program P_i which computes f, and a polynomial $p(\ )$ such that $\text{TIME}_i(x) \leq p(|x|)$ for all $x\}$, where $|x|$ denotes the length of the input(s) x. $\mathcal{L}_* = \{$set of strings $A \mid$ the characteristic function f_A of A is in $\mathcal{L}\}$.

The appeal of the class $\mathcal{L}$ lies in the widespread belief that those computations which are "exponential in difficulty" are not "algorithmically feasible." That is, while exponentiality does not rule out the possibility of good heuristics for a large subclass of a problem, it does mean that a "slick solution" is not possible. Whereas physical constraints in the technology indicate that a time bound of $p(y) = y^{100}$ is also not practical,† a time complexity of 2^y represents another dimension of impracticality (see Parikh, 1970). Note, however, that $f(x) = 2^x$ is in $\mathfrak{L}$, assuming a reasonable (nonunary) input–output convention.

The invariance of $\mathfrak{L}$ lies in the fact that the class is not essentially dependent on the use of Turing machines as the model of computation. The following developments will indicate that $\mathfrak{L}$ is stable under a wide class of models.

Time Simulations and Diagonalization

Many of the results that follow hold whether complexity is considered as a function of the input length or input value. Thus we shall make the distinction explicit only when necessary.

FACT 7

Let $GR+ = [X \leftarrow Y \pm Z,$ **if** $X = 0$ **than go to** $\langle label \rangle]$ and let P_i be a program written in $GR+$ which with input register value x executes in $T(x)$ steps. Then there is a multitape T.M. which computes the same function as P_i and executes within $\Theta(|x| \cdot T(x)^2)$ steps. Recall the notation: $|y|$ represents the length of y, and $y =$ contents of register Y.

Sketch. Represent (in binary) the contents of each of the registers on one of the T.M. tapes. Consider only the simulation of an add instruction $X \leftarrow Y + Z$. This will require $\Theta(\max(|y|, |z|))$ steps. If only k steps of the GR program have been executed, then $|y| \le k|x|$ for any register Y (where X is the input register). Thus the Turing machine can simulate the $GR+$ program in $\Theta(\sum_{k=1}^{T} k|x|) = \Theta(|x| \cdot T^2)$ steps.

Cook (1971a) notes that if we extend $GR+$ by allowing multiplication as a basic operation, then the simulation would have to be exponential [i.e., $\Theta(2^{T(\cdot)})$], since a register after k steps could contain a large number y with $|y| = 2^k$, whereas a T.M. would require at least 2^k steps to produce such a large number. Cook presents a strong argument for "charging" more than one step for a basic arithmetic. Since any real machine has only finite size registers, $X \leftarrow Y + Z$ should have a charge of $\max(|y|, |z|)$ to reflect the cost of multiple-precision arithmetic. In light of the recent Schonhage–Strassen algorithm, (see Section 2-4), $\max(|y|, |z|) \times \log \min(|y|, |z|)$ might be a reasonable charge for $X \leftarrow Y \times Z$.

Using such a "charge scheme," $GR+$ could be simulated within $T \log T$ by a multitape T.M. Moreover, in developing a model of computation, mul-

---

†Note that 2^{100} operations at 10^{-12} seconds each would take over 10^7 years.

tiplication need not be included as a basic operation, since it can be implemented efficiently (at the proper asymptotic cost) within GR+.

A number of models having random-access capabilities can be found in the literature (Shepherdson and Sturgis, 1963; Hartmanis, 1970). Cook's RAM model is basically GR+ with random access introduced by allowing one level of indirect addressing (i.e., $X_{X_i} \leftarrow X_{X_j} + X_{X_k}$). Using the "logarithmic" or "length" charging scheme (including a charge $|x|$ to input a number x), Cook (1971a) shows

FACT 8

A RAM program whose total charge is $T(\ )$ can be simulated within $\Theta(T^2)$ by a multitape T.M.

Sketch. Represent the nonzero registers of the RAM on one main tape of the T.M. (i.e., register number, contents of register, register number, contents of register, etc.) and use other tapes to update the main tape. It is not difficult to show that in simulating the RAM

1. The main tape length is $\leq c$ RAM charge thus far for some constant c.
2. The number of steps to update the main tape is proportional to its length.

Then we have again (as in Fact 1) a T^2 simulation.

This type of simulation was first employed by Hartmanis and Stearns (1965) in their T^2 simulation of a multitape T.M. by a one-tape T.M. A very clever encoding and simulation is used by Hennie and Stearns (1966) in their $T \log T$ simulation of a multitape T.M. by a two-tape T.M. It seems fair to conclude, then, that any T.M. model is appropriate for studying whether or not certain problems are of polynomial difficulty with respect to a realistic total time charge.

In general, it is not known whether or not these simulations can be improved. That is, can a multitape T.M. simulate a RAM within a $T \log T$ (or perhaps even a linear) factor? If this were the case, then multitape T.M. would even be appropriate for asking whether a problem was of quadratic or cubic difficulty. For the one-tape simulation of a multitape T.M., we do know that, strictly speaking, a better simulation is not possible. For the set of palindromes $= \{x_1 \ldots x_n \# x_n \ldots x_1 \,|\, x_i$ in some finite, nonunary alphabet$\}$ is recognizable in "real time" $[T(n) = $ time to recognize string of length $n = n]$ by a two-tape T.M., whereas the time required by a one-tape T.M. must be $\Theta(n^2)$. On the other hand, for all T such that $T(n) \geq n^2$, a linear simulation by a one-tape T.M. is still possible.

Simulations are not only important in describing the relative complexity power of various models, they play an integral part in establishing specific hierarchy theorems for resource-bounded classes. The following theorem concerns multitape T.M. and time bounds as a function of the input length.

THEOREM 7
(*Hartmanis and Stearns, 1965; Hennie and Stearns, 1966*)

Let t_2 be linearly honest with respect to a multitape T.M. [For our present purposes, we need the property that $t(n)$ squares can be marked off on a tape within $\Theta(t(n))$ steps]. Then if $\inf(t_1 \log t_1)/t_2 = 0$, it follows that there is a set recognizable in time $\Theta(t_2)$ but not in time $\Theta(t_1)$.

Sketch. Consider an input of length n to represent two tracks:

"input"	$w = x_1 x_2 \ldots x_n$
$0 \ldots 0$	description of some T.M. program i

We construct a "diagonalizing" machine D which will run in $t_2(n)$ steps. D first lays off $t_2(n)$ squares and then begins to simulate program i on w. If the simulation can be accomplished within $t_2(n)$ steps, then the output of D is made different from the output of program i.

If program i is running within $\Theta(t_1)$ steps, then since the simulation can be performed on two tapes within $\Theta(t_1 \log t_1)$, eventually the output of D will differ (on some input) from program i.

Let us comment on Theorem 7. The cost of diagonalization derives basically from the cost of the simulation ($T \log T$) plus the cost of incorporating a timer (essentially no cost for Theorem 7). The gap theorem (see section 2-2) shows that the honesty condition for t_2 is essential. Measuring complexity as a function of input length allowed us to encode input w and program i description within the length of w. Measuring complexity as a function of the input itself (and recalling the notation from Section 2-2) we can easily modify the argument to show:

COROLLARY 3

If $\lim t_1^2/t_2 = 0$ and t_2 is linearly honest, then there is a 0–1 function in $R_{t_2}^{\text{TIME}} - R_{t_1}^{\text{TIME}}$ (and, of course, $R_{t_1} \subset R_{t_2}$).

Sketch. The program i can be extracted from the input x by some standard "pairing" function $\pi_1 : N \longrightarrow N$ satisfying

$$(\forall i) \text{ (there exist infinitely many } j) \ \pi_1(j) = i.$$

We see then that if the Hennie–Stearns simulation could be improved, the hierarchy would be more refined. For RAMs, Cook and Reckhow (1972) show that such a refinement is possible.

COROLLARY 4

If $\lim t_1/t_2 = 0$, then there is a set recognizable within time $\Theta(t_2)$ by some RAM but not in time $\Theta(t_1)$ for any RAM.

Sketch. The idea is to show that random access enables a fixed RAM to simulate an arbitrary RAM program P_i running in time T within $c_i T$ (for some constant c_i depending on the program P_i). Anyone familiar with an interpreter would agree that such a simulation is not difficult. This theorem applies whether or not one wishes to charge for the basic operations. However, in the case of charging, one must be careful to show that the "timer" can be incorporated without too much cost. Finally, we note that with regard to T.M. models, the "Θ" can usually be omitted by appealing to a linear time reduction made possible by "packing" tape symbols.

Memory Simulations and Diagonalization

Memory measures have received almost as much attention as time measures. For Turing machine computation, the memory measure is usually taken to be the number of tape squares used in a computation. Memory is perhaps the most "stable" of any of the specific measures studied.

Suppose that we are considering GR or RAM programs. Then a reasonable candidate for memory would be $\sum_{j=1}^{N} |x_j|$, where N is the largest register used in the computation, and $|x_j|$ is the (binary) length of the largest number x_j occurring in register j. Cook argues, and we again concur, that if $x_j = 0$, $|x_j|$ should be defined $= 1$, for "holes" in the memory should be reflected somehow in the measure. We then have the following equivalences.

FACT 9

Function f is computable (alternatively, set S is recognizable)

a. By an $\Theta(T(\quad))$ MEMORY-bounded GR program.
b. By an $\Theta(T(\quad))$ MEMORY-bounded RAM program.
c. By an $\Theta(T(\quad))$ tape-bounded multitape T.M.
d. By an $\Theta(T(\quad))$ tape-bounded one-tape T.M.

Sketch. b $\Rightarrow$ c. Represent the RAM memory on one tape.

---

contents of register 1 $\#$ contents of register 2 . . .

It is still an open question whether a linear memory simulation and quadratic time simulation can be achieved simultaneously. The time simulation of Fact 8 produces a $T \log T$ memory simulation; the above simulation produces an exponential time simulation.

c $\Rightarrow$ d. To simulate a k-tape machine, treat the one tape as having k tracks. That is, each tape symbol is thought of as a k-tuple. Obviously, the size of the tape alphabet must be greatly increased, and it is not hard to argue that a "true" memory measure should be (size of tape alphabet) $\times$ (length of tape used).

In any case, the above results allow us to formulate our memory results with respect to T.M. computation. In considering the amount of tape, it is customary to consider T.M. models which have a separate read-only input tape, and count only the number of squares used on the "work" tapes. In this way, it is possible to consider tape bounds $t(n) < n$ (e.g., $\log n$). The tape measure is probably the "easiest measure to work with" and it is often used to establish general properties for dynamic complexity measures. One of the nice features is that tape or memory is a "reusable" resource, unlike time or tape-head reversals.

The same packing of symbols used to show (c $\Rightarrow$ d) in Fact 9 also permits a linear reduction for tape. Finally, the tape hierarchy is as refined as possible.

THEOREM 8
(*Stearns, Hartmanis, and Lewis, 1965*)

Let $t_2(n) \geq \log n$ be linearly honest with respect to tape. That is, we can mark off t_2 tape without exceeding $\Theta(t_2)$ tape. Then if inf $t_1/t_2 = 0$ and t_2 is linearly honest, there is a set recognizable in $\Theta(t_2(n))$ tape but not in $\Theta(t_1(n))$ tape. And similar to the time case, the linear reduction allows us to omit the Θ.

Sketch. The simulation and the incorporating of the timer can be achieved essentially without cost.

Theorem 8 holds even if we consider tape measured as a function of the input rather than input length, but the argument must be substantially changed.

When In Doubt, Diagonalize?

In the absence of techniques for establishing good lower bounds for "problems of natural interest," the previous diagonalizations at least provide some reassurances. Moreover, just as diagonalization can be a subtle and unsuspected cause of undecidability (e.g., Hilbert's tenth problem), in the same way diagonalization can be a subtle and unsuspected cause of complexity for a decidable problem.

Meyer and Stockmeyer (1972) have demonstrated that regular expressions over a finite alphabet Σ can be used to describe bounded T.M. computations. Specifically, given a linearly tape-bounded T.M. and an input w, a regular expression α_w of length $\Theta(|w|)$ can be "efficiently" constructed such that α_w represents Σ^* if and only if w is not accepted by the T.M. The construction is based on the ability to express succinctly the conditions for an invalid computation. Furthermore, if the language of regular expressions is augmented with "more powerful" operators, then in the augmented language a short expression can describe long strings. The the language can "talk about" computations with fast-growing tape bounds. In particular, Meyer has shown that the addition of the negation operator and an operator $\gamma(x) = \{y \mid |y| = |x|\}$ are sufficient to talk about $t_k(n)$ bounded computations for all k, where $t_1(n) = 2^n$ and $t_{k+1}(n) = 2^{t_k(n)}$. (Stockmeyer subsequently showed that γ is not even needed). Using Theorem 8, it then follows that we cannot decide emptiness for such "γ expressions" within tape (and hence time) bounded by $t_k(n)$ for any fixed k. That is, for all k there are infinitely many expressions α for which we cannot decide within $t_k(n)$ if α represents the empty set. Thus by the R. Ritchie (1963) characterization of ε, "γ emptiness" is a non-elementary decidable problem.

Although such results are of obvious interest to automata theory, we might still try to deny the "naturalness" of these problems. But Meyer goes beyond automata theory and shows that this type of descriptive power is also embedded in the language of many decidable theories. In this regard, Meyer first showed that the emptiness problem for γ expressions could be *efficiently reduced* to deciding truth in the weak second-order theory of one successor (WS1S). Hence, the Büchi–Elgot (1958) decision procedure for WS1S is inherently non-elementary. More recent results involve direct but very sophisticated encodings to establish lower bounds for many first-order theories. For example, we have: satisfiability in the first-order theory of a linear order is non-elementary (Meyer), and truth in Presburger arithmetic is at least of nondeterministic, single exponential difficulty (Rabin) and no worse than deterministic, triple exponential difficulty (Oppen).[†]

Again, we should caution that in all these theories there may be many sentences which are easy to decide. But to emphasize the importance of these results, consider the phrase used at the beginning of this subsection: "in the absence of techniques for establishing good lower bounds for problems of natural interest." The reader must now make his or her own choice—either accept diagonalization as a viable technique or restrict one's interpretation of "natural."

It is erroneous to believe, however, that diagonalization can always be used to exhibit a set or function in class A but not in class B. In general, class A may not be "powerful enough" to diagonalize over class B and yet one can feel strongly that class B is properly contained in class A.

Although the concept "can*not* diagonalize" is vague, there are many

---

[†]M. Fischer and A. Meyer have shown it to be of at least nondeterministic, double exponential difficulty.

situations where this seems to be the case. For example, in the next section we shall discuss the "determinacy problem" for both time and memory.

Another well-known problem concerns diagonalization over linear bounded automata. Does there exist a set S recognizable in linear space and perhaps exponential time, which is not recognizable in linear space and linear time? In light of the relationship between bounded cellular automata and linear bounded automata, this inability to diagonalize is the reason we do not know if there are sets recognizable by a cellular automaton but not in linear (perimeter) time (Beyer, 1970; Smith, 1970).

Nondeterministic Computations

Having (we hope) persuaded the reader to accept T.M. computations as an appropriate model for studying complexity, we shall jeopardize whatever confidence has been established and proceed to discuss nondeterministic T.M. computations. We argue that nondeterminism should be thought of as a "conceptual aid" rather than as a purely hypothetical feature of no practical significance. For surely, nondeterminism has afforded us valuable insight into the understanding of context-free and context-sensitive languages. We shall see that many problems lose their complexity in the presence of nondeterminism. The question then becomes: How much does nondeterminism help? This "determinacy" question with respect to both time and memory has been one of the fundamental questions in computational complexity, the source and substance of many well-known (at least in computer science) open questions.

A nondeterministic (nondet) T.M. is one for which there is a finite number of "moves" possible for every configuration or instantaneous description the T.M. is in. (A deterministic machine has only one possible move.) A nondeterministic machine accepts a set L in time or tape $T(n)$ if for every string x in L there is some computation path which outputs YES for x within $T(|x|)$ time or tape, but for x not in L there is no accepting computation.

For example, it is well known that the class of context-sensitive languages (see Chapter 1) is composed precisely of those languages recognizable in linear bounded space by some nondeterministic T.M. (Myhill, 1960). That is, every string w in L is accepted within $c|w|$ for a constant c. Again, the c can be removed by expanding the tape alphabet.

Most theoretically oriented computer scientists are familiar with the so-called LBA problem. That is, is every context-sensitive language recognized by a deterministic linear tape-bounded automaton (LBA) or, equivalently, are deterministic LBA's as powerful as nondeterministic LBA's? In general, the determinacy question for tape is then: Are $L(\ )$ det tape-bounded machines equivalent to $L(\ )$ nondet tape-bounded T.M.? Since there is a trivial "exponential simulation," the gap theorem tells us that for many bounding functions L, the models are equivalent. However, these are "uninteresting" bounds, and the question should really be restricted to linearly honest (tape-constructible) bounds. Savitch (1970) has shown that the exponential simulation can be substantially improved.

THEOREM 9

If S is accepted by an $L(n) \geq \log n$ tape-bounded, $T(n)$ time-bounded nondet T.M., then S is accepted by an $L(n) \log T(n)$ tape-bounded det T.M.

Sketch. The proof is based on a clever recursion (which, of course, must be explicitly implemented on a T.M.). Consider a nondet computation on an input w, using l tape and $2^r + 1$ time. The T.M. tape is divided into blocks, each containing an instantaneous description of the T.M. at some time. The length of each block, therefore, can be made $\leq l$. We want to show that an accepting computation can be discovered by using only $r + 2$ blocks.

initial config.		midpoint = time $2^{r-1} + 1$	final config. $=$ time $2^r + 1$

The idea is to guess systematically (by trying each possibility) what the final configuration will be. We verify that there is a path from the initial to the final configuration, using only $r - 1$ more blocks, by systematically guessing at the midpoint configuration. We then determine that it is indeed the midpoint by verifying that there is a path from the initial to the midpoint configuration (do this using only $r - 2$ other blocks) and from the midpoint to the final configuration (using the same $r - 2$ other blocks). We continue recursing in this manner.

1				9

1			5	9

1		3	5	9

1	2	3	5	9

Verify that 1 and 2, 2 and 3 are possible successive descriptions. This verifies the path from 1 to 3.

1	3		5	9

1	3	4	5	9

The path from 3 to 5 can now be verified. Therefore, the path from 1 to 5 has been verified. And so on. Whenever a guess fails, update the most recent guess. Either every guess at a final configuration will fail or a complete path will be verified in space $(r + 2) l \approx L(n) \log T(n)$.

COROLLARY 5
(*Savitch, 1970*)

An $L(n)$ tape-bounded nondet T.M. can be simulated by an $\Theta(L(n)^2)$ tape-bounded det T.M.

Sketch. This follows because there is a constant c (depending on the nondet T.M.) such that $T(n) \leq c^{L(n)}$.

The Savitch proof makes explicit an idea embedded in the proof that every CFL is recognizable within space $\log^2 n$ (Lewis, Stearns, and Hartmanis, 1965). Savitch (1970) has also shown that if $L(n) = \log n$ nondeterministic and deterministic tape-bounded machines are equivalent in power, then $L(n)$ bounded nondeterministic and deterministic machines are equivalent for all constructable (linearly honest) bounds $L(n)$. In spite of Savitch's theorem, most researchers in this area still believe that nondeterminism does afford extra power with respect to space bounds. The fundamental problem is that there are no techniques (except for diagonalization) for proving that a set is not recognizable within $\Theta(\log n)$ tape.

The determinacy problem for time is even more frustrating. For here the best simulation known is the obvious exponential simulation (check all $k^{T(n)}$ possible paths). In contrast to space, many believe that this may be "close" to the best simulation possible. In particular, Cook (1971c) has recently presented some persuasive evidence that a polynomial simulation may not be possible. Recall Cobham's class of polynomial computable "problems" $\mathcal{L}_*$, and let $\mathcal{L}_*^{ND}$ refer to those problems (sets) acceptable in polynomial time by a nondet T.M.

THEOREM 10

The following are equivalent:

    a. $\mathcal{L}_* = \mathcal{L}_*^{ND}$.

    b. $A = \{w \,|\, w$ represents a satisfiable formula in the propositional calculus$\}$ is in $\mathcal{L}_*$.

    c. $B = \{\langle w_1, w_2\rangle \,|\, w_1$ represents a graph isomorphic to a subgraph of the graph represented by $w_2\}$ is in $\mathcal{L}_*$.

Sketch. We must first describe an encoding over a finite alphabet for the sets A and B. A sentence in the propositional calculus can be transformed to a string by numbering all the variables and encoding the ith variable P_i by $p\bar{i}$, $\bar{i}$ being the binary representation of i. Thus an informal sentence (written using an infinite alphabet) of length n can be transformed to a formal string of length $\leq n \log n$. A graph can be represented by its edges: $e_{ij} = 1$ if there is an edge from node i to node j and 0 otherwise. An N-node graph can then be represented by the string $e_{11}e_{12}\ldots e_{1N} * e_{21}e_{22}\ldots e_{2N} * \ldots * e_{N1} \ldots e_{NN}$. Thus the length of the encoded string is approximately N^2.

The proof that a $\Rightarrow$ b and a $\Rightarrow$ c is relatively straightforward, since it is not difficult to show that A and B are both in $\mathcal{L}_*^{ND}$. Specifically, w is satisfiable iff there is an assignment of truth values of the variable which satisfies the sentence w represents. This assignment can be made non-deterministically and verified easily within polynomial time. Similarly, for the subgraph problem a nondeterministic machine can guess at the isomorphism and then verify it in polynomial time. b $\Rightarrow$ a: The proof is based on Wang's (1962) construction of a formula (in first-order predicate calculus) for each T.M. computation which is satisfiable if the computation halts. Similarly, suppose that S is accepted by a single-tape nondet T.M. M in time $T(n)$, for some polynomial $T(n)$. Then for each input w, a formula A_w in the propositional calculus can be constructed such that A_w is satisfiable iff w is accepted within $T(|w|)$. Moreover, the conversion to A_w and the length of A_w can be realized within $p(|w|)$, for some polynomial p. Stated another way, every S in $\mathcal{L}_*^{ND}$ is *polynomial time reducible* to the {satisfiable formulas}.

A stronger result is actually proved in Cook (1971c): that only formulas in conjunctive normal form (CNF)—in fact, only those having three variables per conjunct—need be considered. c $\Rightarrow$ b: A clever idea shows how to construct from any formula A (in CNF with only three variables per conjunct), a pair of graphs G_1, G_2 such that G_1 is a subgraph of G_2 iff A is satisfiable.

Thus, while the basic time-determinacy question has not been answered, a strong equivalence has been shown with standard problems in computer science. In a sense, the satisfiability or tautology problem is a canonical problem. In addition to Theorem 10, Karp (1972) and others have found a number of further equivalences (e.g., determining the chromatic number of a graph, deciding whether an undirected or directed graph has a Hamilton circuit, determining if a set of integers can be partitioned into two subsets whose sums are equal, and many other combinatorial problems). Moreover, many other problems are shown (Cook, 1971c) to be "easy," given a deterministic polynomial recognition of the satisfiable formulas. These problems include the graph-isomorphism problem and the recognition of primes. Since the prevailing view is that these problems are indeed very complex (specifically, not polynomial and "probably" exponential), it is conjectured that nondeterminism does significantly increase the time-bounded computing power. But it is just possible that the work of Cook and Karp will be the first step in showing that all these problems are really of polynomial difficulty.

Equivalence of Some Resource-Bounded Classes;
Time–Space Tradeoffs

The issue of time–space tradeoffs is a natural question for computational complexity. Unfortunately, a satisfactory treatment of this question has not yet been achieved. Consider either a T.M. or RAM model of computation.

As noted before, a simple "counting-of-all-configurations" argument tells us that $R_{t(\ )}^{\text{MEMORY}} \subseteq$ union of $\{R_{ct(\ )}^{\text{TIME}} \mid c \geq 1\}$. As for the converse, we only know that $R_t^{\text{TIME}} \subseteq R_t^{\text{MEMORY}}$. Is it possible that $R_t^{\text{MEMORY}} =$ union of $\{R_{ct(\ )}^{\text{TIME}} \mid c \geq 1\}$. Although this seems unlikely,[†] there are some "less standard" models of computation for which we can establish this kind of equivalence. In general, a number of equivalences can be shown for these models. We prove equivalence, of course, by exhibiting simulations for each direction of the equivalence.

To illustrate this type of result, we shall discuss briefly two particular models. The strength of these results may be a good indication that the models are not really "appropriate" general models of computation. On the other hand, it is again possible that the equivalences established will "transfer" difficult problems to the proper framework for solution.

The first model is that of a counter machine (C.M.) introduced by Minsky (1967) and studied extensively with respect to complexity by Fischer, Meyer, and Rosenberg (1968). A C.M. has an input tape and has counters instead of work tapes (equivalently, its work tapes have a unary alphabet). G_3 (see Section 2-2) can be viewed as a programming model realization for counter machines. The most serious deficiency of a C.M. is, of course, the inefficient unary representation of its memory. However, some reasonably interesting computations (e.g., recognition of postfix expressions) can be performed in real time by C.M., and we have the following results (Fischer, Meyer, and Rosenberg, 1968).

FACT 10

For all increasing $t(n) \geq n$ and polynomials p,

$$R_{p(t)}^{\text{C.M.SPACE}} = R_t^{\text{C.M.SPACE}} = R_{\log t}^{\text{T.M.TAPE}}$$

THEOREM 11

For all $t(n) \geq n$,

a. $R_t^{\text{C.M.SPACE}} =$ union of $\{R_{p(t)}^{\text{C.M.TIME}} \mid p \text{ is a polynomial}\}$.

b. The set of palindromes $S = \{w \neq w^R\}$ is recognizable in real time on a one-tape T.M., but S is not recognizable in time $t(n) \leq 2^{n/2k}$ by any k-counter C.M.

There are a number of other ways in which C.M. results differ drastically from what is known about T.M. For example, one counter is not sufficient

[†]A more "serious" conjecture is that the union of $\{R_{ct(\ )}^{\text{TIME}} \mid c \geq 1\} \subseteq R_{g(\ )}^{\text{MEMORY}}$, where $g(x) = t(x)^2$. Motivation for this conjecture can be found in the $\log^2 n$ tape recognition algorithm for (n^3 time recognizable) context-free languages. But there are also good reasons to believe that this algorithm cannot be generally extended.

for the study of C.M. space bounds, and C.M. with a "one-way" input can be exponentially inefficient in TIME as compared to a "two-way" C.M.

The second model is Cook's auxiliary pushdown machine. An auxiliary PDM is a multitape T.M. with one additional pushdown tape on which the space used is considered "free." That is, in analyzing the tape used by the auxiliary PDM, we do not count the pushdown tape. This extra storage, even with its limited access, yields a number of strong relationships. There is, of course, no difference with respect to TIME for APDM and T.M.

THEOREM 12
(*Cook, 1969*)

The following statements are equivalent:

a. S in $R_t^{\text{det APDM SPACE}}$
b. S in $R_t^{\text{nondet APDM SPACE}}$
c. S in $R_{2^{ct_{(\cdot)}}}^{\text{det T.M. TIME}} = R_{2^{ct_{(\cdot)}}}^{\text{det APDM TIME}}$

Indeed, this formulation did provide the missing link for a number of open problems related to formal languages, concerning the relative computing power of devices such as det and nondet two-way stack automata. It also yields another formulation for Cobham's class $\mathcal{L}_*$ as those sets accepted by two-way multihead pushdown automata. The open question now is whether or not the auxiliary tape actually increases the computing power.

While the true nature of time–space tradeoffs is still in question, R. Book has made an interesting observation relating to this issue. By exploiting language homomorphisms, he has shown that deterministic (nondet) linear-space-bounded T.M. are not equivalent to deterministic (respectively, nondet) polynomial time-bounded T.M. The curious thing about Book's observation is that we still don't know if one class is a proper subset of the other, or (as seems more likely) if the classes are incomparable.

Real-Time Computation

Although the emphasis in computational complexity has been on asymptotic behavior, there has been a considerable body of research concerning real-time computation. That is, in view of the present limitations in proving "nonlinear lower bounds," it is understandable that we try to differentiate further the linear computations.

Specifically, one distinguishes between set recognition within $t(n) = n$ and within $t'(n) = (1 + \epsilon)n$. A significant number of results have been established in this regard, and in the next section we shall discuss certain sets that are not real-time-recognizable by T.M. models. Real-time computation has analogues in both sequence generation and function computation. A (binary) sequence $\alpha_0 \alpha_1 \ldots$ is real-time-generable if there is a T.M. which outputs α_i

on the ith step. A monotone-increasing function is "real-time countable" if the characteristic sequence $\{\alpha_i\}$ of its range (i.e., $\alpha_i = 1$ iff i in the range of f) is real-time generable. In contrast to recognition problems, linear-time and real-time sequence generation are equivalent.

Real-time countable functions were introduced by Yamada (1962), and they played the role of the "timer" in the original proof of Theorem 7. Yamada observed that many "common functions" are real-time countable [e.g., n, n^k, poly(n), and 2^n]; it is also not hard to see that there are arbitrarily fast-growing real-time countable functions. In our terminology, the real-time countable functions are a set of very honest functions.

A number of trivial linear simulations become sophisticated problems when one attempts to see if real-time recognition can be preserved. For example, Fischer, Meyer, and Rosenberg (1972) show that:

THEOREM 13

If a set S is recognizable in time t by a T.M. with many heads per tape, then it is recognizable in precisely time t by a T.M. with only one head per tape (but using many more tapes).

On the other hand, if one is allowed to leave tabs or pebbles on a T.M. tape, and be able to return to a tab in one operation, then the real-time recognition power is increased.

THEOREM 14
(*Cole, 1969*)

Let $L = \{\mu_1 \# \mu_2 \# \ldots \mu_n \$^i \mu_{n-i+1}^R \mid$ where the μ_i are strings over $\{0, 1\}$ and μ^R indicates μ reversed$\}$. Then L is not real-time recognizable by any T.M. but is real-time recognizable by a "tab machine."

Real-time computation has also been studied with respect to iterative arrays of finite automata and (the closely related) cellular automata. These models can be viewed as highly parallel devices, and thus it is reasonable that they should be able to process more efficiently in some cases. In fact, we have the important result:

THEOREM 15

Multiplication cannot be performed in real time by a T.M. (Cook and Aanderaa, 1969) but can be performed in real time by an iterative array (Atrubin, 1965).

Time Considerations for a Subrecursive Formalism

In Section 2-2 we observed that a subrecursive language such as LOOP might be arbitrarily wasteful with respect to size. We now ask: How inefficient with respect to TIME can such a language be when compared to a general recursive model of computation? From the Ritchie–Cobham property, we know that every primitive recursive function is computable in LOOP or GR using $\leq f_n^p(\ \ )$ steps, where the $\{f_i\}$ are the functions introduced in Fact 6. Thus we can say informally that $(f_n^{p-1} + 1, f_n^p)$ is the maximum range of improvement that can be expected if we compute in a general recursive language.

Unfortunately, the above range is quite large if n is big. However, an efficient simulation is possible.

THEOREM 16
(*Constable and Borodin, 1970*)

Let P_i be any GR program which computes a primitive recursive function f. Let us assume that LOOP is augmented to include the arithmetics of the given GR language. Then there is a LOOP program P_j computing f such that for all x, $\text{TIME}_j(x) \leq c_i \cdot \text{TIME}_i(x)$ for some constant c_i (depending on the program P_i).

Sketch. We can assume without loss of generality that $\text{TIME}_i(x) \leq f_n^p(x)$ for all x. The obvious simulation would be

$$[\, Y \leftarrow f_n^p(x)$$
$$\begin{bmatrix} \text{DO} & Y \\ Z \leftarrow r(I, X, Y) \\ \text{END} \end{bmatrix}$$
$$\text{OUTPUT } Z$$

where $r(i, x, y)$ is the simulation function introduced in Section 2-2. This program would require more than $f_n^p(x)$ steps, whereas $\text{TIME}_i(x)$ might be much less. The idea is to replace $r(i, x, y)$ with a "direct simulation" and compute f_n^p in "parallel" with this direct simulation. Also, when the simulation is complete, an efficient exit from nested loops must be made.

$$\text{DO } X$$
$$\cdot \text{DO } X$$
$$\left. \begin{array}{c} \vdots \\ \vdots \end{array} \right\} \text{ direct simulation}$$
$$Z \leftarrow Z + 1 \quad Z \text{ is accumulating } f_n^p$$
$$\text{END}$$
$$X \leftarrow \begin{cases} Z & \text{if simulation not complete} \\ 0 & \text{otherwise} \end{cases}$$
$$\cdot \text{END}$$
$$\text{END}$$

The simulation embodied in Theorem 16 is applicable to a wide range of subrecursive classes and measures (i.e., not just LOOP versus GR). However, a general statement of this result must first await the notion of an "acceptable subrecursive formalism."

Whatever Happened to Size?

Having fulfilled our promise to concentrate on dynamic measures, let us attempt a mild defense of our failure to consider size. Our emphasis in this section has concerned mostly general recursive models of computation. In this regard, the question of size simulations is not a formally interesting question. For given any two reasonable models, each will possess a universal function for the other. Thus there is a constant c (= size of universal program) such that any function computable in size s in model 1 is computable in size $s + c$ in model 2.

One can certainly argue that whether or not a computation can be expressed within m units of size is of practical significance. If possible, we don't want the program itself to use up too much of main memory. But granting this important consideration, the questions of time and dynamic storage utilization seem to be much more the limiting factors. Certainly, the formal interest has been more in this direction.

We must mention, however, two papers dealing with the computation of finite tables and computation on finite input segments. Young (1969) and Symes (1971) are both concerned with the tradeoffs between run-time complexity on a finite number of input values and the size of the program. Their results may indicate a direction in discussing size–structure–time tradeoffs.

Exit Gracefully from Section 2-3

Section 2-3 contained a number of simulations. A general question then is: Which of these simulations can be improved? In a few instances we are assured that the best result has been obtained (e.g., linear tape simulation). But many open questions remain: How efficiently can MEMORY be utilized in simulating a TIME-bounded computation? Can random access be simulated linearly ("unlikely") or within a $T \log T$ factor ("possible") by a static access machine? Can two (or ten) tapes linearly simulate any fixed number of tapes? Of course, saying that the simulation cannot be improved is equivalent to exhibiting a function or set computable in one model and bound but not in another. It is this "proof of not being computable in some bound" which continues to be the fundamental question and barrier for computational complexity.

2-4. COMPLEXITY OF SPECIFIC FUNCTIONS, SETS, AND PROBLEMS

We are now ready to discuss the third and final of our subareas of computational complexity. Anyone who has sought after the "intrinsic difficulty of a function" recognizes just how elusive this concept can be. Obviously, for any computable function f, a computing device can be hypothesized for which f is considered a basic operation. Thus, it seems only reasonable to approximate the question of "intrinsic difficulty" by choosing a general class of computing devices and then investigating how properties of a function or set affect complexity on that class of machines. It is our belief that the other subareas (Sections 2-2 and 2-3) have helped to establish the nature and scope of this investigation.

One of the most satisfying experiences in computer science is to invent a clever algorithm. At times, there seems to be almost as much joy in this endeavor as discovering a new application. "Clever" often means suprisingly efficient; that is, a "good" upper bound is obtained on the complexity of the problem. In computational complexity, we are at least as interested in establishing a "good" lower bound. The best of all worlds is a proof of optimality: exhibiting an efficient algorithm, and showing that there cannot be a more efficient algorithm. As previously indicated, it is this latter part, "impossibility proofs," for which we have few techniques. We know that diagonalization and simple counting arguments (list all cycles in a graph) do establish the existence of exponentially difficult problems. But apart from diagonalization, there are no "non-trivial natural" problems for which we can prove that a polynomial bound is not possible. In fact, it is mainly counting or growth arguments which provide the few examples we have of nonlinear lower bounds. It should not be surprising, then, that our emphasis in this section will be on linear and polynomial problems. For the other choice is to list problems which seem to be exponential and then try to analyze the better-known methods for these problems [e.g., the Corneil and Gotlieb (1970) algorithm for graph isomorphism, or the Davis and Putnam (1960) algorithm for tautologies].

Turing Machine Results

There are a number of results concerning provable lower bounds, mostly concerned with real-time set recognition. A basic "information-theoretic" argument yields:

THEOREM 17
(*Hartmanis and Stearns, 1965*)

The set

$$L_1 = \{w_1 \mathrel{\#} w_2 \mathrel{\#} \ldots \mathrel{\#} w_r \, \$ \, w_i^R \mid 1 \leq i \leq r, \, w_j \text{ in } (0, 1)^*\}$$

is not real-time recognizable by any multitape T.M.

Sketch. A T.M. is limited in the number of past configurations it can distinguish in the next i moves. Specifically, for an m-tape, k-symbol, d-state machine, at most $dk^{2(i+1)m}$ configurations can be distinguished in i moves. However, there are $2^{2^{i-1}}$ subsets of words of length i which must be distinguished when the T.M. sees the \$. Obviously, L is linearly recognizable by a T.M., and is real-time recognizable by a nondet T.M.

A more sophisticated information-theoretic argument is avilable for one-tape T.M. computations. "Crossing sequence" arguments involve how much information can be transferred across the "boundary between tape squares."

THEOREM 18
(*Hennie, 1965*)

If a one-tape T.M. P_1 recognizes the palindromes $L_2 = \{w \# w^R \,|\, w$ in $(0, 1)^*\}$, then

$$\text{TIME}_i(n) = \Theta(n^2) \qquad n = \text{input length}$$

More precisely, for n odd, $\lim [\text{TIME}_i(n)/n^2] > 0$.

Sketch. A *crossing sequence* between two tape squares

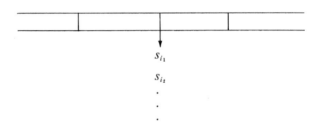

is the ordered sequence of states that the one-tape T.M. was in as it crossed the boundary. It is not difficult to show (by "splicing" computations together) that the indicated crossing sequences

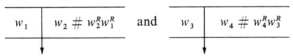

cannot be the same if $w_1 \neq w_3$.

It then follows that the length of the crossing sequence after the initial segment of i symbols must be $\geq ci$ on the average. And thus, for n odd, $T(n) \geq \sum_{i=1}^{n/2} ci = \Theta(n^2)$. This establishes the optimality of the one-tape simulation.

A technique similar to the crossing-sequence argument is that of bottleneck squares.

THEOREM 19
(*Rabin, 1963*)

Consider a T.M. with a separate read-only input tape and one work tape. Then

$$L_3 = \{u \# v2u^R\} \cup \{u \# v3v^R\}$$

is not recognizable in real time by such a machine. However, L_3 is real-time recognizable using two work tapes, thus establishing that two tapes are better than one at least for real-time recognition.†

Perhaps the most extensive use of these information-theoretic arguments appears in the Cook and Aanderaa 1969 proof that multiplication is not real-time computable.

THEOREM 20

Consider a T.M. model with two input tapes (to be read in tandem):

a_1	a_2	a_3	a_4	$\cdots$
b_1	b_2	b_3	b_4	$\cdots$

where a_1 and b_1 are the low-order digits of the numbers being represented. The T.M. is to produce a sequence of output digits $c_1 c_2 \ldots$ which is to be the product of the inputs. The machine is said to be "on line" if c_i is output before $\langle a_{i+1}, b_{i+1} \rangle$ is read. It is shown that any on-line machine requires $\Theta(n \log n / \log \log n)$ to produce c_n. If the on-line condition is dropped, then it only follows that the product cannot be output in real time.

This difficult result yields formal evidence that multiplication is indeed more difficult than addition. In the next subsection we will discuss the Schonhage–Strassen algorithm for multiplication.

The crossing-sequence argument can also be used to establish lower bounds for the tape measure.

THEOREM 21
(*Cobham, 1966a*)

Again, let $L_2 = \{w \# w^R\}$. If a multitape T.M. P_i recognizes L_2, then $\text{TAPE}_i(n) = \Theta(\log n)$; more precisely, for n odd, $\lim [\text{TAPE}_i(n)/\log n] > 0$.

Sketch. Without loss of generality, assume a read-only input tape and one work tape. Assume that there are q work-tape symbols and s states in the

---

†In a seminar at the University of Waterloo (June 1970), Aanderaa presented a proof that $n + 1$ tapes are better (again with respect to real time) than n tapes.

finite control. The number of total memory configurations possible is then $p = L \cdot q^L \cdot s$, where L is the length of the work tape. If we let a crossing sequence (c.s.) now refer to the record of total memory configurations (rather than just internal states), it follows that the length of this longest c.s. is $\leq p$ (in order to avoid looping), and the number of distinct c.s. of length $\leq p$ is $\sum_{i=0}^{p} p^i \leq p^{p+1}$. And again, if $w_1 \neq w_2$, every crossing sequence on $w_1 \neq w_1^R$ must be different from those for $w_2 \neq w_2^R$. If $|w_1| = |w_2| = n$, this implies that $2^{(n-1)/2} < p^{p+1}$, and consequently $L > c \log n$ for some constant c.

Cobham actually is concerned not only with this asymptotic result but also with determining precise lower bounds on the "memory capacity" ($=$ tape length $\times \log q$) required for recognition. He shows that L_2 requires memory capacity $C(n) > \log n$ for n odd.

The Hartmanis and Stearns (1965) paper issued a challenge to relate number theory and computational complexity. In their still-unanswered conjecture, they asked whether every number real-time-generable by a T.M. must be either rational or transcendental. A number of interesting results concerning bounds for the recognition of perfect squares and primes have been established using ideas from both number theory and computational complexity. In particular, Cobham (1966b) has shown

$$\inf \frac{\text{CAPACITY}(N)}{\log_2 \log_2 N} \geq 1$$

and

$$\sup \frac{\text{TIME}(N) \, \text{CAPACITY}(N)}{(\log N)^2} \geq \frac{1}{4 \log_2 b}$$

as lower bounds for recognizing $P = \{N \mid N \text{ is a perfect square in } b\text{-ary nota-}$ tion$\}$, and he has exhibited T.M. programs for recognizing P in either $\text{CAPACITY}(N) \approx \log_2 N$, $\text{TIME}(N) = \Theta((\log N)^2)$ or $\text{CAPACITY}(N) \approx 4 \log_2 \log N$, $\text{TIME}(N) = \Theta((\log N)^3)$. (Note: here complexity is being measured as a function of the input value N rather than its length n.) Hartmanis and Shank (1969) have shown a lower bound for the amount of tape required by an off-line T.M. to recognize the set of primes: namely, $\lim [\text{TAPE}(n)/\log n] > 0$. A straightforward T.M. program uses $\Theta(n)$, and it has been conjectured that this might be the best possible bound. As previously mentioned, it is not known whether $\{p \mid p \text{ is a prime in binary notation}\}$ is polynomial-TIME-recognizable.

A lack of space (in our case, page constraints are the limiting factor) prevents us from even indicating the extent of research with regard to specific T.M. recognition problems. We should at least note, however, the short but lucid exposition of some results in Hopcroft and Ullman (1969), and the older but comprehensive survey in Fischer (1965).

The Basic Arithmetics

The operations of $(+, -, \times, \div)$ are so prominent in both hand and machine computing that they can justifiably be called the *basic arithmetic operations*. The complexity of these operations, therefore, deserves some special attention.

With respect to single-precision computation, it is quite proper to consider each of these operations as requiring only one step of computation on a "realistic" computing device. On the other hand, actual computers have a fixed word size, and single-precision arithmetic is not adequate for many problems. We therefore wish to explore the asymptotic difficulty of the basic operations. With regard to asymptotic difficulty, it is immaterial whether we study complexity relative to the amount of precision or to the number of digits in b-ary notation ($b \geq 2$). For definiteness, let all representations be binary and $|v| = \lceil \log_2 v \rceil =$ number of binary digits in v.

Addition and subtraction can be dealt with immediately. Since every digit must be looked at, $u \pm v$ requires $\Theta(\max(|u|, |v|))$ and, of course, this bound can be realized trivially. In fact, we have already noted that $u + v$ can be realized in real time by a T.M.

Multiplication is a much more substantial problem. We have already mentioned the Cook–Aanderaa result concerning a lower bound. As for upper bounds, there is a history of methods which we shall bypass in favor of the best known method (at the time of this writing). The Schonhage–Strassen method for multiplying two n-digit numbers is "nearly" an $n \log n$ algorithm. (Recall that the conventional method is an n^2 algorithm.) The Schonhage–Strassen techniques rely heavily on the concept of a fast Fourier transform.†

LEMMA

Let $u(x) = \sum_{i=0}^k a_i x^i, v(x) = \sum_{i=0}^k b_i x^i$. Then the coefficients $\{c_i\}$ of $w(x) = u(x) \times v(x)$ can be "approximated" in $\Theta(k \log k)$ complex arithmetic operations and if the coefficients are integers can be computed exactly in $\Theta(k \log k)$ arithmetic operations mod m, where $m \approx \max_i c_i = \sum_{j=0}^i a_j b_{i-j}$ (and thus the precision required is approximately that of the coefficients).

Sketch. The discrete Fourier transform can be viewed as a transformation (by evaluation) of a polynomial in "coefficient representation" to

†Cooley, Lewis, and Welch (1967) study the impressive history of the fast Fourier transform. Major credit goes to Runge and Konig in 1924, to Danielson and Lanczo in 1942, and to Cooley and Tukey (1965). Knuth (1969) discusses the fast transform and describes how to use modular techniques to achieve an $\Theta(n \log n)$ method for integer polynomial multiplication (see the answer to problem 14 of Section 4.6.4). I am indebted to M. Fischer and J. Lipson for their discussions about the FFT and its application to fast number multiplication.

"point value" representation in such a way that the inverse transform (i.e., interpolation) can also be realized as an evaluation. The fast Fourier transform results by exploiting the symmetry of the "Fourier evaluation points."

Specifically, if we evaluate $w(x_i) = u(x_i) \times v(x_i)$ at $r \geq 2k + 1$ distinct points, interpolation will result in a unique polynomial $w(x)$ of degree $2k$. The points $x_i = \omega^i$, where ω is a primitive rth root of unity, allow us to perform the fast transform. In traditional Fourier transforms, one chooses the field of complex numbers, and ω as the appropriate complex root of unity (e.g., i is a primitive fourth root of unity since $i^4 = 1$ and $i^p \neq 1$ for $1 \leq p < 4$). Using this choice of points, $w(x)$ can be approximated in $\Theta(k \log k)$ complex operations. We say approximated because complex (or real) arithmetic can only be approximated using finite rational representations.

In the method, one assumes that $r = 2^s$ for some s. The condition that ω is a primitive root of unity in a field can be weakened somewhat. For the forward transform, all that is needed is that ω is an rth root of unity in some ring with unity. For the inverse transform (interpolation), we need to know that r^{-1} exists and that

$$\sum_{0 \leq s < r} \omega^{s\alpha} = \begin{cases} r & \text{if } \alpha = 0 \bmod r \\ 0 & \text{otherwise} \end{cases}$$

These conditions ensure that the interpolation can be viewed as an evaluation at the points $x_i = \omega^{-i}$.

In order to do exact number-theoretic computation for the coefficients of $w(x)$, we choose a finite field having the appropriate roots of unity (e.g., {integers mod $m \mid m = cr + 1$ is prime}). The modulus m is chosen as close to $\max_i c_i$ as possible. In practice, J. Lipson has shown that a "good" choice of the modulus can always be made. Furthermore, modular techniques could be used to reduce the cost of the arithmetic operations.

Perhaps a few words on "fast algorithms" are in order. Many of these algorithms are based on a simple strategy: split the problem into equal parts, work on each part (recursively), put the pieces back together. The simplest example of this strategy is a recursive merge-sort algorithm. The FFT works by splitting nth degree polynomial evaluation at n points into two $n/2$-degree evaluations, each at $n/2$ points. By the same strategy (and with the aid of fast polynomial multiplication), we can do polynomial division within $\Theta(n \log^2 n)$ arithmetic operations (Moenck and Borodin, 1972).

Returning to n-bit number multiplication, we have:

THEOREM 22
(*Schonhage and Strassen, 1971*)

Let u and v be n-bit numbers. Then $u \times v$ can be evaluated in $\Theta(n \log n \log \log n)$ "bit operations" (i.e., steps on a T.M. model).

Sketch. Consider u (and similarly v) as K segments, each segment of length L (and then $KL = n$): that is, $u = \sum_{i=1}^{K} a_i x^{i-1}$ evaluated at $x = 2^L$, where a_i is the value of the ith segment. For example, $u = 100001 = 10\ 00\ 01 = 2x^2 + 1$ evaluated at $x = 4$. We want the value of $w = w(x) = u(x) \times v(x)$ evaluated at $x = 2^L$. The polynomial multiplication is essentially performed via a fast transform with the approximation error dealt with either by careful analysis of the complex arithmetic or by carrying out the transform relative to some finite ring.

To fascilitate a recursive algorithm, one assumes (without loss of generality) that $K = 2^k$, $L = 2^l$, $n = 2^r$, and that multiplication is to be performed mod $(2^n + 1)$. Since the coefficients $\{w_i\}$ of $w(x)$ are $\leq k \cdot 2^{2L}$, we can choose two relatively prime moduli $M_1 = K$ and $M_2 = 2^{2L} + 1$ and then calculate each w_i mod M_1 and mod M_2 (recovering w_i by a Chinese Remainder algorithm). The dominant part of the analysis is to compute the w_i mod $(2^{2L} + 1)$. This is accomplished by a fast Fourier transform with respect to the ring of integers mod $(2^{2L} + 1)$. The cost is $\Theta(K \log K)$ steps of mod $(2^{2L} + 1)$ arithmetic $= \Theta(L)$. $\Theta(K \log K) = \Theta(nk)$ bit operations, and K multiplications of the transforms mod $(2^{2L} + 1)$ which are done recursively. Setting $k = \lceil r/2 \rceil$ and $l = \lfloor r/2 \rfloor$ yields the desired bound.

Schonhage and Strassen point out that their method can be translated to the design of logical nets realizing n-bit number multiplication with the number of two-input logic elements being $\Theta(n \log n \log \log n)$. Obviously, addition–subtraction can be realized using only $\Theta(n)$ elements.

The depth of a logical net is the number of delays through the net to produce the output (assuming a unit delay for the operation of each circuit element). Suppose that we wish to add or multiply two n-bit numbers. Assuming the standard encoding (i.e., binary representation) and using elements with at most r inputs, it is easy to see that the required depth is $\geq \log_r n$. This follows since the carry "depends" on each digit and hence the "fan-in delay" yields the $\log_r n$ bound. Schonhage and Strassen claim that their method when translated to this setting also yields an $\Theta(\log n)$ depth.

Winograd (1965, 1967) has elegantly generalized the question of depth in a logical net. In his d–r model, each element has r input lines and one splittable output line, and each line has d possible values. The model permits an arbitrary encoding of both input and output. Informally speaking, Winograd shows that $\log \log N$ depth is required for both addition and multiplication modulo $N(= 2^n)$ and that these lower bounds can be "nearly" achieved. Winograd, however, is not concerned with the number of circuit elements for the realization. Winograd also shows that $\log \log \log N$ is a lower bound for multiplying (not modulo) $u \times v$ for $u, v \leq N$, and the bound is nearly achieved by a prime encoding.†

---

†Winograd is not concerned with the cost of performing the encoding–decoding.

The remaining operation to be considered is division. Knuth (1969) describes an idea due to S. Cook which shows how to realize $u \div v$ ($=$ the quotient of u divided by v) in the same asymptotic bound as for $u \times v$ [i.e., in $\Theta(n \log n \log \log n)$]. The idea is to get an n-digit approximation for $1 \div v$ and then multiply by u. The reciprocal approximation can be realized in the time for multiplication by using a Newtonian iteration. This is the method by which division was simulated in early computing machines. As in the situation for large numbers, Strassen shows how to use fast polynomial multiplication to achieve a fast polynomial (with real coefficients) division algorithm [i.e., using $\Theta(n \log n)$ arithmetic operations to find the quotient and remainder polynomials].

We leave this section by mentioning some other asymptotically fast algorithms based on fast number multiplication. Schonhage (1971) uses a recursive technique involving continued fraction expansion to achieve an $\Theta(n \log^2 n \log \log n)$ algorithm for finding the GCD of two n-bit numbers. Schonhage's algorithm is actually an extended GCD algorithm, and Heindel and Horowitz (1971) show how to use this to construct an $\Theta(n \log^2 n \log \log n)$ Chinese remainder algorithm; that is, to reconstruct an n-precision number $u \equiv u_i \bmod P_i$ ($1 \leq i \leq n$, P_i a single-precision prime) from the u_i. Finally, it can also be shown that the modular representation $\{u_i \mid 1 \leq i \leq n\}$ of an n-precision number u can be obtained in $\Theta(n \log^2 n \log \log n)$ single-precision operations by using fast number division. It must be emphasized, however, that polynomial manipulations via the Fourier transform, and fast number multiplication with all its applications, are still in an experimental stage with regard to practical application.

The Number of Arithmetics for Computing
Certain Functions

A popular area of current research is [partially borrowing a title from Winograd (1970a)] the study of the number of arithmetics ($+$, $-$, $\times$, $\div$) required to compute certain "functions." The types of problems we have in mind are evaluating polynomials in one or more variables, matrix multiplication and inversion, finding the transitive closure of a (directed) graph. For each of these problems, there are "standard parameters" relevant to which we measure the difficulty. For polynomials, it is the degree; for matrix problems, the dimension; for graph problems, the number of nodes or the number of edges. If we fix the standard parameter, it should be obvious that the indicated computations can be performed using a straight-line program.

DEFINITION 9

A (*straight-line arithmetic*) *program* is a sequence of statements $s_1, s_2, \ldots,$ s_k, where each statement is of the form $p_i \leftarrow q_{i_1} \text{ op } q_{i_2}$, where p_i is a new variable name; q_{i_1} and q_{i_2} are previous variables p_j ($j < i$), "inputs" of the problem, or constants. A program computes a function, $f(x_1, \ldots, x_n)$ if there is a p_i such that $p_i \equiv f$. (A program computes a set of functions $\{f_j\}$ if there are $\{p_{j_i}\}$ such that $p_{j_i} \equiv f_i$).

That is, we have a program as in Sections 2-2 and 2-3, with a limited set of binary operations and no control statements. For the polynomial and matrix problems to be considered, there will be no loss of generality in not allowing branching instructions, since we can "unwind" more general random-access machine programs. This claim will become clearer as we proceed. We will now count the number of arithmetics required (relative to the standard parameter) for the previously mentioned problems using this straight-line-program model.

For both this and the next subsection, we shall primarily be assuming either symbolic computation or computation over the reals. In actual computing, of course, we are doing either exact integer arithmetic or approximating computation over the reals by "reasonably accurate" floating-point ($=$ ⟨integer exponent, integer significant digits⟩) arithmetic. Thus the complexity of all problems considered should be modified by appropriate (depending on accuracy desired) charging for each arithmetic or comparison operation. Unless explicitly stated otherwise, all results mentioned in these two subsections do hold for computation over the integers or rationals (although the arguments may require some modification).

Polynomial evaluation is perhaps the most extensively studied problem in this area. We shall say that we are evaluating an nth-degree "general polynomial" $p(x) = \sum_{i=0}^{n} a_i x_i$ when we treat the $\{a_i\}$ as well as x as inputs for the computation.

THEOREM 23

The evaluation of an nth-degree general polynomial requires

    a. n statements involving $+$ or $-$ (Ostrowski, 1954; Belaga, 1958).
    b. n statements involving $\times$ or $\div$ (Garsia, 1962; Pan, 1966).

In fact, at least n $\times$ or $\div$ operations are required which "actively" involve the $\{a_i\}$. Since Horner's rule achieves these bounds, it is an optimal method (with respect to the number of arithmetics required) for evaluating a general polynomial.

Sketch.

    a. It is easy to argue that n $+$ or $-$ operations are required just to compute $\sum_{i=0}^{n} a_i$ if we did not have $\div$. Kirkpatrick (1972) has shown the above allowing $\div$.

b. It is easier to prove the result by considering

$$p(\vec{a}, x) = \sum_{i=0}^{n} l_i(a_0, \ldots, a_n)x^i + r(x)$$

where $r(x)$ is a rational function of x and each l_i is a linear combination $\sum_{j=0}^{n} c_j a_j$ with c_j in $F = \{\text{reals}\}$. We then prove by induction on u that if there are u linearly independent $\{l_{i_j}\}$ (i.e., $\sum_{j=1}^{u} d_j l_{i_j}(\vec{a}) = 0 \Rightarrow$ all $d_j = 0$), then at least $u - 1$ "active" $\times$ or $\div$ operations are required. The induction step is based on making an appropriate substitution

$$a_i = l'(a_0, \ldots, a_{i-1}, a_{i+1}, \ldots, a_n) \pm r'(x)$$

which effectively eliminates the first active $\times$ or $\div$ operation and reduces the linear independence of the resulting function $p(\vec{a}, x)|_{a_i = l'(\vec{a}) \pm r(x)}$ by at most one.

This active operation and substitution argument has been productively generalized by Winograd (1970a). Let $H = F(x_1, \ldots, x_n)$ be the rational extension of F (i.e., the field of rational functions in $x_1, \ldots, x_n$ with coefficients in F). Suppose that we wish to compute $\psi_i(a_1, \ldots, a_n)$, $1 \leq i \leq t$, and

$$\begin{bmatrix} \psi_1 \\ \psi_2 \\ \cdot \\ \cdot \\ \cdot \\ \psi_t \end{bmatrix} = \Phi_{t \times n} \begin{bmatrix} a_1 \\ \cdot \\ \cdot \\ \cdot \\ a_n \end{bmatrix} + \Phi_{1 \times t}$$

where the elements of Φ and ϕ are in H and hence ψ_i in $H[a_1, \ldots, a_n]$.

THEOREM 24

Suppose that there are u columns $\Phi_1, \ldots, \Phi_u$ of Φ which are "nondependent" with respect to F (there does not exist $d_1, \ldots, d_u$ in F such that $\sum_{i=1}^{n} d_i \Phi_i$ in F'). Then to compute $\psi_1, \ldots, \psi_t$ at least $u \times$ or $\div$ operations are required which "actively" involve the $\{a_i\}$.

COROLLARY 6

a. Theorem 23 is a corollary of Theorem 24, since

$$p(a_0, \ldots, a_n, x) = (1 \ x \ \ldots \ x^n) \begin{pmatrix} a_0 \\ \cdot \\ \cdot \\ \cdot \\ a_n \end{pmatrix}$$

and $x, x^2, \ldots, x^n$ are nondependent with respect to F.

b. The evaluation of t general polynomials p_i of degree n_i, $1 \leq i \leq t$,

$$
\begin{pmatrix}
1\,x \ldots x^{n_1} & & & \\
& 1\,x \ldots x^{n_2} & & \\
& & \ddots & \\
& & & 1\,x \ldots x^{n_t}
\end{pmatrix}
\begin{pmatrix}
a_0^1 \\ \vdots \\ a_{n_1}^1 \\ \vdots \\ a_0^t \\ \vdots \\ a_{n_t}^t
\end{pmatrix}
$$

requires $\sum_{i=1}^{t} n_i \times$ or $\div$ operations. Thus repeated application of Horner's rule is optimal in this regard.

c. To multiply a matrix $A_{r \times n}$ by a vector $v_{n \times 1}$ requires at least $rn \times$ or $\div$ operations, since

$$
Av = \begin{pmatrix}
v_1 \ldots v_n & & & \\
& \ddots & & \\
& & v_1 \ldots v_n
\end{pmatrix}
\begin{pmatrix}
a_{11} \\ a_{12} \\ \vdots \\ a_{1n} \\ \vdots \\ a_{r1} \\ \vdots \\ a_{rn}
\end{pmatrix}
$$

The obvious matrix $\times$ vector algorithm realizes this bound.

An extension of this formulation appears in Fiduccia (1971), where the "independence" of both rows and columns is considered. In particular, Fiduccia's formulation yields, as an easy corollary, the fact [first proved in Winograd (1970b)] that multiplication of two complex numbers requires three real multiplications.

In spite of the elegant extensions (see also Strassen, 1972), arguments based on algebraic independence are certainly limited. For example, a polynomial and its first derivative can be evaluated in n active $\times$ or $\div$ operations but requires more (at least $n + 1$) $\times$ or $\div$ operations totally. Munro (1971) has exhibited an algorithm which requires $n + \sqrt{n}$ $\times$ or $\div$ operations (and $2n + \sqrt{n}$ $+$ or $-$ operations). Kirkpatrick (1972) has shown that (without $\div$) at least $2n - 1 +$ or $-$ operations are required, and this bound can obviously be achieved. Many other problems appear to be such that entirely new techniques will be needed: for example, how many real arithmetic operations are required to evaluate a complex polynomial (complex indeterminant and either real or complex coefficients), how many operations are required to evaluate a general nth-degree polynomial at $n + 1$ unrelated points, and how many operations to interpolate back to an nth-degree polynomial. As a corollary of fast polynomial division (Moenck and Borodin, 1972), evaluation at $n + 1$ points and interpolation can be performed in $\mathcal{O}(n \log^3 n)$ arithmetic operations ($\mathcal{O}(n \log^2 n)$ using Strassen's fast division algorithm). Strassen has also shown that $\mathcal{O}(n \log n)$ multiplications/divisions is optimal, using concepts from algebraic geometry.

Also, there is a lack of techniques for handling tradeoffs between arithmetic operations. For example, an nth-degree polynomial can be evaluated at two points (without preconditioning—see below) in less than $2n$ $\times$, $\div$ operations but seemingly only at the expense of $+$, $-$ operations.

There is another, equally important, formulation for discussing polynomial evaluation. Suppose we know that a polynomial is to be evaluated at many points. Then we may consider operations involving only the coefficients $\{a_i\}$ to be essentially free (since they need be done only once). Motzkin (1955) introduced the concept of "preconditioning," and the following results are known with regard to this concept.

THEOREM 25

a. Without counting the cost of preconditioning, $n +$ or $-$ and $\lceil n/2 \rceil + 1 \times$ or $\div$ operations are still required for "most" nth-degree polynomials (Motzkin, 1955; Pan, 1966). Of course, there are some special polynomials for which special methods can be derived.

b. With respect to integer and rational computation, only $\mathcal{O}(\sqrt{n})$ multiplications are required if we allow an unbounded number of additions (Paterson and Stockmeyer, 1971).

c. Allowing analytic preconditioning functions of the coefficients, an nth-degree polynomial can be "approximately" evaluated in $\lfloor n/2 + 2 \rfloor \times$ operations and $n +$ operations (Motzkin, 1955; Pan, 1966). We say approximately again, because unlimited precision arithmetic is required.

d. Allowing only rational preconditioning functions of the coefficients, Rabin and Winograd (1971) have shown that an nth-degree polynomial can be evaluated in $n/2 + \mathcal{O}(\log n) \times$, $\div$ operations and $n + \mathcal{O}(n) +$, $-$ operations.

The analytic preconditioning schemes cut the number of operations per point to about $\frac{3}{2}$. If the evaluations must be performed iteratively (which is the usual case), then these schemes are the best way to evaluate a general polynomial at many points.

One of the most compelling and important problems in this area is the number of arithmetics required to perform matrix multiplication. There are many reasons for the interest in this problem. Strassen (1969) has exhibited an algorithm which is asymptotically more efficient than the standard method. It can be said that Strassen's method has been a major factor (among "theoretical types") in the present emphasis on "practical algorithms."

THEOREM 26

Two $n \times n$ matrices can be multiplied together in $\mathcal{O}(n^{\log_2 7}) \approx \mathcal{O}(n^{2.81})$ total arithmetic operations.

Sketch. The method is based on a clever (and not obvious) way to multiply two 2×2 matrices in seven (rather than eight) "element" multiplications without using commutativity of the elements. A recursion can then be used to achieve the general bound. That is, multiplying

$$\left(\begin{array}{c|c} A_1 & A_2 \\ \hline A_3 & A_4 \end{array}\right)_{2^k \times 2^k} \qquad \left(\begin{array}{c|c} B_1 & B_2 \\ \hline B_3 & B_4 \end{array}\right)_{2^k \times 2^k}$$

can be viewed as multiplying two 2×2 matrices, each of whose elements are $2^{k-1} \times 2^{k-1}$ matrices. Because the recursion is based on multiplication, it is not important (for the asymptotic bound) that 18 addition-subtractions are used in the 2×2 case.

As far as a lower bound is concerned, in spite of substantial efforts, precious little is known. From Theorem 24, it is immediate that n^2 multiplication or division operations (and $n(n - 1)$ addition or subtaction operations) are required. Kirkpatrick has raised the lower bounds to $2n^2 - n$ multiplication/ division operations and to $2n^2 - 3n + 1$ addition/subtraction operations [see Kirkpatrick (1972) for the $+$, $-$ result]. To be sure, these lower bounds are $\mathcal{O}(n^2)$, whereas the Strassen result is $\approx \mathcal{O}(n^{2.81})$. A good deal of effort has been spent on trying to improve Strassen's method by finding (for example) a 21-multiplication method for the 3×3 case. The fact that strictly more than n^2 multiplications are needed implies that an $\mathcal{O}(n^2)$ bound cannot be achieved by a Strassen-like recursion. The difficulty of this problem is perhaps best indicated by the complicated proofs needed in the following results.

THEOREM 27

a. *Hopcroft and Kerr (1971).* Without assuming commutativity, $n/2$ applications of Strassen's method is optimal (with respect to scalar multiplications) for a (2×2) by $(2 \times n)$ matrix multiplication. Assuming commutativity, this bound can be improved (thus commutativity helps), but as Winograd observes, commutativity can at best cut the number of scalar multiplications in half.

b. *Winograd (1970b).* Seven scalar multiplications are required for the (2×2) by (2×2) case, even assuming commutativity.

The importance of the matrix multiplication problem is magnified (like the tautology problem) by the number of applications and related problems. Strassen shows that matrix inversion can be performed within (asymptotically) the number of arithmetics required for matrix multiplication [i.e., $\Theta(n^{\log_2 7})$ to invert an $n \times n$ matrix]. Unfortunately (as Strassen recognizes) this method for inversion will not be "well defined" for every invertible matrix. Consider

$$A_{2^k \times 2^k} = \begin{pmatrix} A_1 & A_2 \\ A_3 & A_4 \end{pmatrix}$$

The idea is to invert A by performing Gaussian elimination. Counting the number of order 2^{k-1} inversions and multiplications, and recursing, yields the result. The hitch is that A_1, A_2, A_3, and A_4 may all be singular even though A is nonsingular.

Another application relates to the transitive closure problem.

THEOREM 28

Let $A_{n \times n} = (a_{ij})$ be the adjacency matrix of an n-node directed graph ($a_{ij} = 1$ iff there is an edge from i to j) and let $A^*_{n \times n} = (a^*_{ij})$ be its transitive closure ($a^*_{ij} = 1$ iff there is a path from i to j).

a. *Munro (1971b).* A^* can be found using a number of "bit operations" proportional to the number of operations required for one $n \times n$ Boolean matrix multiplication ($+$ is "or," $\times$ is "and").

b. *Fischer and Meyer (1971).* $n \times n$ Boolean matrix multiplication can be performed in a number of operations proportional to that needed for $n \times n$ transitive closure.

c. *Fischer and Meyer (1971).* If $m(n)$ is the number of arithmetics required for ordinary $n \times n$ matrix multiplication, and $b(k)$ is the number of bit operations to perform k-bit arithmetic [i.e., from last section $\Theta(k \log k)$ would be a reasonable approximation], then $n \times n$ Boolean matrix multiplication can be accomplished in $\Theta(m(n) \cdot b(\log n))$ bit operations.[†]

We should note that the importance of fast matrix multiplication does not lie in its immediate practicality. An implementation of the method will show that standard matrix multiplication is distinctly better for $n \leq 50$, and there are questions of roundoff behavior and characteristics of the operating system (e.g., paging) to be considered. On the other hand, surprising algo-

---

[†]It is interesting to note that $n \times n$ Boolean matrix multiplication is performed in less than $\Theta(n^3)$ operations by allowing arithmetic operations and $y(x) = \min(1, x)$. If the computation had to be performed using only "or" and "and," then $\Theta(n^3)$ operations would be required (Kerr, 1970).

Munro's result assumes that the cost function for $n \times n$ Boolean matrix multiplication has the property that cost $(2n) \geq (2 + \epsilon)$ cost (n).

rithms do make us challenge our acceptance of standard methods, stressing the need for theoretical lower bounds. Moreover, fast multiplication may someday be sufficiently improved to come into use for certain applications.

Counting the Number of Comparisons

Counting the number of basic arithmetics for straight-line programs is obviously a limited aspect of complexity. To be sure, it is a reasonable framework for a large class of problems. However, in attempting to study the difficulty of many problems (e.g., with regard to searching and sorting), it is appropriate to investigate the number of "compare and branch" instructions required. If only a bounded number of arithmetic operations occur between execution of comparisons (as would be the case for a "uniform method"), it follows that the total number of steps is proportional to the number of comparisons executed in a computation. In any event, the number of comparisons affords a machine-independent criterion for discussing various problems.

To be specific, let us consider only binary comparisons ($\leq, >$). We should expect that the number of comparisons required for a given problem will depend on the allowable set of arithmetics. For indeed, if $\max(x_1, x_2)$ is an allowable arithmetic operation, then comparisons can be avoided in any given instance of the problem. That is, for any n we can write a straight-line program (using max but no explicit comparisons) which will sort n numbers. Reingold (1971) calls a set B of functions "ignorant" if the function max cannot be realized from B. We shall assume that the arithmetics used are indeed ignorant.[†] One usually considers having only the basic arithmetics and most often no arithmetics at all.

A standard framework for analysis is the use of a *computation tree*.[‡] Each interior node of a rooted tree is associated with an operation, and output takes place at the leaves of the tree. Comparison operations have two branches, arithmetic operations have one branch. As in the straight-line program, a new variable name can be associated with the result of each arithmetic operation. A comparison is then the form $q_{i_1} : q_{i_2}$, where q_{i_1} and q_{i_2} are previously computed variables, inputs, or constants. As before, we describe a problem relative to a standard parameter n (i.e., length of a list, number of nodes or edges in a graph, etc.). For each n there is a finite tree to describe the computation. Computation obviously begins at the root and proceeds from node to node until a leaf is reached. The path of greatest length (or

---

†Perhaps "innocent" would be more complimentary.

‡As Knuth reminds us, trees have been in existence since the third day of creation. Computation trees were probably discovered soon after. For this reason, it is hard to give exact credit for many of the simple but important information theoretic (counting) arguments based on the number of leaves in a computation tree [although Steinhaus (1958) was probably the first to make these ideas explicit for sorting and insertion into a sorted list].

having the most comparisons) indicates a worst-case difficulty, and the average length (or number of comparisons) over all paths indicates "average" difficulty. (Of course, "average" will have its intuitive meaning only if a weighting is given to each path, reflecting the input distribution.) Like the straight-line program (which is a special case), the finite computation tree yields lower bounds for general problems by viewing the tree as unwinding a general program for each particular n.

We shall first discuss some problems under the more traditional assumption that only comparisons (and no arithmetics) are allowed. The following is a well-known basic property of binary trees:

LEMMA

The longest (average) path length of a strictly binary tree with k leaves is greater than or equal to $\lceil \log k \rceil$ ($\lfloor \log k \rfloor$). (All logs are base 2.)

As an immediate corollary, we have the following worst-case lower bounds (bounds in the "average" sense can be one less when using this basic counting argument).

THEOREM 29

a. $\lceil \log n! \rceil = n \log n - \Theta(n)$ comparisons are required to sort n distinct numbers, since there are $n!$ different possible permutations.

b. $\lceil \log \binom{n+m}{m} \rceil$ comparisons are required to merge a sorted list of m elements into a sorted listed of n elements ($m \leq n$), since there are $\binom{n+m}{m}$ distinct orderings possible. In particular, for $m = 1$ (single insertion) $\lceil \log(n + 1) \rceil$ comparisons are required, and for $m = 2$ (two-element insertion) $\lceil \log \binom{n+2}{2} \rceil \approx 2 \log n$ comparisons are required.

As we all know, these bounds are optimal or "near optimal." The familiar merge sort uses $\sum_{i=1}^{n} \lceil \log i \rceil \leq n \lfloor \log n \rfloor + 1$ comparisons, and the Ford and Johnson (1959) merge-insertion algorithm, which has not yet been beaten for any n, uses $\sum_{i=1}^{n} \lceil \log \frac{3}{4}i \rceil$ comparisons.†

The binary search method obviously realizes the $\lceil \log(n + 1) \rceil$ bound for single insertion. For two-element insertion, the double application of binary insertion is very near optimal and optimal results have been established by Graham and by Hwang and Lin (1971). As m gets larger, successive insertion becomes inefficient. Karp has observed that for $n - 1 \leq m \leq n$, the standard tape merge is optimal.

Perhaps the most studied problem with respect to the number of comparisons is "finding the kth largest (or smallest) in a set of n numbers." It

---

†For $n = 12$ (the first n for which $\log n! < \sum_{i=1}^{n} \lceil \log \frac{3}{4}i \rceil$, Mark Wells (1965) has shown by computer searching that the information-theoretic bound $\lceil \log 12! \rceil = 29$ is not attainable.

was only recently that an asymptotically optimal algorithm was found for the general problem.

THEOREM 30
(*Worst-case analysis for kth-of-n problem*)

a. For $k = 1$, we are finding the best or the MAX of n numbers, and $n - 1$ comparisons is easily seen to be optimal. In fact, every path in the computation tree must have length $\geq n - 1$.

b. For $k = 2$, we are finding the second best, and this is equivalent to finding the first and second best. Schreier (1932) and Slupecki (1951) have shown that $n - 1 + \lfloor \log_2(n - 1) \rfloor$ comparisons are required. The proof technique is a prime example of "the adversary approach." For every algorithm, there is a strategy for choosing an ordering of the n elements so as to force the worst case. Kislicyn (1964) has shown that the bound is attainable, and his algorithm is aptly referred to as a tournament-elimination bout. The name suggests the method: Find the MAX; the second best is one of the $\lceil \log n \rceil$ contestants to lose directly to the MAX.

c. For general $k \leq \lceil n/2 \rceil$, Hadian and Sobel (1969) showed that $n - k + (k - 1) \lceil \log(n - k + 2) \rceil$ comparisons are sufficient. But for $k = n/2$ this bound is $\Theta(n \log n)$. Until recently, many people believed that finding the MEDIAN required sorting at least half the list, and hence that $\Theta(n \log n)$ was asymptotically optimal. Blum, Floyd, Pratt, Rivest, and Tarjan (1972) have developed a linear algorithm; that is, there is a constant c (≈ 5.7) such that the kth largest of n can be found in $\leq cn$ comparisons. With hindsight, the basic idea of their recursive method is relatively simple: Find the "sample median" of each group of 15 elements, and find recursively the median MM of the sample medians; by comparing each element with MM we are able to discard at least $4n/15$ elements which cannot be the kth largest, and finally recurse again to find the jth largest, where j depends on which elements were discarded. As for a lower bound on this problem, we have Blum's observation that a simple adversary strategy yields a worst-case bound of $n - 1 + k$. In particular, then, we have that $3n/2 \leq$ comparisons for median of n numbers $\leq 6n$.

There are two other optimal results which are of related interest. Pohl (1970) has shown that $\lceil 3n/2 \rceil - 2$ comparisons is optimal for finding MAX and MIN in the same computation (the first round of the bout separates the potential winner MAX and loser MIN). Spira (1971b) discusses the ranking problem, given some partial knowledge about the rank of x_i in $\{x_1, \ldots, x_n\}$. For example, if we know that x_1 is either the jth or kth largest of n numbers, then $n - |j - k|$ comparisons are necessary and sufficient to determine the relative rank of x_1 in $\{x_1, \ldots, x_n\}$.

Most of the theoretical interest has been with respect to this type of worst-case analysis. Rather than defend the "mathematical appeal" of worst-case analysis, let us only remark again that "average" behavior implies knowledge about the distribution of the inputs. In the case of a set of n distinct numbers, it seems reasonable to assume that the $n!$ orderings are equally likely. But in many cases (e.g., graph problems), it is hard to say what "average" really means.

THEOREM 31
(*Floyd, 1970*)

a. On the average, the kth largest of n can be found in $n + k - \Theta(n)$, where $\lim \Theta(n)/n = 0$.

b. $5n/4 \leq$ average number of comparisons to find the median of n numbers $\leq 3n/2 + \Theta(n)$.

Let us now consider some of the same problems when arithmetics are allowed in the computation. Even the simplest problems can become extremely difficult to analyze in this framework. For the remainder of this section, assume that computation takes place over the real numbers (i.e., $\vec{x} = \langle x_1, \ldots, x_n \rangle$ is a point in real n space).

THEOREM 32
(*Rabin, 1971*)

Suppose that we want to verify that a point $\vec{x}$ is in $L^+ = \{\vec{x} \mid l_i(x_1, \ldots, x_n) \geq 0, 1 \leq i \leq m\}$, where the l_i are linear functions. For example, proving the statement $x_1 = \text{MAX}(x_1, \ldots, x_n)$ is equivalent to verifying that $\vec{x}$ is in $\{x_1 - x_i \geq 0 \mid 2 \leq i \leq n\}$.

A *line* of a verification proof is a set of allowable functions $p_1(x_1, \ldots, x_n)$, $\ldots, p_r(x_1, \ldots, x_n)$ with the property that

$$[p_i(\vec{x}) \geq 0 \mid 1 \leq i \leq r] \Rightarrow [l_i(\vec{x}) \geq 0 \mid 1 \leq i \leq m]$$

We say that r is the *width* of the line. That is, a line verifies the desired positivity of L^+ for some set of points. A *complete proof for* L^+ *on a set* C is a set of lines such that every point $\vec{x}$ in $C \cap L^+$ is verified by some line.

Rabin defines a set $\{l_i\}$ to be *sign independent on* C if all 3^m possible combinations are possible for

$$\{\langle s_1(\vec{x}), \ldots, s_m(\vec{x}) \rangle \mid \vec{x} \text{ in } C\} \qquad s_i(\vec{x}) = \begin{cases} 1 & l_i(\vec{x}) > 0 \\ 0 & l_i(\vec{x}) = 0 \\ -1 & l_i(\vec{x}) < 0 \end{cases}$$

Rabin shows that if we want to verify $L^+ = \{l_i(\vec{x}) \geq 0 \mid 1 \leq i \leq m \leq n\}$ on some convex set C and if (1) all the allowable functions $\{p_i\}$ are analytic, and (2) the $\{l_i\}$ are sign independent on C, then any complete proof for L^+ on C must have some line with width $\geq m$.[†]

Rabin's formulation has an immediate application to comparison problems (for example, the kth-of-n problem).

COROLLARY 32.1

Consider computations with comparisons and some set of allowable functions. If the composition of allowable functions is always analytic (or the quotient of analytic functions), then at least $n - 1$ comparisons are required for the kth-of-n problem. This follows because a shorter computation would yield a verification proof that x_1 is the kth largest on C ($=$ real n-space) with maximum line width $< n - 1$.

In particular, $\{+, -, \times, \div\}$ cannot reduce the number of comparisons required to compute $\text{MAX}(x_1, \ldots, x_n)$. On the other hand, Reingold (1971) has shown how to find $\text{MAX}(x_1, \ldots, x_n)$ in log n comparisons by allowing comparisons of the type

$$n^{dx_1} + \ldots + n^{dx_{n/2}} : n^{dx_{n/2+1}} + \ldots + n^{dx_n}$$

where $d = \sum_{i>j}(x_i - x_j)^2 + 1/(x_i - x_j)^2$ is chosen so that whichever side contains the max will be greater.

In light of Rabin's result, we can see that Reingold's method depends on the nonanalytic functions used. Of course, the $\Theta(n^2)$ arithmetics ($+, -, \times, \div$, exponentiation) used dominate the complexity of the method, but the example is only meant to show how the number of comparisons can be reduced by an ignorant set of arithmetics.

Spira (1971a), working in Rabin's framework has proved some additional results when $+$ and $-$ are the only allowable arithmetics. By restricting the allowable arithmetics, the requirement of sign independence can be eased. As a corollary Spira can show that $n - 1$ comparisons would still be needed to verify that $x_1 = \text{MAX}(x_1, \ldots, x_n)$ even if we knew, a priori, that x_1 is the first or second best.

The Rabin–Spira development is necessarily based on concepts and results from analytic geometry. As such, it represents a level of "mathematical sophistication" not present in our previous examples. Unfortunately, their techniques are limited to producing lower bounds $\leq$ the standard parameter (e.g., the number of elements in the list).

Reingold (1971) also studies the effect of $+$ and $-$ operations on various

---

[†]See Spira (1971a) for a precise statement of Rabin's theorem. Rabin also proved a converse to this theorem; roughly speaking, it states that a complete proof with maximum line width $\leq n + 1$ can always be found using only polynomials as the allowable functions.

comparison problems. Using a more algebraic approach, Reingold seems to have been the first to show that $+$ and $-$ could not reduce the number of comparisons for MAX, and he also shows that $\lceil \log n! \rceil$ comparisons are required to test if two n-element sets are equal even when $+$ and $-$ operations are allowed.

In a sense, counting arguments are very "stable." For the problems and model discussed, the leaves of the computation tree output some sequence of the inputs $\{x_i\}$. In this framework, N. Friedman has shown that if only analytic functions are used at the output leaves, then the number of required leaves cannot be reduced, and hence the information-theoretic bound is not affected. We are even tempted to conjecture that no ignorant set of functions can affect the number of required leaves.

A word of caution before leaving this section. The number of comparisons required is a well-motivated, mathematically important issue. With regard to practical significance, it suggests what order method is obtainable and sometimes leads us to "good" algorithms. But a good searching or sorting algorithm is not just based on the number of comparisons, but rather on the total number of operations (including replacement statements), the size and structure of the required program, and memory requirements. For example, a simple merge–sorting algorithm is easy to program, but uses $2n$ registers (i.e., n more than the space required for the set itself). The Ford–Johnson algorithm, the king of the methods with respect to comparisons only, is relatively difficult to program and the number of replacements is prohibitive.

On the other hand, Floyd's (1964b) Treesort 3 is an easily programmable $\Theta(n \log n)$ method ($2n \log n$ comparisons) which does not require extra space. Briefly stated, there is no one "best" sorting method.

The computation tree has some obvious deficiencies. It is tempting to see whether one could define a formal model which would yield (for example) meaningful lower bounds on the size of program or the number of replacements plus comparisons required. Finally, there are some simple cases where arithmetics $(\times, -)$ do reduce the number of comparisons required (e.g., determining if all the input numbers are distinct). For such tradeoff situations, we do not have lower bounds on the total (arithmetics plus comparisons) complexity.

But What About . . .

Once again, it seems time for another apology. Why didn't we discuss . . . ? Obviously, we could not even begin to survey all those results which relate to the "complexity of practical computation." Fortunately, the number of ingenious algorithms seems to be "unbounded." Let me just list some of the more obvious omissions.

In the previous two subsections, we have restricted ourselves to a few "simple" arithmetic and searching problems, concentrating on complexity considerations ultimately related to TIME. To a much lesser extent, some of these same problems have been analyzed with respect to MEMORY considerations. From a practical point of view, one is often interested in the number of storage locations required for a computation. If this is the case, then one needs to be careful to avoid "degenerate" results obtained by "encoding" all information in one register. Assuming that only one number may be stored in a location, Pohl has shown that $n + 1$ locations are required to find the median of $2n + 1$ numbers which are to be input once sequentially.

A more serious omission might be the vigorous amount of activity concerning efficient "graph algorithms." We have only briefly mentioned the isomorphism problem and some of the Cook–Karp class of problems as good candidates for nonpolynomial (possibly exponential) problems. While many continue to work on different (often heuristic) aspects of these problems, the recent activity to which we refer concerns improved polynomial algorithms. In particular, one could fill up an entire page of references with shortest-path algorithms or with the efficient algorithms of Hopcroft, Karp, Tarjan, and others. A good example of this work is the $\Theta(n \log n)$ algorithm (Hopcroft and Tarjan, 1971) and an improved $\Theta(n)$ algorithm (Tarjan) for planarity testing of an n-node graph represented by an appropriate listing of edges. Clever and efficient manipulation of stacks (as well as graph-theoretic properties) is a central part of these algorithms. Generally speaking, nontrivial lower bounds or proofs of optimality have not been considered for graph problems; of course, if there are e edges and n nodes, then an $\Theta(e)$ or $\Theta(n^2)$ lower bound, depending on the graph presentation, is usually immediate. A good theoretical model for graph problems would be an important contribution. For example, if one knows that the difficulty of a graph problem is $\Theta(e)$, what can be said about the required constants?

We have also failed to mention the large number of results concerning switching-circuit models. Lawler (1971), in his short but interesting survey of combinatorial computations, discusses the limitations, pitfalls, and benefits of three abstract computation models: the computation tree, the switching circuit, and the idealized programming model.

We have generally kept a promise by avoiding aspects of complexity which are particular to some specific field (e.g., numerical analysis and pattern recognition). The results presented here could all be classified as combinatoric problems, although analytic techniques (e.g., Theorem 32) are sometimes required. In numerical analysis or approximation theory the important optimality questions are rarely combinatoric. Traub (1971) discusses one example of noncombinatoric complexity in his survey: he studies the tradeoff between the number of function evaluations and the order of an iterative method for finding roots. Although the techniques are completely different, the title and substance of his survey is of a "common spirit" with our presentation.

An indication of the activity in the general area of "efficient and optimal algorithms" is reported in the March 1972 IBM Symposium on Complexity of Computer Computations. In addition to other topics, there are discussions of efficient graph algorithms, polynomial and matrix evaluation, parallelism, list merging, and iterative processes. Paterson (1972) proves a result which relates to Traub's consideration of iteration efficiency. He defines the efficiency V of an iteration to be [$\log_2$(order)/number of multiplications other than by a constant] and then shows that Newton's method yields the best possible efficiency ($V = 1$) for calculating $\sqrt{A}$. Kung (1972) shows that this result can be obtained in a purely algebraic manner, but once again there are indications that number theory and analysis will become more and more important in computational complexity.

2-5. CONCLUSION

By now, I am sure that the reader is convinced that I am (at best) an incurable empire builder. But I must confess that, to me, many diverse issues appear essentially as questions of complexity. Perhaps I should have practiced some self-control and restricted this effort to one major aspect or area. In any event, I am left with one last opportunity to establish the relatedness of all that I have paraded forth, and conjecture about the direction of future research.

If I must have a central thesis, then the following will have to do: We would like to understand why certain problems seem to be "difficult." The difficulty that we perceive often seems to be independent of the choice of computing model. What do we mean by "difficult"? Can we formulate precisely why certain problems are "intrinsically" difficult? If we are to make progress toward answering these admittedly vague questions, then we must understand the limitations of our concepts, the invariant and the non-invariant notions, the techniques now available, the problems beyond our present capabilities, and so on. To this end, Section 2-2 outlined our theoretical foundation; Section 2-3 analyzed, in more depth, models and measures of interest and set forth some of the invariant notions and limitations of the present "state of the art;" and finally Section 2-4 investigated a few specific and practical problems within our present capabilities. I have no illusions (or wildly optimistic predictions) about the present state of computational complexity. Given the short span of active interest, I do believe that the results indicate a very successful development. But any assessment must be tempered by the fundamental inadequacies; in particular, the inability to prove that many "natural" recognition problems are of nonpolynomial (or even nonlinear) complexity. And then there are the many versions of tradeoff questions. There is no reason to believe that these central issues will be resolved in the near future. On the other hand, I do not believe that these are the only issues worth any effort.

A number of open problems have been suggested throughout this paper. The present vogue seems to favor both "low-level" complexity (upper and lower bounds for practical problems of linear or near linear complexity), and "seemingly" or provably difficult (non-polynomial) combinatoric problems. Although it may be fashionable to say that the theory of complexity is "dead," I am far from convinced that all the important issues have been resolved. In particular, I would like to see some more theory for the "medium and low levels." But to quote Minsky and Papert: "Good theories rarely develop outside the context of a background of well-understood real problems and special cases."

In this survey, I have only attempted to indicate the scope of computational complexity, referring to only a small subset of the relevant publications. My choice of topics and references does not in any sense represent a consensus; I have tried to include not only "fundamental" results, but also some results of perhaps less importance, which are either obscured in (or absent from) the literature.

I would like to thank Professors R. Constable and S. Cook (as well as many others), from whom I have freely stolen ideas. I am also indebted to the National Research Council of Canada for their generous support.

3 PROGRAM SCHEMAS

Zohar Manna†
Computer Science Department
Stanford University

3-1. INTRODUCTION

Substantial effort has recently been devoted toward developing methods for proving properties of programs. It turns out that one can often prove properties of a given program independent of the exact meaning of its functions and predicates; only the control structure of the program is really important in this case. For example, in order to show that a given program always terminates, it is sometimes easier to show the stronger result that any program having that control structure always terminates.

This is one of the main reasons for introducing the notion of *program schemas*. A program schema is a program in which the variables are not declared (their domain is indicated by the symbol D), and the functions and predicates are unspecified (they are denoted by the function symbols f_1, $f_2, \ldots$ and the predicate symbols $p_1, p_2, \ldots$).

Thus a program schema may be thought of as representing a family of real programs. A real program of the family is obtained by providing an interpretation for the symbols of the program schema, i.e., a specific domain for D and specific functions and predicates for the symbols f_i and p_i.

Since our purpose in this chapter is to introduce only the basic notions and basic results regarding program schemas, we restrict our discussion to a very simple class of program schemas: flowchart-like schemas.

†Present address: Applied Mathematics Department, The Weizman Institute of Science, Rehovot, Israel.

3-2. BASIC NOTIONS

Syntax

An *alphabet* Σ_S of a program schema S is a finite subset of the following set of symbols:

1. Constants
    a. *n*-ary *function constants* f_i^n ($i \geq 1$, $n \geq 0$); f_i^0 is called an *individual constant* and also denoted by a_i.
    b. *n*-ary *predicate constants* p_i^n ($i \geq 1$, $n \geq 0$); p_i^0 is called a *propositional constant*.
2. Individual variables
    a. Input variables $x_1, x_2, \ldots$.
    b. Program variables $y_1, y_2, \ldots$.
    c. Output variables $z_1, z_2, \ldots$.

The number of input variables $\bar{x}$, program variables $\bar{y}$, and output variables $\bar{z}$ in Σ_S is denoted by $|\bar{x}|$, $|\bar{y}|$, and $|\bar{z}|$, respectively, where $|\bar{x}|, |\bar{y}|, |\bar{z}| \geq 0$. The subscripts of the symbols are used for enumerating the symbols and will be omitted whenever their omission can cause no confusion. The superscripts of f_i^n and p_i^n are used only to indicate the number of arguments and therefore will always be omitted.

A *term* τ *over* Σ_S is constructed in the normal sense by composing individual variables, individual constants, and function constants of Σ_S. An *atomic formula* A *over* Σ_S is a propositional constant p_i^0 or an expression of the form $p_i^n(t_1, \ldots, t_n)$, $n \geq 1$, where $t_1, \ldots, t_n$ are terms over Σ_S. We shall write $\tau(\bar{x})$ and $A(\bar{x})$ to indicate that the term τ and the atomic formula A contain no individual variables other than members of $\bar{x}$; similarly, we shall write $\tau(\bar{x}, \bar{y})$ and $A(\bar{x}, \bar{y})$ to indicate that the term τ and the atomic formula A contain no individual variables other than members of $\bar{x}$ and $\bar{y}$.

A *statement over* Σ_S is of one of the following five forms:

1. START statement

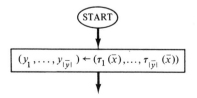

2. Assignment statement

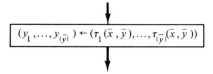

3. Test statement

4. HALT statement

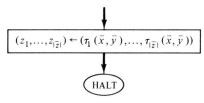

5. LOOP statement

where all the terms and atomic formulas are over Σ_S.

A *program schema* S over a finite alphabet Σ_S (*schema*, for short) is a finite flow diagram constructed from statements over Σ_S with one START statement.

Example 1

In the sequel we shall discuss the program schema S_1 described in Figure 1. Σ_{S_1} consists of the individual constant a, the unary function constant f_1, the binary function constant f_2, the unary predicate constant p, the input variable x, the program variables y_1 and y_2, and the output variable z. Each statement of S_1 is enclosed by a dashed line.

Semantics (Interpretations)

An *interpretation* $\mathscr{I}$ of a program schema S consists of

1. A nonempty set of elements D (called the *domain* of the interpretation).

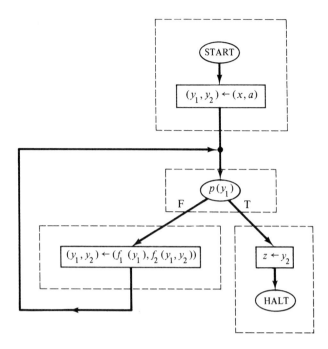

Fig. 1 The program schema S_1.

2. Assignments to the constants of Σ_S:
   a. To each function constant f_i^n in Σ_S we assign a total function mapping D^n into D (if $n = 0$, the individual constant f_i^0 is assigned some fixed element of D).
   b. To each predicate constant p_i^n in Σ_S we assign a total predicate mapping D^n into $\{T, F\}$ (if $n = 0$, the propositional constant p_i^0 is assigned the truth value T or F).

The pair $P = \langle S, \mathcal{I} \rangle$, where S is a program schema and $\mathcal{I}$ is an interpretation of S, is called a *program*. Given initial values $\bar{\xi} \in D^{|\bar{x}|}$ for the input variables $\bar{x}$ of S, the program can be executed.

The *computation of* $\langle S, \mathcal{I}, \bar{\xi} \rangle$ proceeds in the normal sense, starting from the START statement with $\bar{x} = \bar{\xi}$. The values of $(y_1, \ldots, y_{|\bar{y}|})$ are first initialized in the START statement to $(\tau_1(\bar{\xi}), \ldots, \tau_{|\bar{y}|}(\bar{\xi}))$. Note that if an assignment statement of the form $(y_1, \ldots, y_{|\bar{y}|}) \leftarrow (\tau_1(\bar{x}, \bar{y}), \ldots, \tau_{|\bar{y}|}(\bar{x}, \bar{y}))$ is reached with $\bar{y} = \bar{\eta}$ for some $\bar{\eta} \in D^{|\bar{y}|}$, the execution of the statement results in $(y_1, \ldots, y_{|\bar{y}|}) = (\tau_1(\bar{\xi}, \bar{\eta}), \ldots, \tau_{|\bar{y}|}(\bar{\xi}, \bar{\eta}))$; in other words, the new values of $y_1, \ldots, y_{|\bar{y}|}$ are computed simultaneously. Thus to interchange, for example, the values of y_1 and y_2, one can simply write $(y_1, y_2) \leftarrow (y_2, y_1)$.

The computation terminates as soon as a HALT statement is executed or a LOOP statement is reached. In the first case, if the execution of the HALT statement results in $\bar{z} = \bar{\zeta} \in D^{|z|}$, we say that $val\langle S, \vartheta, \bar{\xi}\rangle$ is *defined* and $val\langle S, \vartheta, \bar{\xi}\rangle = \bar{\zeta}$. In the second case (i.e., if the computation reaches a LOOP statement) or if the computation never terminates, we say that $val\langle S, \vartheta, \bar{\xi}\rangle$ is *undefined*. Thus a program P represents a partial function mapping $D^{|\bar{x}|}$ into $D^{|z|}$.

Example 2

Consider the program schema S_1 (Figure 1) with the following interpretations.

Interpretation ϑ_A: $D = \{$the natural numbers$\}$, a is 1, $f_1(y_1)$ is $y_1 \dot{-} 1$ (where $0 \dot{-} 1 = 0$), $f_2(y_1, y_2)$ is $y_1 \cdot y_2$, and $p(y_1)$ is $y_1 = 0$. The program $P_A = \langle S_1, \vartheta_A \rangle$, represented in Figure 2A, clearly computes the factorial function $z = factorial(x)$.

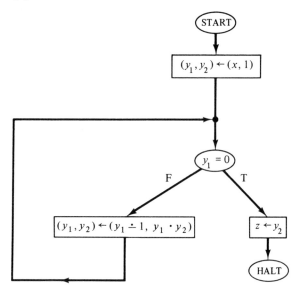

Fig. 2A   The program $P_A = \langle S_1, \vartheta_A \rangle$ for computing $z = factorial(x)$.

The second interpretation, ϑ_B, uses as domain the set Σ^* of all finite strings over the finite alphabet $\Sigma = \{A, B, \ldots, Z\}$ including the empty string Λ. We shall make use of three basic functions defined over Σ^*:

$h(x)$ gives the head (first letter) of the string x
$t(x)$ gives the tail of the string x (i.e., x with its first letter removed)
$a \cdot x$ concatenates the letter a to the string x

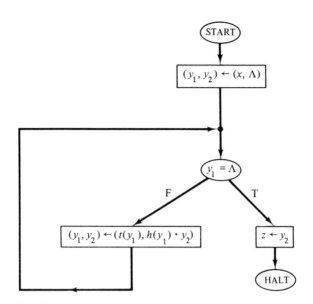

Fig. 2B   The program $P_B = \langle S_1, \mathcal{I}_B \rangle$ for computing $z = reverse(x)$.

For example, $h(ABC) = A$, $t(ABC) = BC$, and $A \cdot BC = ABC$. We agree that $h(\Lambda) = t(\Lambda) = \Lambda$ (the empty string). The interpretation $\mathcal{I}_B$ can then be defined as follows: $D = \{A, B, \ldots, Z\}^*$, a is Λ, $f_1(y_1)$ is $t(y_1)$, $f_2(y_1, y_2)$ is $h(y_1) \cdot y_2$, and $p(y_1)$ is $y_1 = \Lambda$. The program $P_B = \langle S_1, \mathcal{I}_B \rangle$, represented in Figure 2B, clearly reverses the order of letters in a given string, i.e., $z = reverse(x)$.

Example 3

Consider the program schema S_3 (Figure 3), where $y_1 \leftarrow f(y_1)$ abbreviates $(y_1, y_2) \leftarrow (f(y_1), y_2)$.

Note that S_3 does not contain any input variable. Thus for a given interpretation $\mathcal{I}$ of S_3, the program $\langle S_3, \mathcal{I} \rangle$ can be executed without indicating any input value. We therefore discuss the value of $val\langle S_3, \mathcal{I} \rangle$ rather than $val\langle S_3, \mathcal{I}, \bar{\xi} \rangle$ in this case.

S_3 contains a dummy output variable (we always assign the individual constant a to it). The reason is that in this example, we would like to know just whether $val\langle S_3, \mathcal{I} \rangle$ is defined rather than the value of $val\langle S_3, \mathcal{I} \rangle$.

Let us consider the following interpretation $\mathcal{I}^*$ of S_3:

a. The domain D consists of all strings of the form† "a", "$f(a)$", "$f(f(a))$", "$f(f(f(a)))$", ...

---

†For clarity we enclose the strings within quotation marks.

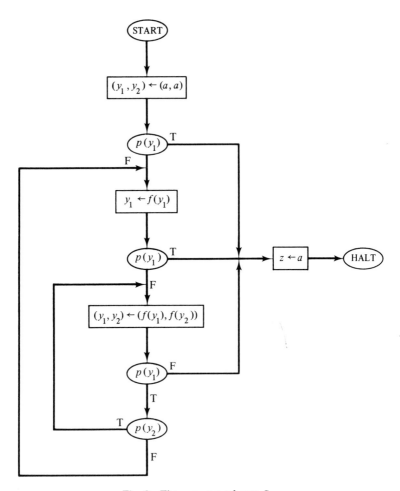

Fig. 3 The program schema S_3.

b. The individual constant a of Σ_{S_3} is assigned the element "a" of D.

c. The unary function constant f of Σ_{S_3} is assigned an unary function mapping D into D as follows.† Any element "$f^n(a)$" of $D, n \geq 0$, is mapped into "$f^{n+1}(a)$", which is also an element of D.

d. The unary predicate constant of Σ_{S_3} is assigned a unary predicate mapping D into $\{T, F\}$ as follows: $p("f^n(a)")$, $n \geq 0$, takes the values

$$n: 0 \;\; 1 \;\; 2 \;\; 3 \;\; 4 \;\; 5 \;\; 6 \;\; 7 \;\; 8 \;\; 9 \;\; 10 \;\; 11 \;\; 12 \;\; 13 \;\; 14 \;\; 15$$

$$p("f^n(a)"): \;\; F, F, \underbrace{T}, F, \underbrace{T, T}, F, \underbrace{T, T, T}, F, \underbrace{T, T, T, T}, F, \ldots$$

The computation of $\langle S_3, \mathscr{I}^* \rangle$ is best described by the following sequence of elements of $D \times D$ indicating the successive values of (y_1, y_2):

†Here $f^0(a)$ stands for a, $f^1(a)$ for $f(a)$, $f^2(a)$ for $f(f(a))$, $f^3(a)$ for $f(f(f(a)))$, and so on.

$$("a", "a") \to ("f(a)", "a") \to ("f^2(a)", "f(a)") \to ("f^3(a)", "f(a)")$$
$$\to ("f^4(a)", "f^2(a)") \to ("f^5(a)", "f^3(a)")$$
$$\to ("f^6(a)", "f^3(a)") \to \cdots$$

It can be proved (by induction) that $val\langle S_3, \mathcal{I}^* \rangle$ is undefined. Interpretations similar to $\mathcal{I}^*$ are of special interest and will be discussed later.

One can further show that $val\langle S_3, \mathcal{I} \rangle$ is defined for every interpretation $\mathcal{I}$ with finite domain, and it is also defined for every interpretation $\mathcal{I}$ with infinite domain unless $p("f^n(a)")$, $n \geq 0$, takes the following values under $\mathcal{I}$:

$$\text{F, F, T, F, T, T, F, T, T, T, F, T, T, T, T, F, }\ldots$$

Basic Properties

Our next step after defining the syntax and the semantics of program schemas is to introduce a few basic properties of program schemas which will be discussed in the rest of this chapter.

Halting and Divergence. For a given program $\langle S, \mathcal{I} \rangle$ we say that

1. $\langle S, \mathcal{I} \rangle$ *halts* if for every input $\bar{\xi} \in D^{|\bar{x}|}$, $val\langle S, \mathcal{I}, \bar{\xi} \rangle$ is defined.
2. $\langle S, \mathcal{I} \rangle$ *diverges* if for every input $\bar{\xi} \in D^{|\bar{x}|}$, $val\langle S, \mathcal{I}, \bar{\xi} \rangle$ is undefined.

Note that a program $\langle S, \mathcal{I} \rangle$ may neither halt nor diverge if for some $\bar{\xi}_1 \in D^{|\bar{x}|}$, $val\langle S, \mathcal{I}, \bar{\xi}_1 \rangle$ is defined and for some other $\bar{\xi}_2 \in D^{|\bar{x}|}$, $val\langle S, \mathcal{I}, \bar{\xi}_2 \rangle$ is undefined.

For a given program schema S we say that

1. S *halts* if for every interpretation $\mathcal{I}$ of S, $\langle S, \mathcal{I} \rangle$ halts.
2. S *diverges* if for every interpretation $\mathcal{I}$ of S, $\langle S, \mathcal{I} \rangle$ diverges.

Example 4

The program schema S_4 in Figure 4 halts (for every interpretation). One can observe that (a) the LOOP statement can never be reached, since whenever we reach test statement α, $p(a)$ is F; and (b) we can never go through the loop more than once, since whenever we reach test statement β, either $p(a)$ is T, or $p(a)$ is F and $p(f(a))$ is T.

Example 5 (*Paterson*)

The program schema S_5 in Figure 5 also halts (for every interpretation). However, it is very hard to prove it: We shall never test $p(f^i(a))$, where $i > 140$, but there are some interpretations for which we do have to test $p(f^{140}(a))$.

Equivalence. The next property we introduce is the equivalence of two

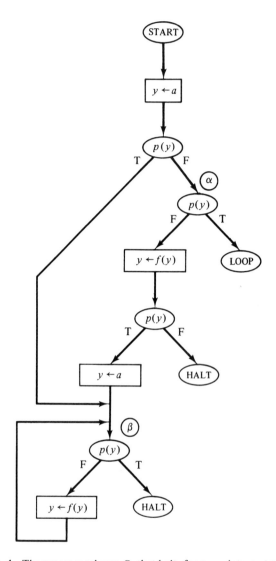

Fig. 4   The program schema S_4 that halts for every interpretation.

program schemas, which is certainly the most important property considered among program schemas.

Two program schemas S and S' are said to be *compatible* if they have the same set of input variables $\bar{x}$ and the same set of output variables $\bar{z}$. Two programs $\langle S, \mathcal{I} \rangle$ and $\langle S', \mathcal{I}' \rangle$ are said to be *compatible* if the program schemas S and S' are compatible, and the interpretations $\mathcal{I}$ and $\mathcal{I}'$ have the same domain.

For two given compatible programs $\langle S, \mathcal{I} \rangle$ and $\langle S', \mathcal{I}' \rangle$, we say that $\langle S, \mathcal{I} \rangle$ *and* $\langle S', \mathcal{I}' \rangle$ *are equivalent* (notation: $\langle S, \mathcal{I} \rangle = \langle S', \mathcal{I}' \rangle$), if for every

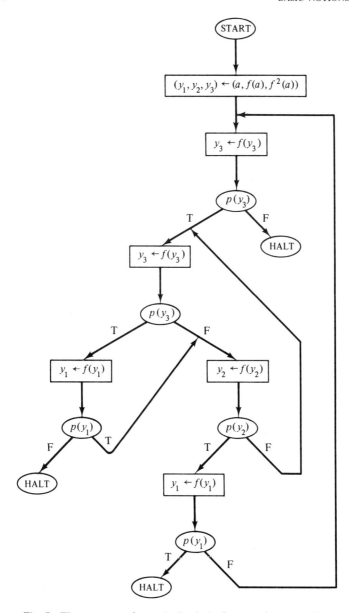

Fig. 5 The program schema S_5 that halts for every interpretation.

input $\bar{\xi} \in D^{|\bar{x}|}$, $val\langle S, \mathcal{G}, \bar{\xi}\rangle \overset{*}{=} val\langle S', \mathcal{G}', \bar{\xi}\rangle$; i.e.,† either (1) both $val\langle S, \mathcal{G}, \bar{\xi}\rangle$ and $val\langle S', \mathcal{G}', \bar{\xi}\rangle$ are undefined or (2) both $val\langle S, \mathcal{G}, \bar{\xi}\rangle$ and $val\langle S', \mathcal{G}', \bar{\xi}\rangle$ are defined and $val\langle S, \mathcal{G}, \bar{\xi}\rangle = val\langle S', \mathcal{G}', \bar{\xi}\rangle$.

† $\overset{*}{=}$ is the extension of the regular $=$ relation for handling undefined values; it is true if either both arguments are undefined or both are defined and equal, and it is false otherwise. (Thus the value is false if only one of the arguments is undefined.)

For two given compatible program schemas S and S', we say that S and
S' are equivalent, (notation: $S = S'$), if for every interpretation† $\mathcal{I}$ of S and
S', $\langle S, \mathcal{I} \rangle$ and $\langle S', \mathcal{I} \rangle$ are equivalent.

Note that the above notion of equivalence is not only reflexive and symmetric but also transitive (i.e., it is really an equivalence relation). Thus one
way to prove the equivalence of two program schemas is by passing from one
to the other by a chain of simple transformations, each of which obviously
preserves equivalence. Some examples of such transformations are shown
below. It should be clear in each case that they do preserve equivalence.

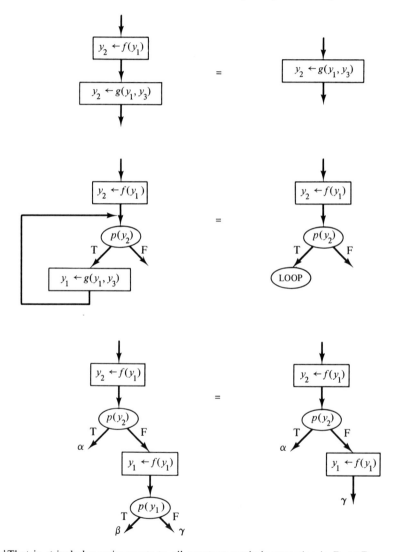

†That is, $\mathcal{I}$ includes assignments to all constant symbols occurring in $\Sigma_S \cup \Sigma_{S'}$.

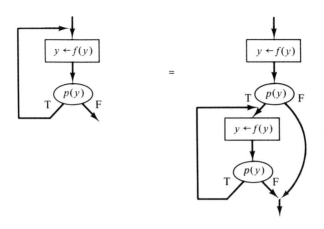

Example 6 (*Paterson*)

We will now try to apply some of those transformations to the program schema S_{6A} (Figure 6A) to show that it is equivalent to the program schema S_{6E} (Figure 6E). We proceed in four steps (see Figures 6B to 6D).

a. $S_{6A} = S_{6B}$. Consider the program schema S_{6A}. First note that if we take at some stage the F branch of statement 7, i.e., $p(y_4) = $ F, the schema gets into an infinite loop since the value of y_4 is not changed in statements 3, 4, and 6. Also note that after execution of statements 2 and 3, we have that $y_1 = y_4$. Thus, the first time we take the F branch of statement 5 we either get into an infinite loop through statements 3 and 4, or if we get out of the loop, we will get into an infinite loop when $p(y_4)$ is tested. Hence, let us replace the F branch of statement 5 by a LOOP statement. Now, whenever we reach statement 5 we have $y_1 = y_4$. Thus whenever we reach statement 7 we must take its T branch. Statement 7 can therefore be removed. Since at statement 4 we always have $y_1 = y_4$, we can replace y_4 by y_1 in this statement. Now, since y_4 is not used any longer, we can remove statement 2. Finally, we introduce the extra test statement 8′ just by unwinding once the loop through statements 8 and 9.

b. $S_{6B} = S_{6C}$. Consider the program schema S_{6B}. Since y_2 and y_3 are assigned the same values at statement 4, we have $y_2 = y_3$ when we first test $p(y_2)$ in statement 8. Therefore, (1) if we take the T branch of $p(y_2)$ we can go directly to statement 11, (2) if we take the F branch of $p(y_2)$ and later take the T branch of statement 8′, since $p(y_3)$ is F (y_3 has not been modified) Figure 6C) and y_3 can be replaced by y_2 in statement 6. Finally, since y_3 is now redundant, it can be eliminated.

c. $S_{6C} = S_{6D}$. Consider the program schema S_{6C}. Leaving the inner loop (8′–9), the value of y_2 is not used in statement 3, while we reset y_2 in statement

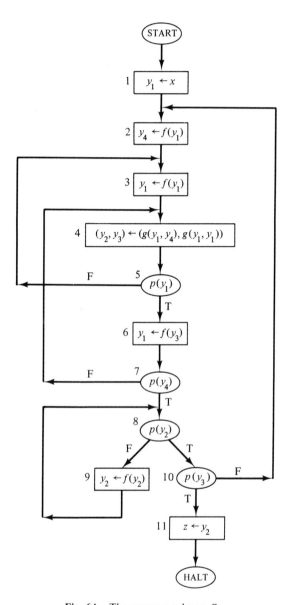

Fig. 6A   The program schema S_{6A}.

we get back to statement 3. So, statement 10 can be removed (as shown in 4. Thus the value of y_2 created in statement 9 serves no purpose. This suggests that we can remove the inner loop. There is, however, the chance that we

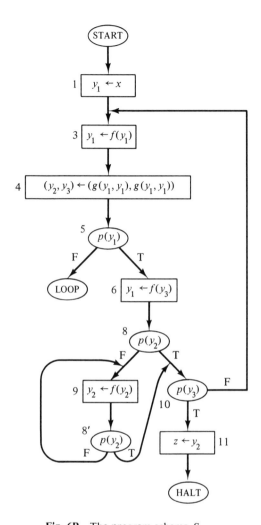

Fig. 6B The program schema S_{6B}.

could loop indefinitely through statements 9 and 8′. In this case, if we reach statement 8 with some value $y_2 = $ "η", then $p(\text{"}f^i(\eta)\text{"}) = $ F for all i and especially $p(\text{"}f^2(\eta)\text{"}) = $ F. Now, if we remove the inner loop, in statement 6 we set $y_1 = $ "$f(\eta)$", and then in statement 3 we set $y_1 = $ "$f^2(\eta)$". So $p(y_1)$ in statement 5 will be F leading to the LOOP statement. Thus, since the only possible use of statements 9 and 8′ is covered by the LOOP statement, the inner loop can be removed. Finally, since the value of y_2 is not used in statement 5 we can execute statement 4 after testing $p(y_1)$. Similarly, since

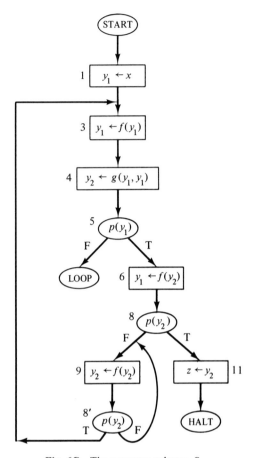

Fig. 6C   The program schema S_{6C}.

the value of y_1 is not used in statement 8, we can execute statement 6 after testing $p(y_2)$.

d. $S_{6D} = S_{6E}$. Considering statements 4 and 6 in S_{6D}, we realize that y_2 is merely a dummy variable and can be replaced by y_1. Dropping therefore the subscript and modifying statements 1, 3, and 6, we get S_{6E}.

Isomorphism. Sometimes we would like to know not only if two program schemas S and S' yield the same final value for the same interpretation, but in addition whether or not both compute this value in the same manner. We therefore introduce the stronger notion of equivalence, called *isomorphism*.

Two compatible program schemas S and S' are said to be *isomorphic* (notation: $S \equiv S'$) if for every interpretation $\mathscr{g}$ of S and S' and for every input $\bar{\xi} \in D^{|\bar{x}|}$, the sequence of statements executed in the (finite or infinite)

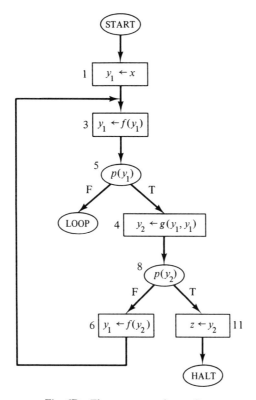

Fig. 6D The program schema S_{6D}.

computation of $\langle S, \mathcal{g}, \bar{\xi} \rangle$ is identical to the sequence of statements executed in the computation of $\langle S', \mathcal{g}, \bar{\xi} \rangle$.

Example 7

The three program schemas S_{7A}, S_{7B}, and S_{7C} (Figure 7) are compatible. It is clear that $S_{7A} = S_{7B} = S_{7C}$, but $S_{7A} \equiv S_{7B} \not\equiv S_{7C}$.

Herbrand Interpretation

The basic properties of program schemas, such as halting, divergence, equivalence, or isomorphism, depend by definition on their behavior for all interpretations (over all domains). It would clearly be of great help in proving properties of program schemas if we could fix on one special domain such that the behavior of the program schemas for all interpretations over this domain characterize their behavior for all interpretations over any domain. Fortunately, for any program schema S, there does exist such a domain; it is called the *Herbrand universe of S* and is denoted by H_S. H_S consists of all strings of the following form: (1) If x_i is an input variable and

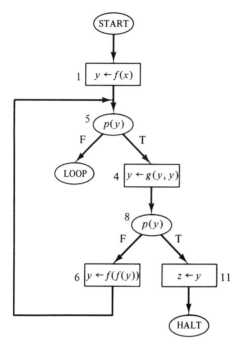

Fig. 6E   The program schema S_{6E}.

a_i is an individual constant occurring in S, then "x_i" and "a_i" are in H_S; (2) if f_i^n is an n-ary function constant occurring in S and "t_1", "t_2", ..., "t_n" are elements of H_S, then so is "$f_i^n(t_1, \ldots, t_n)$".

Example A

For the program schema S_1 (Figure 1), H_{S_1} consists of the strings

$$\text{``}a\text{''}, \text{``}x\text{''}, \text{``}f_1(a)\text{''}, \text{``}f_1(x)\text{''}, \text{``}f_2(a, a)\text{''}, \text{``}f_2(a, x)\text{''}, \text{``}f_2(x, a)\text{''},$$
$$\text{``}f_2(x, x)\text{''}, \text{``}f_1(f_1(a))\text{''}, \ldots$$

For the program schema S_3 (Figure 3), H_{S_3} consists of the strings

$$\text{``}a\text{''}, \text{``}f(a)\text{''}, \text{``}f(f(a))\text{''}, \text{``}f(f(f(a)))\text{''}, \ldots$$

Now, for any given program schema S, an interpretation over the Herbrand universe H_S of S consists of assignments to the constants of S, as follows: (1) To each function constant f_i^n which occurs in S we assign an n-ary function over H_S (in particular, each individual constant a_i is assigned some element of H_S); and (2) to each predicate constant p_i^n which occurs in S we assign an n-ary predicate over H_S (in particular, each propositional constant is assigned the truth value T or F).

Among all those interpretations over H_S we are interested in a special

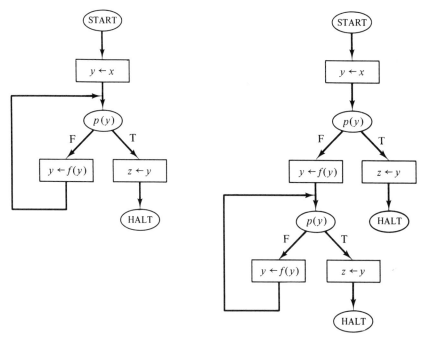

program schema S_{7A} program schema S_{7B}

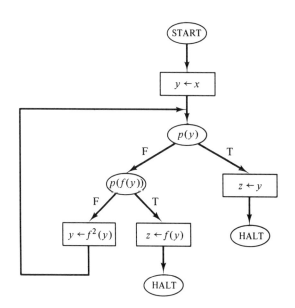

program schema S_{7C}

Fig. 7

subclass of interpretations, called *Herbrand interpretations of S,* which satisfy the following conditions: (1) Each individual constant a_i in S is assigned the string "a_i" of H_S; and (2) each constant function f_i^n occurring in S is assigned the n-ary function over H_S which maps the strings "t_1", "t_2", ..., "t_n" of H_S into the string "$f_i^n(t_1, t_2, \ldots, t_n)$" of H_S. Note that there is no restriction on the assignments to the predicate constants of S.

Example B

The interpretation $\mathcal{I}^*$ described in Example 3 is a Herbrand interpretation of the program schema S_3.

Note that H_S contains the strings "x_i" for all input variables x_i occurring in S. We let "$\bar{x}$" denote the vector of strings ("x_1", "x_2", ..., "$x_{|\bar{x}|}$"). In general, among all possible computations of a program schema S with Herbrand interpretation $\mathcal{I}^*$, the most interesting computation is the one of $\langle S, \mathcal{I}^*, "\bar{x}" \rangle$, i.e., the one in which the strings "x_i" of H_S are assigned to the input variables x_i.

The most important property of Herbrand interpretations is that for any interpretation $\mathcal{I}$ of a program schema S and input $\bar{\xi} \in D^{|\bar{x}|}$, there exists a Herbrand interpretation $\mathcal{I}^*$ such that the (finite or infinite) computation of $\langle S, \mathcal{I}^*, "\bar{x}" \rangle$ follows exactly the "trace" (path on the flow diagram) of the computation of $\langle S, \mathcal{I}, \bar{\xi} \rangle$. The appropriate Herbrand interpretation $\mathcal{I}^*$ of S is obtained by defining the truth value of $p_i^n("\tau_1", \ldots, "\tau_n")$ as follows: If under interpretation $\mathcal{I}$ and input $\bar{\xi}$, $(\tau_1, \ldots, \tau_n) = (d_1, \ldots, d_n)$, where $d_i \in D$, and $p(d_1, \ldots, d_n) = T$, then we let $p("\tau_1", \ldots, "\tau_n") = T$ under interpretation $\mathcal{I}^*$; and if $p(d_1, \ldots, d_n) = F$, we let $p("\tau_1", \ldots, "\tau_n") = F$.

This implies that many properties of program schemas can be described and proved just by considering Herbrand interpretations rather than all interpretations, as suggested by the following theorem.

THEOREM 1 (*Luckham–Park–Paterson*)
"Herbrand's Theorem" for program schemas

a. For every program schema S, S halts/diverges *if and only if* $val\langle S, \mathcal{I}^*, "\bar{x}" \rangle$ is defined/undefined for every Herbrand interpretation $\mathcal{I}^*$ of S.

b. For every two compatible program schemas S and S', S and S' are equivalent *if and only if* $val\langle S, \mathcal{I}^*, "\bar{x}" \rangle \overset{*}{=} val\langle S', \mathcal{I}^*, "\bar{x}" \rangle$ for every Herbrand interpretation $\mathcal{I}^*$ of S and S'.

c. For every two compatible program schemas S and S', S and S' are isomorphic *if and only if* for every Herbrand interpretation $\mathcal{I}^*$ of S and S', the sequence of statements executed in the computation of $\langle S, \mathcal{I}^*, "\bar{x}" \rangle$ is identical to the sequence of statements executed in the computation of $\langle S', \mathcal{I}^*, "\bar{x}" \rangle$.

Proof. Let us sketch the proof of part b. The proof of parts a and c are similar. It is clear that if S and S' are equivalent then $val\langle S, \mathcal{I}^*, "\bar{x}"\rangle \overset{*}{=} val\langle S', \mathcal{I}^*, "\bar{x}"\rangle$ for every Herbrand interpretation $\mathcal{I}^*$. To prove the other direction, we assume that S and S' are not equivalent. Then there must exist an interpretation $\mathcal{I}$ of S and S' and an input $\bar{\xi} \in D^{|\bar{x}|}$ such that $val\langle S, \mathcal{I}, \bar{\xi}\rangle \overset{*}{\neq} val\langle S', \mathcal{I}, \bar{\xi}\rangle$. For this interpretation $\mathcal{I}$ and input $\bar{\xi}$, there exists a Herbrand interpretation $\mathcal{I}^*$ of S and S' such that the computations of $\langle S, \mathcal{I}^*, "\bar{x}"\rangle$ and $\langle S', \mathcal{I}^*, "\bar{x}"\rangle$ follow the same traces as the computations of $\langle S, \mathcal{I}, \bar{\xi}\rangle$ and $\langle S', \mathcal{I}, \bar{\xi}\rangle$, respectively. Thus we clearly have that $val\langle S, \mathcal{I}, "\bar{x}"\rangle \overset{*}{\neq} val\langle S', \mathcal{I}^*, "\bar{x}"\rangle$.†

Q.E.D.

Normal Form

In this section we discuss a class of program schemas restricted by the form of their flow diagram, called *normal form*. We present two equivalent definitions of normal form: the "graph definition" and the "block definition." This class of program schemas is of special interest because every program schema can be transformed effectively into an isomorphic program schema in normal form; the block definition can then be used to prove properties of the normal-form program schema by induction on its block structure.

DEFINITION 1
The "graph definition"

A program schema is in *normal form* if its flow diagram has the form of a tree (the root is the START statement and the terminals are HALT and LOOP statements) in which branches may bend back but only to ancestors.

Example 8

The flow diagram in Figure 8 represents a program schema in normal form. Here the root node stands for the START statement, each terminal node stands for a HALT or LOOP statement, each single-exit node stands for an assignment statement, while each two-exit node stands for a test statement. Note that if arc α, for example, had led to statement B rather than to statement A, the program schema would not have been in normal form.

THEOREM 2 (*Cooper and Engeler*)
The normal-form theorem

Every program schema S can be transformed effectively into an isomorphic program schema S' which is in normal form.

†Note that $val\langle S, \mathcal{I}, \bar{\xi}\rangle \overset{*}{\neq} val\langle S', \mathcal{I}, \bar{\xi}\rangle$ implies that $val\langle S, \mathcal{I}^*, "\bar{x}"\rangle \overset{*}{\neq} val\langle S', \mathcal{I}^*, "\bar{x}"\rangle$ but not necessarily vice versa!

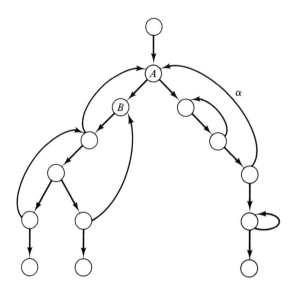

Fig. 8 A flow diagram representing a program schema in normal form.

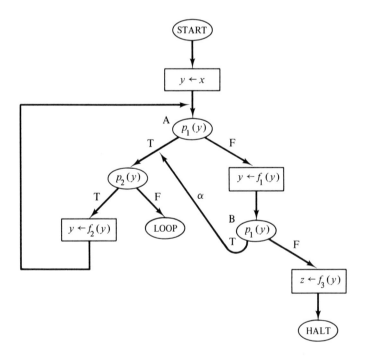

Fig. 9A The program schema S_{9A} (not in normal form).

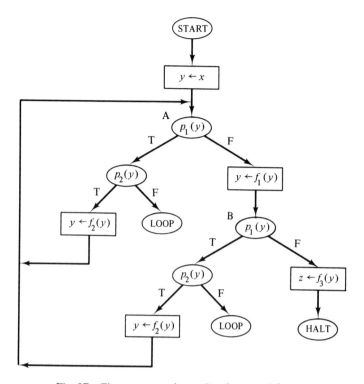

Fig. 9B The program schema S_{9B} (in normal form).

Proof. First, label all statements in S to distinguish between multiple occurrences of the same statement in S. Then, start to construct a "tree schema" corresponding to S by unwinding the loops of S, but, whenever you reach a "labeled" statement which occurs already in that branch (path) of the tree, loop back to the previous occurrence of that statement. Note that the process must always terminate since the depth of the tree (i.e., the length of the longest path) cannot exceed the number of statements in S. This tree is the desired program schema S'.

Example 9

The program schema S_{9A} (Figure 9A) is not in normal form because arc α bends back from a statement on the right branch to a statement on the left branch. Applying the above procedure we obtain the program schema S_{9B} (Figure 9B), which is in normal form and clearly isomorphic to the given program schema S_{9A}.

DEFINITION 2
The "block definition"

A program schema is in *normal form* if it is of the form

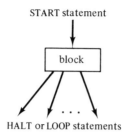

where a *block* is defined recursively as follows:

    a. *Basic blocks:* Any test or assignment statement is a block. The "empty block" with no statements at all is also considered to be a basic block.

    b. *Composition:*

If

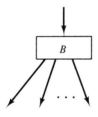

and

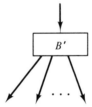

are blocks, then so is

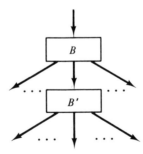

Note that by composition of basic blocks it follows that every program schema with no loops in its structure (without the START, HALT, and LOOP statements) is a block.

c. *Looping*

If

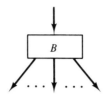

is a block, then so is

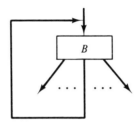

Example 10

The structure of blocks of program schema S_{9B} which is in normal form is illustrated in Figure 10. Blocks B_1, B_2, and B_3 are obtained by composition of basic blocks. Blocks B_4 and B_5 are obtained by looping, while block B_6 is obtained by applying the composition operation twice.

Both definitions of normal form are equivalent in the sense that they define exactly the same class of program schemas. It is straightforward to see that every program schema satisfying the block definition must also satisfy the graph definition. We proceed to verify the converse, i.e., that every program schema satisfying the graph definition also satisfies the block definition. The proof is by induction on the number n of branches bending back.

If $n = 0$, then S is a tree with no loops which can be obtained by composition of basic blocks.

Now, assume that the result is true for $n = 0, \ldots, k$ and consider a tree structure with $k + 1$ branches $\alpha_1, \alpha_2, \ldots, \alpha_{k+1}$ bending back. Suppose that each such branch α_i, $1 \leq i \leq k + 1$ bends back from node a_i to node b_i. Let **b** be a node among all the b_i's with the maximum distance to the root of the tree. Then let **a** be the corresponding a_i. If there is more than one branch bending back to **b**, we take **a** to be the one closest to **b** (see, for example, Figure A). This means that there is no other b_j on the path going down from **b** to **a**, since there is also no loop on this path, it forms a block, B say (see Figure B).† By the "looping" clause in the block-form definition it

---

†Note that the special case of a redundant test statement where both branches are leading to **b** should be treated separately.

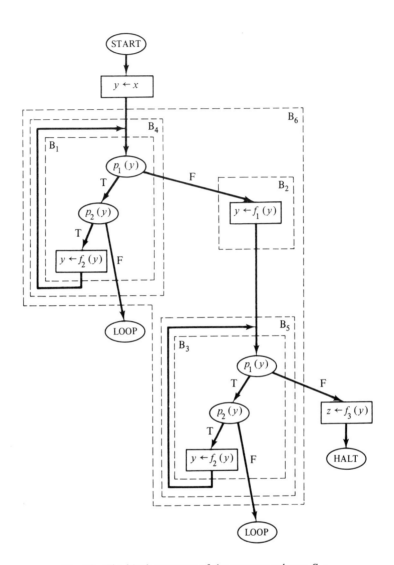

Fig. 10 The block structure of the program schema S_{9B}.

follows that B together with arc α (leading from **a** to **b**) form also a block, B' say. Now treating B' as a node of the tree, we have a tree which has only k branches bending back (see Figure C). By the induction hypothesis, this tree can be put in block form. Thus the original tree is in block form.

By induction, it follows that any tree structure with branches bending back only to ancestors satisfies the block definition.

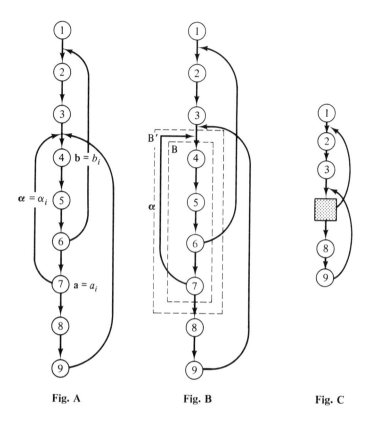

Fig. A   Fig. B   Fig. C

3-3. DECISION PROBLEMS

We say that a class of "yes/no problems" (i.e., a class of problems, the answer to each one of which is either "yes" or "no") is *decidable*, if there exists an algorithm (Turing machine) that takes any problem in the class as input and always stops with the correct "yes" or "no" answer. We say that a class of yes/no problems is *partially decidable*, if there exists an algorithm (Turing machine) that takes any problem in the class as input and: If it is a yes-problem, the algorithm will eventually stop with a yes-answer; otherwise, i.e., if it is a no-problem, the algorithm either stops with a no-answer or loops forever. It is clear that if a class of yes/no problems is decidable, it is also partially decidable.

In this chapter we discuss four classes of yes/no problems:

1. *The halting problem for program schemas*—does there exist an algorithm (Turing machine) that takes any program schema S as input and

always stops with a correct yes-answer (S halts for every interpretation) or no-answer (S does not halt for every interpretation)?

2. *The divergence problem for program schemas*—does there exist an algorithm (Turing machine) that takes any program schema S as input and always stops with a correct yes-answer (S diverges for every interpretation) or no-answer (S does not diverge for every interpretation)?

3. *The equivalence problem for program schemas*—does there exist an algorithm (Turing machine) that takes any two compatible program schemas S and S' as input and always stops with a correct yes-answer (S and S' are equivalent) or no-answer (S and S' are not equivalent)?

4. *The isomorphism problem for program schemas*—does there exist an algorithm (Turing machine) that takes any two compatible program schemas S and S' as input and always stops with a correct yes-answer (S and S' are isomorphic) or no-answer (S and S' are not isomorphic)?

We show that the halting problem for program schemas is undecidable but partially decidable; while the divergence, equivalence, and isomorphism problems for program schemas are not even partially decidable. It is quite surprising that all these undecidability results can actually be shown for a very restricted class of program schemas. For this purpose let us consider the class $\mathcal{S}_1$ of program schemas. We say that a program schema S is in the class $\mathcal{S}_1$ if

1. Σ_S consists of a single individual constant a, a single unary function f, a single unary predicate p, two program variables y_1 and y_2, a single output variable z, but no input variables.

2. All statements in S are of one of the following forms:

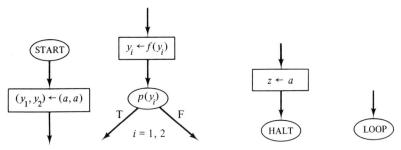

In Section 2.1 we show that

1. The halting problem for program schemas in $\mathcal{S}_1$ is undecidable.
2. The divergence problem for program schemas in $\mathcal{S}_1$ is not partially decidable.
3. The equivalence problem for program schemas in $\mathcal{S}_1$ is not partially decidable.

4. The isomorphism problem for program schemas in S_1 is not partially decidable.

In the rest of this chapter we discuss subclasses of program schemas for which these problems are decidable. It is very interesting to compare, for example, the four decision problems for S_1 with those of a very "similar" class of program schemas, S_2. The two classes S_1 and S_2 differ only in that every program schema in S_2 contains two individual constants a and b, and the START statement is of the form

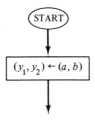

However, it will follow from our discussion later that since every program schema in S_2 is "free," S_2 has entirely different decision properties:

1. The halting problem for program schemas in S_2 is decidable.
2. The divergence problem for program schemas in S_2 is decidable.
3. The equivalence problem for program schemas in S_2 is decidable.†
4. The isomorphism problem for program schemas in S_2 is decidable.

Undecidability of the Basic Properties

The undecidability of the basic properties for the class S_1 of program schemas is proved by using the known result (see, e.g., Davis, 1958) that the *divergence problem of Turing machines is not partially decidable.* That is, there does not exist an algorithm (Turing machine) that takes any Turing machine M and any tape α, over $\Sigma = \{T, F\}$ say, as input, and: if M diverges starting with tape α the algorithm will stop with a yes-answer; otherwise, i.e., if M does not diverge (i.e., halts) starting with tape α, the algorithm either stops with a no-answer or loops forever.

There are two important ideas which are used in our proof:

1. Every Herbrand interpretation $\mathcal{I}^*$ of a program schema S in S_1 can actually be described by an infinite string over $\{T, F\}$, where the ith ($i \geq 0$) letter in the string indicates the value of $p(``f^i(a)")$ under $\mathcal{I}^*$.
2. A computation of a Turing machine M over $\Sigma = \{T, F\}$ starting with tape α can be described by a (possibly infinite) string over $\Sigma = \{T, F\}$:

---

†This follows from a recent (unpublished) work of Malcolm Bird.

$\alpha_0 * \alpha_1 * \alpha_2 * \alpha_3 * \ldots$, where $\alpha_i \in \Sigma^*$ ($i \geq 0$) indicates the "configuration" of M (contents of tape, position of reading head, and current state) after the ith step of the computation (α_0 is α). (Note that the auxiliary symbol $*$ can also be encoded using the $\{T, F\}$ symbols.)

Our main result is:

THEOREM 3 (*Luckham–Park–Paterson*)

The following properties of program schemas in S_1 are not partially decidable:

    a. $(S, \mathcal{I})$ diverges for every interpretation $\mathcal{I}$.
    b. $(S, \mathcal{I})$ diverges for some interpretation $\mathcal{I}$.

Part a is proved by showing that the divergence problem of Turing machines is reducible to the divergence (for every interpretation) problem of program schemas in S_1. That is, there exists an algorithm (Turing machine) that takes any Turing machine M and any tape α over $\Sigma = \{T, F\}$ as input and yields a program schema $S_A(M, \alpha)$ in S_1, such that M diverges starting with tape α if and only if $S_A(M, \alpha)$ diverges for every (Herbrand) interpretation. Thus since the divergence problem of Turing machines is not partially solvable, neither is the divergence (for every interpretation) problem of program schemas in S_1. The construction of $S_A(M, \alpha)$ is given in detail in Luckham, Park, and Paterson (1970) (see also Paterson, 1968).

Part b of the theorem is proved similarly by showing that the divergence problem of Turing machines is reducible to the divergence (for some interpretation) problem of program schemas in S_1. That is, there exists an algorithm (Turing machine) that takes any Turing machine M and tape α over $\Sigma = \{T, F\}$ as input and yields a program schema $S_B(M, \alpha)$ in S_1 such that M diverges starting with tape α if and only if $S_B(M, \alpha)$ diverges for some (Herbrand) interpretation.

From the theorem we get the following important corollary:

COROLLARY

    1. The halting problem for program schemas in S_1 is undecidable.[†]
    2. The divergence problem for program schemas in S_1 is not partially decidable.
    3. The equivalence problem for program schemas in S_1 is not partially decidable.

[†]From our discussion later it will actually follow that the halting problem of program schemas is in general partially decidable.

4. The isomorphism problem for program schemas in $\mathcal{S}_1$ is not partially decidable.

Proof. Part 1 follows from part b of the theorem, since if the halting problem is decidable so should be its complement: the divergence problem for some interpretation.

Part 2 is actually part a of the theorem.

Part 3 follows from part 2, since a program schema S of $\mathcal{S}_1$ is equivalent to the following program schema of $\mathcal{S}_1$ if and only if S diverges:

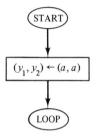

Part 4 also follows from part 2. For any program schema S of $\mathcal{S}_1$, let $\bar{S}$ be the program schema of $\mathcal{S}_1$ obtained by replacing all HALT statements in S by LOOP statements. Then S is isomorphic to $\bar{S}$ if and only if S diverges.

In the following sections we discuss subclasses of program schemas for which the four problems are decidable.

Free Schemas

"Freedom" is an important notion since it is usually substantially simpler to prove properties of free program schemas rather than of nonfree program schemas. Let us consider first the following example.

Example 11

Consider the program schema S_{11A} described in Figure 11A. Note that no computation of S_{11A} includes a sequence of statements of the form . . . –1–2–4–7– . . . , or a sequence of statements of the form . . . –1–2– 5–8– . . . , or a sequence of statements of the form . . . –5–1–3– . . . . In addition, no finite computation of S_{11A} includes the sequence of statements 1–2–5–1. It therefore follows that the program schema S_{11B} (Figure 11B) is equivalent to S_{11A}.

The program schema S_{11A} had impossible sequences of statements in the sense that no computation could follow those sequences; program schemas with such impossible sequences are said to be nonfree. The program schema S_{11B} has no such impossible sequences and therefore is said to be free.

Formally, a *program schema S is said to be free if every finite path through its flow diagram from the START statement is an initial segment of some computation.*

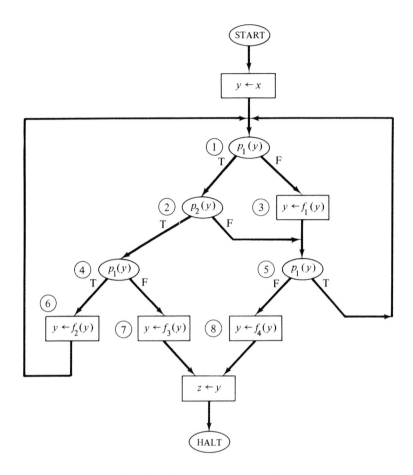

Fig. 11A   The program schema S_{11A}.

Example 12

The program schema S_{12} (Figure 12) is not free. Note that among all possible finite paths from the START statement to the HALT statement, only those that go through loop α the same number of times as through loop β describe possible computations of S_{12}.

The following are several interesting properties of the class of free program schemas:

1. *The halting problem for free program schemas is decidable.* Follows from the fact that a free flowchart schema does not halt if and only if it contains a LOOP statement or its flow diagram contains a loop in its structure.

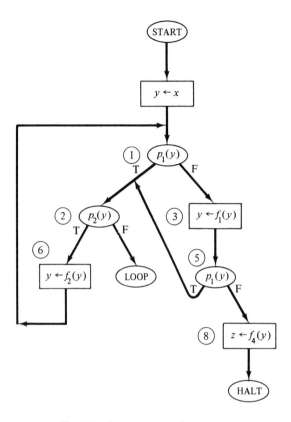

Fig. 11B The program schema S_{11B}.

2. *The divergence problem for free program schemas is decidable.* Follows from the fact that a free flowchart schema does not diverge if and only if it contains a HALT statement.

3. *It is not partially decidable whether or not a program schema is free* (*Paterson, 1967*).

To prove this, we shall show that for every Post's Correspondence Problem (PCP) C it is possible to construct a program schema $S(C)$ s.t. $S(C)$ is free if and only if C has no solution. Then, since it is not partially decidable whether or not an arbitrary PCP does not have a solution (see, e.g., Davis, 1958), it is also not partially decidable whether or not an arbitrary program schema is free.

Let C be a PCP which consists of a set of n pairs of strings $\{(u_i, v_i)\}_{1 \leq i \leq n}$ over an alphabet Σ. Then the corresponding program schema $S(C)$ is constructed as follows: The function constants used in $S(C)$ are f_σ for every

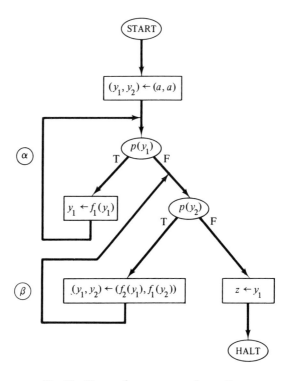

Fig. 12   The nonfree program schema S_{12}.

$\sigma \in \Sigma$. For any word $w = \sigma_1\sigma_2 \ldots \sigma_k \in \Sigma^*$, we let

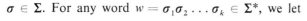

| $w^{(1)}$ | denote | $y_1 \leftarrow f_{\sigma_1}(f_{\sigma_2}(f_{\sigma_3}(\ldots(f_{\sigma_k}(y_1))\ldots)))$ |

and

| $w^{(2)}$ | denote | $y_2 \leftarrow f_{\sigma_1}(f_{\sigma_2}(f_{\sigma_3}(\ldots(f_{\sigma_k}(y_2))\ldots)))$ |

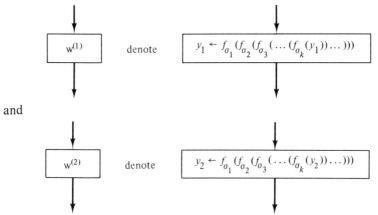

The program schema $S(C)$ (see Figure D) is constructed in such a way that the program variable y_1 simulates the composition of the u_i's while the program variable y_2 simulates the composition of the v_i's. Nonfreedom can only result from reaching α with $y_1 = y_2$, in which case the path $\ldots \alpha\beta\gamma$ is

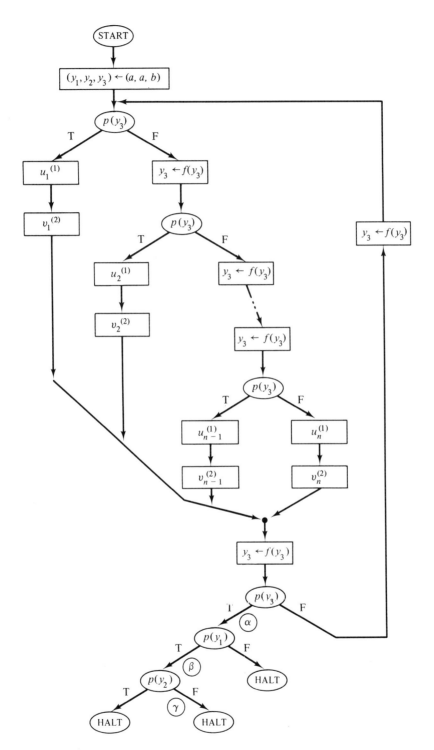

Fig. D The program schema $S(C)$ corresponding to Post's Correspondence Problem C.

impossible. Thus $S(C)$ is not free if and only if the **PCP** C has a solution; or equivalently, $S(C)$ is free if and only if C has no solution.

4. *It is unknown yet whether or not the equivalence problem for free program schemas is decidable.*

5. *The isomorphism problem for free program schemas is decidable.*

To show this it is very convenient to express a program schema by a regular expression which consists of "statements" rather than "letters," as illustrated below.

Example 13

The regular expression $\mathcal{R}(S_{13A})$ representing the program schema S_{13A} (Figure 13) is

$$\text{START}\,[y \leftarrow x]([p(y) = \text{F}][y \leftarrow f(y)])^*[p(y) = \text{T}][z \leftarrow y]\,\text{HALT}$$

and the regular expression $\mathcal{R}(S_{13B})$ representing the program schema S_{13B} is

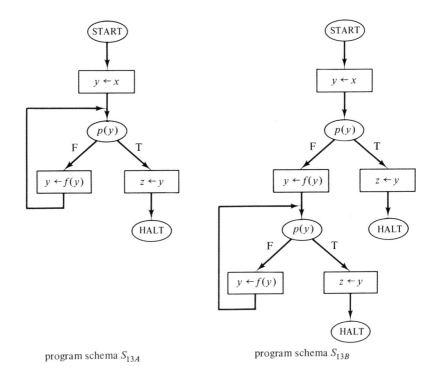

program schema S_{13A} program schema S_{13B}

Fig. 13   The isomorphic program schemas S_{13A} and S_{13B}.

START $[y \leftarrow x]([p(y) = T][z \leftarrow y]$ HALT

$+ [p(y) = F][y \leftarrow f(y)]([p(y) = F][y \leftarrow f(y)])^*[p(y) = T][z \leftarrow y]$ HALT)

For any free program schema S, every "word" in $\mathcal{R}(S)$ represents a sequence of statements of some *finite* computation $\langle S, \mathcal{I}^*, "\bar{x}" \rangle$ and vice versa. We leave to the reader to conclude from this that two compatible free program schemas S and S' are isomorphic if and only if $\mathcal{R}(S) = \mathcal{R}(S')$. Since it is decidable whether or not two regular expressions define the same set of words (see, e.g., Ginzburg, 1968), it follows that it is decidable whether or not two free program schemas are isomorphic.

For example, $\mathcal{R}(S_{13A})$ above has the form $ab(cd)^*efg$, while $\mathcal{R}(S_{13B})$ has the form $ab(efg + cd(cd)^*efg)$. Since $ab(efg + cd(cd)^*efg) = ab(\Lambda + cd$ $(cd)^*)efg = ab(cd)^*efg$, and since S_{13A} and S_{13B} are free program schemas, it implies that $S_{13A} \equiv S_{13B}$.

6. *The nonfree program schema S_{12} (Figure 12) has no equivalent free program schema (Chandra, 1973).*

Suppose there exists a free program schema, S' say, which is equivalent to S_{12}. It can be shown that there must exist a free program schema S'' which is equivalent to S' and contains no function constants other than the unary functions f_1 and f_2 and the individual constant a. Then, since S'' is free and contains only unary function constants, it can be shown that the set of all final terms generated by S'', under all possible Herbrand interpretations, can be expressed by a regular expression. But the set of all final terms generated by S_{12} is "$f_2^i(f_1^i(a))$", $i \geq 0$, which cannot be expressed by any regular expression (see e.g., Ginzburg, 1968); this is a contradiction.

The last result clearly implies that there cannot exist in general an algorithm for transforming a given program schema into an equivalent free program schema. The best we can do is to construct for a given program schema an equivalent free "tree schema." We discuss in the next section the class of tree schemas.

Tree-Program Schemas

A *tree schema* T over a finite alphabet Σ_T is a (*possibly infinite*) tree-like flow diagram constructed from statements over Σ_T such that

1. There is exactly one START statement.
2. For each statement, there is exactly one way it can be reached from the START statement.
3. Each terminal statement is a HALT or a LOOP statement.

Note that every finite tree schema (i.e., a tree schema with finitely many statements) is a program schema, therefore also called *tree-program schema*.

It is straightforward to show that

1. The halting problem for tree-program schemas is decidable.
2. The divergence problem for tree-program schemas is decidable.
3. The equivalence problem for tree-program schemas is decidable.
4. The isomorphism problem for tree-program schemas is decidable.

We illustrate the method for deciding whether two compatible tree-program schemas are equivalent or not in the following example.

Example 14

Consider the tree-program schema S_{14A} (Figure 14A) and S_{14B} (Figure 14B). Here e_1 is "$f(x_1, x_2)$", e_2 is "$g(x_2)$", and e_3 is "$f(f(x_1, x_2), g(x_2))$". The final value of z obtained by S_{14A} can be described by

$$if \ p(e_2) = p(e_3) = F \ then \ "a" \ else \ "b"$$

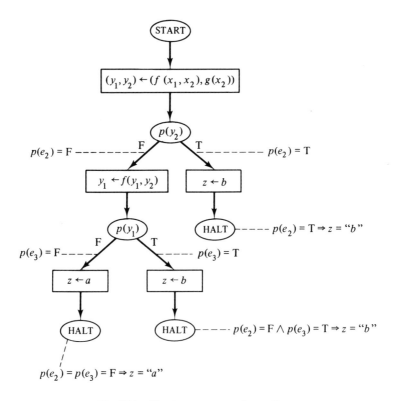

Fig. 14A   The tree-program schema S_{14A}.

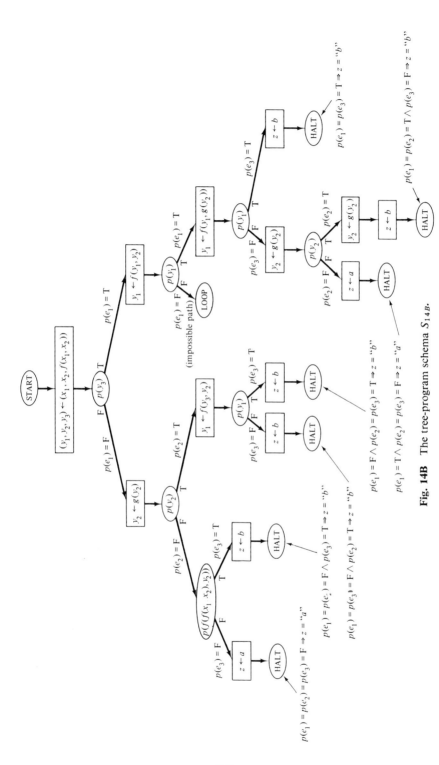

Fig. 14B The tree-program schema S_{14B}.

127

The final value of z obtained by S_{14B} can be summarized by the following table:

$p(e_1)$	$p(e_2)$	$p(e_3)$	z
T	T	T	"b"
T	T	F	"b"
T	F	T	"b"
T	F	F	"a"
F	T	T	"b"
F	T	F	"b"
F	F	T	"b"
F	F	F	"a"

or equivalently,

$$\textit{if } p(e_2) = p(e_3) = \text{F } \textit{then } \text{"}a\text{" } \textit{else } \text{"}b\text{"}$$

This implies that $val(S_{14A}, \vartheta^*, \text{"}\bar{x}\text{"}) \stackrel{*}{=} val(S_{14B}, \vartheta^*, \text{"}\bar{x}\text{"})$ for every Herbrand interpretation ϑ^*. Thus, S_{14A} and S_{14B} are equivalent.

Tree schemas and program schemas are computed in the same manner and therefore one can naturally define freedom of tree schemas and discuss equivalence between compatible program schemas and tree schemas. Further, Theorem 1 holds for tree schemas as well as for program schemas.

The key point about tree schemas is that *for any given program schema S one can construct an equivalent free tree schema T(S)*, called the *tree schema of S*. Rather than giving a detailed algorithm, we illustrate the construction of $T(S)$. Note that by Theorem 1 it suffices to consider only Herbrand interpretations.

Example 15

Consider again the program schema S_3 (Figure 3). We can "unwind" the loops of S_3 to produce an equivalent infinite tree. While unwinding we systematically look for impossible paths, which can be pruned. In this way we construct for S_3 the infinite tree described in Figure 15A. The FAILURE statements indicate impossible computations (i.e., no computation can reach these points). In the part of the tree that is shown in Figure 15A we have two FAILURE statements, since

a. Whenever we reach the test statement α, $(y_1, y_2) = (\text{"}f^2(a)\text{"}, \text{"}f(a)\text{"})$ and $p(\text{"}f(a)\text{"}) = \text{F}$; therefore, it is impossible to take the T branch.

b. Whenever we reach the test statement β, $(y_1, y_2) = (\text{"}f^4(a)\text{"}, \text{"}f^2(a)\text{"})$ and $p(\text{"}f^2(a)\text{"}) = T$; therefore, it is impossible to take the F branch.

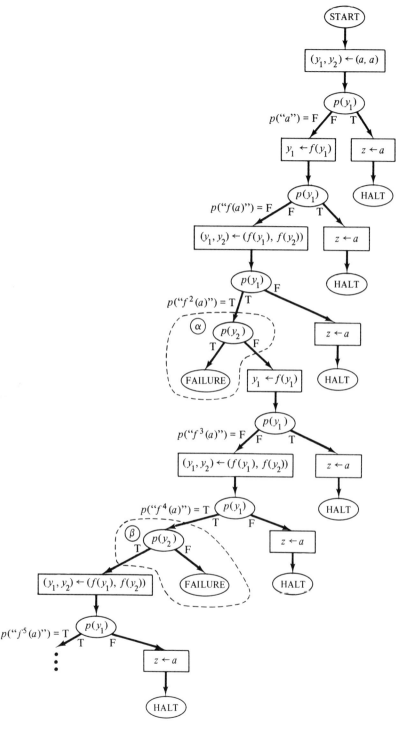

Fig. 15A The intermediate step in the construction of $T(S_3)$.

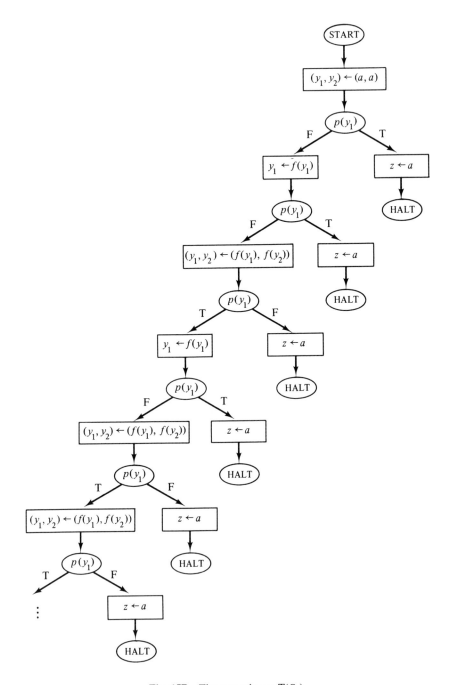

Fig. 15B   The tree schema $T(S_3)$.

The tree is pruned further (by removing those parts enclosed within dashed lines) to get the free tree schema $T(S_3)$ (Figure 15B). $T(S_3)$ is clearly equivalent to S_3.

Suppose we translate in the same way a program schema S which halts (for every interpretation) to get its equivalent free tree schema $T(S)$. Since every path in $T(S)$ corresponds to the trace of some computation of S, and since S halts for every interpretation, it follows that there are no infinite paths in $T(S)$. Moreover, every node (statement) in $T(S)$ has at most two branches leaving it; thus by König's infinity lemma (see, e.g., Knuth, 1968a) it follows that $T(S)$ has only finitely many statements [i.e., $T(S)$ is finite]. We therefore can conclude that *for every program schema which halts for every interpretation one can effectively construct an equivalent free tree-program schema.*†

This is actually quite a strong result; it implies that for every program schema S that halts for every interpretation, there exists a bound $b > 0$ such that no computation of S executes more than b statements. In other words, any program schema S which has the property that for every positive integer i there is a computation of S that executes more than i statements— must have at least one infinite computation.

Example 16

Consider the program schema S_{16A} (Figure 16A) which halts for every interpretation. We first construct the program schema described in Figure 16B. We have three FAILURE statements, since

a. Whenever we reach the test statement α, $(y_1, y_2) = ($"$f(x)$", "$f^2(x)$"$)$ and $p($"$f(x)$"$) = T$; therefore, it is impossible to take the F branch.

b. Whenever we reach the test statement β, $(y_1, y_2) = ($"$f^2(x)$", "$f^3(x)$"$)$ and $p($"$f^2(x)$"$) = F$; therefore, it is impossible to take the T branch.

c. Whenever we reach the test statement γ, $(y_1, y_2) = ($"$f^2(x)$", "$f^3(x)$"$)$ and $p($"$f^3(x)$"$) = F$; therefore, it is impossible to take the T branch.

The tree is pruned further (by removing those parts enclosed within dashed lines) to get the free tree-program schema S_{16B} (Figure 16C).

The results introduced in this section can be used to show that

1. *The equivalence problem for program schemas which halt for every interpretation is decidable.*

---

†We showed earlier that the halting problem for program schemas is undecidable. The above discussion implies, however, that the halting problem for program schemas is *partially decidable.*

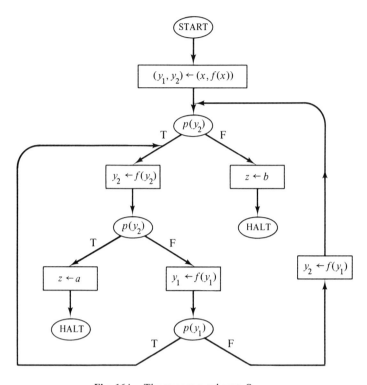

Fig. 16A   The program schema S_{16A}.

2. *The isomorphism problem for program schemas which halt for every interpretation is decidable.*

Ianov Schemas

In the previous section we showed that the equivalence problem is decidable for the class of all program schemas which always halt. In this section we discuss another class of program schemas, known as *Ianov schemas*, for which the equivalence problem is also decidable. The most important feature characterizing Ianov schemas is that they have a single program variable y.

We say that a program schema S is an *Ianov schema* if

1. Σ_S consists of a finite set of unary function constants $\{f_i\}$, a finite set of unary predicate constants $\{p_i\}$, a single input variable x, a *single program variable y*, and a single output variable z. (Note that individual constants are not allowed.)

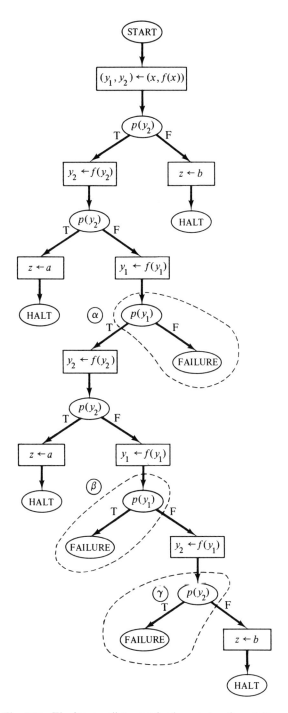

Fig. 16B The intermediate step in the construction of S_{16B}.

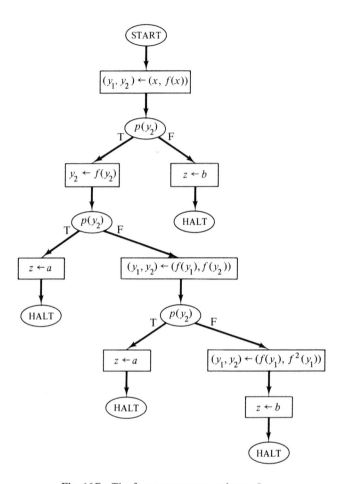

Fig. 16C   The free tree program schema S_{16B}.

2. All statements in S are of one of the following forms:

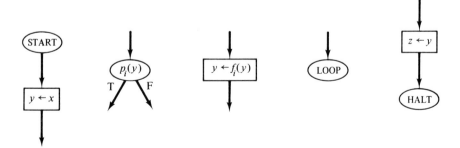

Example 17

The program schemas S_{17A} (Figure 17A) and S_{17B} (Figure 17B) are Ianov schemas.

The following are several interesting properties of the class of Ianov schemas.

1. *It is decidable whether or not an Ianov schema is free.*

Follows from the fact that an Ianov schema is nonfree if and only if it has a path with two identical tests and with no assignment statement between the tests. For example, the Ianov schema S_{17B} (Figure 17B) is free, while S_{17A} (Figure 17A) is not free, because of the paths from α to β and from α to γ.

2. *Every nonfree Ianov schema S can be transformed effectively to an equivalent free Ianov schema S'.*

We leave the proof of this property as an exercise for the reader.

3. *The halting/divergence problems for Ianov schemas are decidable.*

By 2 every nonfree Ianov schema can be transformed effectively to an equivalent free Ianov schema. The result then follows from the fact that these problems are decidable for free program schemas.

4. *The equivalence problem for Ianov schemas is decidable. (Ianov (1960), Rutledge (1964), Kaplan (1969)).*

Suppose that we are given Ianov schema S with a START statement labeled as A_0 and assignment statements $A_1, \ldots, A_k$. Since every Ianov schema can be translated easily to an equivalent Ianov schema which has only one HALT statement, we can assume that S has only one HALT statement, A_{k+1} say. Suppose also that Σ_S consists of n function constants $\{f_1, \ldots, f_n\}$ and m predicate constants $\{p_1, \ldots, p_m\}$.

We shall construct for S a transition graph G_S (see, e.g., Ginzburg, 1968) in such a way that G_S simulates the computations of S.

1. The vertices (states) are†

b_0	(representing the START statement)
a_i and b_i, $1 \leq i \leq k$	(representing the assignment statements)
a_{k+1}	(representing the HALT statement)

---

†Note that we ignore the LOOP statements in S.

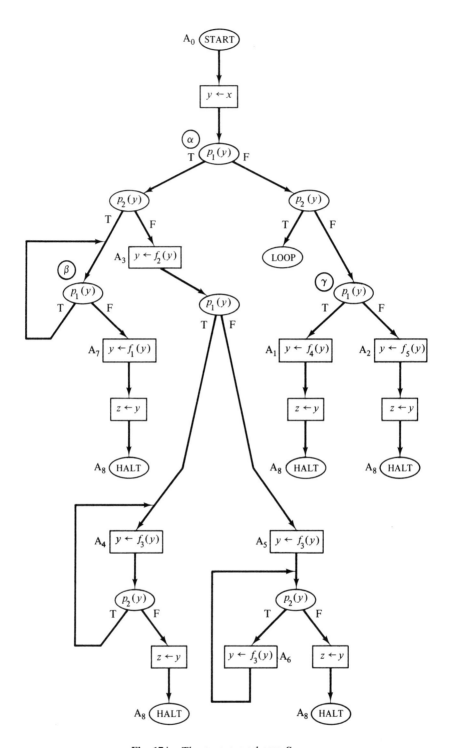

Fig. 17A The program schema S_{17A}.

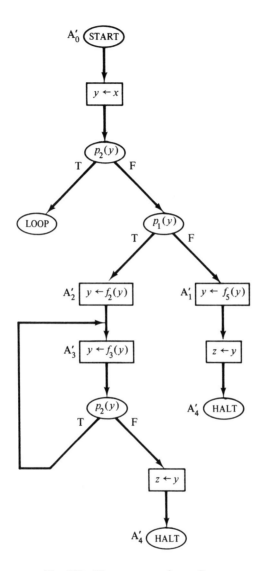

Fig. 17B   The program schema S_{17B}.

The vertex b_0 is the only initial vertex (labeled by $-$) and the vertex a_{k+1} is the only final vertex (labeled by $+$).

2. The alphabet of G_S consists of the function constants $\{f_1, \ldots, f_n\}$ and the 2^m words of $\{T, F\}^m$. Intuitively, each such word (of length m) indicates the possible truth values of the m predicate constants $\{p_1, \ldots, p_m\}$ for a given y.

3. The arrows in G_S are constructed as follows:

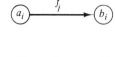

if A_i is $y \leftarrow f_j(y)$

where $w \in \{T, F\}^m$, if there is in S a path from A_i to A_j with no assignment such that the predicate values indicated by w do not contradict the tests along the path.

Now, for two given Ianov schemas S and S', we first construct the corresponding transition graphs G_S and $G_{S'}$. It is clear that S is equivalent to S' if and only if G_S is equivalent to $G_{S'}$. Since the equivalence problem for transition graphs is decidable, so is the equivalence problem of Ianov schemas.

Example 18

Consider again the Ianov schemas S_{17A} (Figure 17A) and S_{17B} (Figure 17B). We would like to prove that S_{17A} is equivalent to S_{17B}. Informally it is easy to see this, since

a.

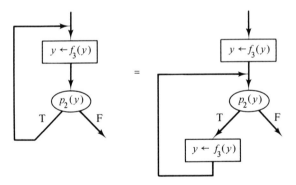

and therefore

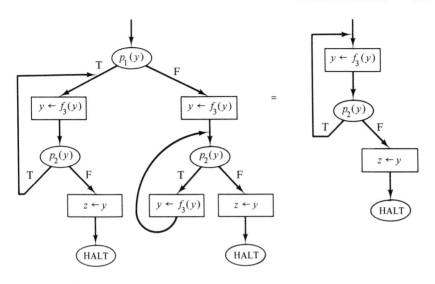

b.

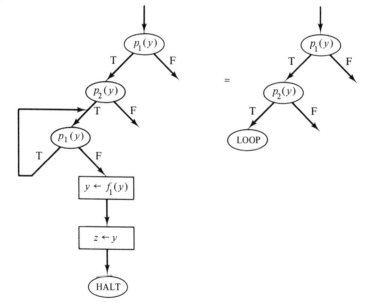

and therefore

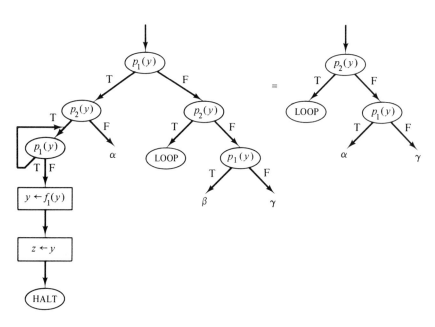

Let us now show the equivalence of S_{17A} and S_{17B} using the algorithm described above. The transition graph G_{17A} for S_{17A} is described in Figure 18A, while the transition graph G_{17B} for S_{17B} is described in Figure 18B. It is straightforward to show that G_{17A} is equivalent to G_{17B} following any one of the known algorithms for proving equivalence of transition graphs.

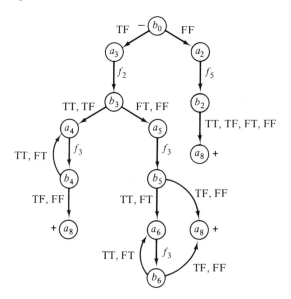

Fig. 18A   The transition graph G_{17A} for S_{17A}.

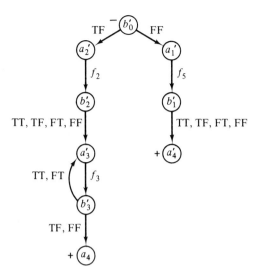

Fig. 18B   The transition graph G_{17B} for S_{17B}.

BIBLIOGRAPHICAL REMARKS

The pioneering work on program schemas was done by Ianov (1960), who proved that the equivalence problem of "Ianov schemas" is decidable. This specific problem has been discussed further by Rutledge (1964) and Kaplan (1969).

The most important works in this area are those of Paterson (1967, 1968) and Luckham, Park, and Paterson (1970). They introduced most of the basic results in this area such as Herbrand's theorem (Theorem 1) and the undecidability of the basic properties (Theorem 3). Similar work has been done for other types of schemas such as parallel schemas (Karp and Miller, 1969) and recursive schemas (Ashcroft, Manna, and Pnueli, 1971). Milner (1970) discussed the decision problems for schemas with "partial interpretations," i.e., interpretations in which functions and predicates may be partial rather than total.

Cooper (1971) and Engeler (1971) introduced independently the notion of normal form and discussed its application.

An excellent survey on the Russians' work in this area was presented by Ershov at IFIP Congress *71*.

Two important topics regarding program schemas have not been discussed in this chapter.

1. *Translation problems.* Some recent work on schemas considered more powerful program schemas than ours, i.e., program schemas with additional programming features, like recursion (Paterson and Hewitt, 1970; Strong, 1971), arrays (Constable and Gries, 1972), pushdown stacks and counters (Garland and Luckham, 1972; Plaisted, 1972), and equality tests (Chandra and Manna, 1972). They were concerned mainly with the problem of translating program schemas from one class to another, in an attempt to compare the "power "of those programming features.

An excellent survey of the above works together with many new results can be found in Chandra's thesis (1973).

2. *Relation to predicate calculus.* Following Floyd's (1967) "inductive assertion method" for proving partial correctness of programs, Manna formulated the basic properties of programs (1969b) and program schemas (1969a) in first-order predicate calculus. Cooper (1969, 1970) formalized the equivalence of program schemas in second-order predicate calculus. The formalization was extended further to various classes of schemas, such as recursive schemas (Manna and Pnueli, 1970). A survey of these extensions is given in Manna (1970).

4 TREE AUTOMATA: AN INFORMAL SURVEY

James W. Thatcher
IBM Thomas J. Watson Research Center
Yorktown Heights, New York

4-1. INTRODUCTION

We present an informal survey of an area of automata and language theory that has come to be known as "tree automata theory." The aim of this informal presentation is to convince the reader that tree automata theory is just conventional automata theory revisited or, more precisely, conventional automata theory in which labeled trees replace strings as inputs and outputs. Starting with the concept of finite-state acceptor, we show with examples how simple introductory results, generalized to trees, yield proofs of familiar theorems in context-free language theory. Put another way, we will be showing how some results in context-free language theory are proved using techniques of finite automata theory.

More important, however, is the connection between "tree automata with output" and concepts in language theory such as semantics, translations, and transformations. It is more difficult to be convincing on this point. The tree automata with output are conceptually more complicated than the acceptors (much more so than in the conventional theory), and both the definitions and the applications depend heavily on formalism, which, in this survey, we are trying to avoid.

The decision to avoid formalism is a painful one, for I believe that it is precisely that formalism [in terms of algebraic theories (Eilenberg-Wright 1967; Lawvere, 1963), for example] that offers the hope of significant application to language theory—even to computer science. The algebraic formulation is important for at least four reasons: (1) the definitions can be made

143

precise, yet simple and general; (2) the proofs about the concepts are direct (i.e., they are algebraic rather than combinatorial); (3) the "naturalness" of definitions can be tested as they are formulated within the algebraic framework; and (4) the algebraic framework suggests generalizations of the concepts so derived. On the other hand, our informal approach better enables us to indicate areas in which the theory of tree automata may find application (i.e., where the algebraic formulation may be of importance) in terms closer to those of the conventional theory.

Although we will not go into any details here, there is a third area of important application of tree automata and that is in the applications to decision problems in logic. There has been a series of papers applying (generalized) finite automata theory to decision problems in higher-order, applied logics starting with Büchi and Elgot's work (Büchi, 1960; Büchi and Elgot 1958; Elgot, 1961) on the weak second-order theory of arithmetic and culminating in the important decision procedure for the monadic second-order theory of multiple successors developed by Rabin (1968, 1970). Intermediate and auxiliary applications are to be found in Büchi (1962). Doner (1965a, 1965b), Landweber (1968), and Thatcher and Wright (1968).

It could be said that "tree automata theory" had its roots in the algebraic approach to the conventional theory taken by Büchi and Wright (1960). The generalizations were a natural outcome of that work and were arrived at independently (Doner, 1965; Thatcher and Wright, 1968). Other general papers in the area include Arbib (1968), Brainerd (1967, 1969), Magidor and Moran (1969), Mezei and Wright (1967), Rounds (1970), and Thatcher (1967, 1969, 1970). Rabin's survey paper (1967) contains a section on tree automata. Arbib and Give'on (1968) generalize the idea of tree automata to automata operating on directed ordered acyclic graphs (DOAGs). Brainerd (1967, 1969), in addition to considering minimal tree automata, generalizes Büchi's (1962) result concerning regular canonical systems.

4-2. TREES

Let Σ be an alphabet. A Σ tree is a tree whose nodes are labeled with elements of the alphabet Σ. Of course, a tree is a rooted, directed graph which is acyclic and ordered in the sense that the successors of any node have a specific order as is necessary when one draws a tree on paper. Figure 1 shows an $\{a, b\}$ tree, which is typical except that it is binary (every node has either two or zero successors). The root of the tree is the top node (in Figure 1) and the phrase "frontier of the tree" will be used ambiguously to mean either the set of nodes at the bottom of the tree (the end opposite the root) or the string of symbols labeling the frontier nodes. For a tree t, $\mathrm{fr}(t)$ will have the latter meaning. The frontier string of the tree in Figure 1 is *abaa*.

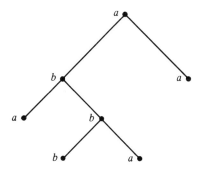

Fig. 1 Typical binary tree over $\{a, b\}$.

There is a well-known correspondence between parenthesized expressions and trees. The tree in Figure 1 can be identified with the expression $a(b(a, b(b, a)), a)$, that in Figure 12 with $c(d(x_2, x_1), c(c, x_2))$.

4-3. TREE AUTOMATA AS RECOGNIZERS

We first consider finite automata as acceptors and later introduce the idea of output so the automata will be viewed as transducers. Of course, as in the Rabin and Scott (1959) theory, the acceptor approach can be considered a special case of the transducer approach, but the latter is considerably more complicated. Simplicity dictates attacking the ideas in two steps.

Let us consider the following informal description of a finite automaton as an acceptor. A *finite automaton* $\mathcal{C}$ consists of a finite set of *states*, S; an *initial state*, s_0; a *transition function* M which maps pairs $\langle$next-symbol, current-state$\rangle$ into next-state; and a designated set F of *final states*,

The automaton $\mathcal{C}$ operates on an input as follows. The automaton starts in its initial state s_0. This state is the current-state and the first symbol of the input is the next-symbol. Then generally, given the current-state and the next-symbol, M determines the next-state of $\mathcal{C}$. This process is continued, producing a state "history" which is a string of states one longer than the input. The last-state of the state history is examined to determine if it is a final state; the input is *accepted* if this is the case. The set of inputs accepted by $\mathcal{C}$ is denoted $T(\mathcal{C})$, and a set U of inputs is *recognizable* if $U = T(\mathcal{C})$ for some automaton $\mathcal{C}$.

The terminology of our informal description may seem strange (current-state, next-symbol, one longer, etc.), but barring that, the reader will probably agree that the description captures the conventional idea of finite-state acceptor. The reason for the strange language is that certain words must be interpreted in the generalization to trees, but the resulting picture serves well to motivate the definition to follow.

We will operate under the simplifying restriction that all trees are binary and write T_Σ for the set of binary Σ trees. This restriction is purely for expositional purposes; the theory applies to trees with arbitrary (nonuniform) branching. In the examples to follow, the input alphabet is $\{a, b\}$.

Under these restrictions the tree illustrated in Figure 1 would be a typical input to an automaton. The first symbol of the input appears to be the symbol "a" at the root of the tree. Considering it to be such gives rise to the *root-to-frontier automaton* (RFA) which was first explicitly discussed in Magidor and Moran (1969). In accord with our informal description of the operation of an automaton, the transition function of an RFA must be defined, at least initially, on $\Sigma \times S$ since the pair $\langle$next-symbol, current-state$\rangle$ is from the set. Similarly, in order to proceed, the "next-state" must be a pair of states, one for each successor of the root. Therefore, we are motivated to require that the transition function be defined on $\Sigma \times S$, taking values in $S \times S$. The beginning of the calculation of the state history is shown in Figure 2. The calculation is continued in Figure 3 and completed in Figure 4. Note that in the process, the state history is forced (for the first time in Figure 3) to be one longer than the input in a generalized sense.

Having indicated how the state history is computed, we are left to interpret "last-state." One natural interpretation is to consider the set of all states

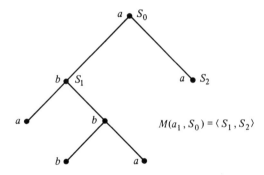

Fig. 2   Beginning the state calculation for RFA.

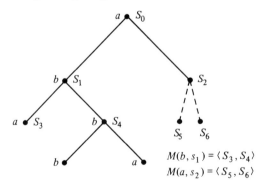

Fig. 3   State calculation (continued).

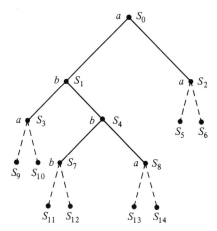

Fig. 4   State calculation (completed).

on the frontier of the state history to comprise the "last-state." Thus the behavioral condition for the input in Figure 1 would be $\{s_9, \ldots, s_{14}, s_5, s_6\}$ $\subseteq F$.

Taking the informal concept of finite automaton, we are led to the following definition of a generalized finite automaton operating on binary trees.

DEFINITION 1

A (deterministic) *root-to-frontier automaton* $\mathfrak{A}$ (RFA) consists of a finite set S of states; a transition function, $M: \Sigma \times S \to S \times S$; an initial state $s_0 \in S$; and a set of final states $F \subseteq S$.

The formation of the state tree is described inductively as follows:

a. The root of the state tree is labeled s_0.

b. Given that any node of the state tree is labeled s, and the corresponding node of the input is labeled σ, then the two successor nodes of the state tree are labeled with the pair $M(\sigma, s)$.

The input is accepted if every state labeling the frontier of the state tree is a final state.

The deterministic RFA are not very powerful. To illustrate this, there are finite sets which are not recognized by any deterministic RFA. For example, the doubleton $\{a(ba), a(ab)\}$ is not recognizable. [In Magidor and Moran (1969) $\{a(aa), a(bb), a(ab)\}$ is given as an example of a nonrecognizable finite set.]

A class of sets of trees recognized by deterministic RFA is obtained as follows. The notion of path in a tree is familiar; a complete linear sequence of nodes from the root to the frontier. We will say that a word $w \in \Sigma^*$ is a Σ path of a Σ tree t if w is the sequence of labels of a path of t. Thus the $\{a, b\}$

paths of the tree in Figure 1 are *aba*, *abbb*, *abba*, and *aa*. Now let R be any regular subset of Σ^* and define T_R to be the set of all trees t which have the property that every Σ path of t is in R. For any regular R the set T_R of Σ trees so defined is recognizable by a deterministic RFA. If $\langle S, M, s_0, F \rangle$ is a conventional finite automaton (Rabin and Scott, 1959) recognizing R, then $\langle S, M', s_0, F \rangle$ is a deterministic RFA recognizing T_R, where $M'(\sigma, s) = \langle M(\sigma, s), M(\sigma, s) \rangle$. Intuitively the RFA mimics the action of the conventional automaton down every path of the input tree; the behavioral condition (all the frontier states of the state tree have to be final) requires that every Σ path of the input tree would be accepted by the original automaton.

For a specific example, if R is the subset of $\{a, b\}^*$ denoted by the regular expression, a^*b^*, then T_R is the set of trees in which all a-labeled nodes precede (in the sense of being closer to the root) all b-labeled nodes.

Looking more closely at the concept of deterministic RFA, one might have the feeling that the class of sets $\{T_R\}$ defined above just might exhaust the power of the deterministic RFA. This feeling is nearly correct as was proved in Magidor and Moran (1969) and outlined below.

Every path in a Σ tree can be represented by a string in $\{l, r\}^*$, where l and r correspond to the left and right branches from a node, respectively. Thus in Figure 1, the paths are: Λll, Λlrl, Λlrr, Λr. For convenience we have added a symbol (not the empty string) for the root of the tree so that the string representing a path will have the same length as the string of labels. A path together with its labels is now represented by a pair $\langle p, x \rangle$, where p is a path (i.e., a string in $\{\Lambda\} \cdot \{l, r\}^*$) and x is a string of labels and p and x have the same length. For example $\langle \Lambda ll, aba \rangle$ is the pair for the leftmost path in Figure 1. Such labeled path pairs can be interpreted in turn as elements of the set $\Delta_\Sigma = (\{\Lambda\} \times \Sigma) \cdot (\{l, r\} \times \Sigma)^*$ under the correspondence

$$\langle \Lambda, \sigma_1 \rangle \langle \beta_2, \sigma_2 \rangle \cdots \langle \beta_k, \sigma_k \rangle \rightleftharpoons \langle \Lambda \beta_2 \cdots \beta_k, \sigma_1 \cdots \sigma_k \rangle.$$

For any regular set R contained in Δ_Σ, let A_R be the set of Σ trees with the property that all label path pairs are in R. Now the characterization theorem of Magidor and Moran (1969) is:

THEOREM 1

A set U is recognizable by a deterministic RFA if and only if $U = A_R$ for some regular subset R of Δ_Σ.

The decision that the label on the root was the first-symbol led to the notion of RFA. If instead we look at the symbols labeling the frontier of the input as "first-symbol," then we arrive at the concept of *frontier-to-root automaton* (FRA) which was first studied in Doner (1965b) and Thatcher and Wright (1968). It is natural, since the state history is to be "one longer" than the input, to begin the automaton's operation as shown in Figure 5.

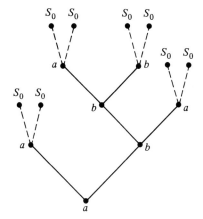

Fig. 5   Starting the FRA.

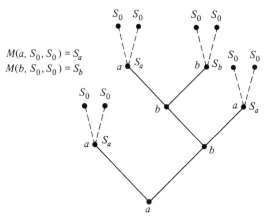

Fig. 6   First step of state calculation.

For each first symbol on the frontier, the current-state is in fact the pair of states labeling the successors of the corresponding node of the state tree. Thus we want the transition function to be defined on $\Sigma \times S \times S$ taking values in S. The first step of the state history calculation is shown in Figure 6 and the completion in Figure 7. The choice of the behavioral condition is obvious. The input is accepted if the state labeling the root of the state tree is final.

The informal definition has thus led us to another definition of generalized finite automaton.

Definition 2

A (deterministic) *frontier-to-root automaton* (FRA) $\mathcal{Q}$ consists of S, s_0, M, and F, where the components are as in Definition 1 with the exception that $M : \Sigma \times S \times S \rightarrow S$. The calculation of the state tree is described inductively by:

   a. The frontier of the state tree is labeled s_0.

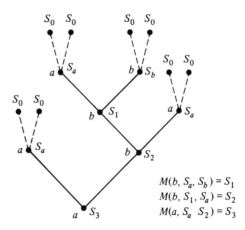

$$M(b, S_a, S_b) = S_1$$
$$M(b, S_1, S_a) = S_2$$
$$M(a, S_a, S_2) = S_3$$

Fig. 7   Completing state calculation.

b. For any node in the input labeled σ, the corresponding node of the state tree is labeled $M(\sigma, s_1, s_2)$, where $\langle s_1, s_2 \rangle$ is the pair of states labeling the successors of that state tree node.

We will write $\bar{M}(t)$ to denote the state labeling the root of the state tree and t is accepted if $\bar{M}(t)$ is a final state.

The frontier-to-root deterministic automata are more interesting than their opposites described above. As the results below show, they mirror very closely conventional finite automata.

We will again use the family $\{T_R\}$ as a source of examples. Let R be a regular subset of Σ^* and let $\hat{R}$ be the set of reversals of strings in R. We know (Rabin-Scott, 1959) that $\hat{R}$ is regular if R is. Now let $\langle S, M, s_0, F \rangle$ be a conventional finite automaton which recognizes the set $\hat{R}$ in Σ^*. We can construct a deterministic FRA, $\langle pS, M', \{s_0\}, pF \rangle$ where $M'(\sigma, u, v) = \{M(\sigma, s) \mid s \in u \cup v\}$ and this FRA recognized T_R. (pS is the set of subsets of S.) The way it works is that at any node of the state tree the FRA has gathered up all states that the original finite automaton would have produced for all paths from the corresponding node of the input to the frontier. When talking about the root of the input, if all those paths are in R (i.e., all those states are final), then the input is in T_R and is accepted by the FRA.

This example makes two points quite clearly. First, one can see that closure of the FRA-recognizable sets under complementation works just as it does for conventional finite automata. The input is not in T_R just in case at least one path is not in R (i.e., just in case the set of states obtained at the root is in $pS\text{-}pF$). Second, the principle of the subset construction that is used to prove the equivalence of the nondeterministic and deterministic automata is implicit in the construction.

Nondeterminism is introduced into these models in the usual way, by making the range of the transition function the power set (set of subsets) of the range in the deterministic case and by allowing a set of initial states. Thus, giving only one of the definitions:

DEFINITION 2′

A *nondeterministic FRA* consists of S, S_0, M, and F, where the components are as in Definition 2 except that $S_0 \subseteq S$ is a set of initial states and $M : \Sigma \times S \times S \rightarrow pS$.

State trees in the nondeterministic case are calculated by selecting one of the elements in the value of the transition function as the next-state. Thus several state trees are possible for one input. An input is accepted if there exists a state tree for the input with the root labeled with a final state.

The nondeterministic FRA and nondeterministic RFA are equipotent because for any nondeterministic RFA $\mathcal{C}$, it is easy to construct the transition function of a nondeterministic FRA $\mathcal{C}'$ ($M'(\sigma, s_1, s_2) = \{s \mid \langle s_1, s_2 \rangle \in M(\sigma, s)\}$) such that upon switching initial and final states ($S_0' = F$, $F' = S_0$) the two automata recognize the same sets of inputs. And similarly, given a nondeterministic FRA $\mathcal{C}$, then a nondeterministic RFA $\mathcal{C}'$ has transition function defined by $M'(\sigma, s) = \{\langle s_1, s_2 \rangle \mid s \in M(\sigma, s_1, s_2)\}$ and also has initial and final sets of states interchanged. [Note that this construction corresponds to the proof that the regular sets are closed under reversal; see Rabin and Scott (1959).]

LEMMA 1

A set U of Σ trees is recognizable by a nondeterministic FRA iff U is recognizable by a nondeterministic RFA.

As suggested above, the subset construction familiar in the conventional theory works for the frontier-to-root automata. That is, given a nondeterministic FRA $\mathcal{C}$ one can construct a deterministic FRA $\mathcal{C}'$ with pS as the set of states such that $T(\mathcal{C}) = T(\mathcal{C}')$. In particular, if $\mathcal{C} = \langle S, M, S_0, F \rangle$, then $\mathcal{C}' = \langle pS, M', S_0, \{u \mid u \cap F \neq \varnothing\} \rangle$, where $M'(\sigma, u_1, u_2) - \bigcup_{s_i \in u_i} M(\sigma, s_1, s_2)$.

LEMMA 2

A set U of Σ trees is recognizable by a nondeterministic FRA iff U is recognizable by a deterministic FRA.

Boolean closure of the FRA recognizable sets is also obtained in a manner identical to that in (Rabin and Scott, 1959). Thus $T_\Sigma - T(\langle S, M, s_0, F \rangle) = T(\langle S, M, s_0, S - F \rangle)$ and the direct product construction yields an FRA which recognizes the intersection of the sets recognized by the component automata. If $\mathcal{Q} = \langle S, M, s_0, F \rangle$ and $\mathcal{B} = \langle T, N, t_0, G \rangle$, then

$$\mathcal{Q} \times \mathcal{B} = \langle S \times T, M \times N, \langle s_0, t_0 \rangle, F \times G \rangle$$

where $M \times N(\sigma, \langle s, t \rangle) = \langle M(\sigma, s), N(\sigma, t) \rangle$; $T(\mathcal{Q}) \cap T(\mathcal{B}) = T(\mathcal{Q} \times \mathcal{B})$.

THEOREM 2

The FRA-recognizable subsets of T_Σ form a Boolean algebra.

Let $hg(t)$ denote the height of the tree t; i.e., $hg(t)$ is the length of the longest path in t. Also, define $T_\Sigma^{(n)}$ to be the set of trees of height less than or equal to n. For any set $U \subseteq T_\Sigma^{(n)}$ define the FRA automaton, $\mathcal{Q}_U = \langle T_\Sigma^{(n)} \cup \{*, \Lambda\}, M, \Lambda, U \rangle$, where

$$M(\sigma, t_1, t_2) = \begin{cases} \sigma(t_1, t_2) & \text{if } t_1, t_2 \in T_\Sigma^{(n-1)} \\ \sigma & \text{if } t_1 = t_2 = \Lambda \\ * & \text{otherwise} \end{cases}$$

The automaton $\mathcal{Q}_U$ recognizes U. For this example we are depending on the identification (mentioned above) between Σ trees and parenthesized expressions (i.e., Σ terms). What is happening with $\mathcal{Q}_U$ is that for any input t with $hg(t) \leq n$, $\bar{M}(t) = t$ and otherwise $\bar{M}(t) = *$. Therefore, an input t is accepted iff $\bar{M}(t) = t \in U$.

Since any finite set is a subset of $T_\Sigma^{(n)}$ for some n, it follows that all finite subsets of T_Σ are FRA-recognizable:

LEMMA 3

All finite subsets of T_Σ are FRA-recognizable.

Now Lemmas 1 and 2 show that every RFA-recognizable set is FRA-recognizable but the converse is not true, as is seen from Lemma 3 together with the example of a finite set (see above) that is not RFA-recognizable.

In the sequel we will use the term "recognizable" without modification to mean FRA-recognizable.

Another important result in the Rabin–Scott theory of finite automata is what might be called the "uv^nw lemma," Lemma 8 (Rabin and Scott, 1959). To state the generalization we do need to introduce some notation.

Consider an FRA with state set S. The set $T_{\Sigma,S} \subseteq T_{\Sigma \cup S}$ is like the set of Σ trees except that in addition, elements of S are allowed to label the frontier nodes of trees in $T_{\Sigma,S}$. The operation of the FRA is extended to $T_{\Sigma,S}$ by requiring that $M(s, s_1, s_2) = s$ for $s, s_1, s_2 \in S$. Thus on the frontier nodes of a tree with labels from S, the corresponding labels of the state tree are identical. (This is closely related to the idea of startable automata [Arbib and Give'on, 1968].)

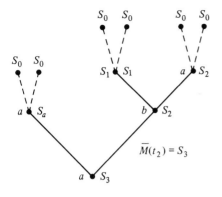

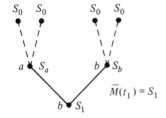

Fig. 8 Substitution of trees.

It should be very clear that if $M(t_1) = s$ and t results from substituting t_1 for any number of occurrences of s in a tree t_2, then $\bar{M}(t) = M(t_2)$. This is illustrated in Figure 8, where t is the tree in Figure 1.

For convenience, consider trees in $T_{\Sigma, S}$ which have at most one occurrence of an element of S on the frontier. Under this circumstance we can write $t_1 t_2$ to mean the result of substituting t_2 for the occurrence of the element of S in t_1.

A generalization of Rabin and Scott's Lemma 8 can now be stated as follows (there is actually a much more general statement of this lemma):

LEMMA 4

If t is accepted by an automaton with r states and $hg(t) > r$, then there exist trees t_1, t_2, r_3 such that

   a. $\text{fr}(t_i) = u_i s v_i; u_i, v_i \in \Sigma^*, s \in S, i = 1, 2; hg(t_2) > 1$.
   b. $\text{fr}(t_3) = w \in \Sigma^*$.
   c. $t = t_1 t_2 t_3$.
   d. $t_1 t_1^n t_3$ is accepted for all n.

This lemma, as is the case in the conventional theory, leads to the decidability of the emptiness and finiteness problems.

THEOREM 3

There exists an effective procedure for determining whether or not $T(\mathcal{Q})$ is empty and there is an effective procedure to determine whether $T(\mathcal{Q})$ is finite.

The notion of substitution necessary for Lemma 4 also gives rise to a theory of regularity (similar to the Kleene theory for recognizable sets of strings) which was developed in Thatcher and Wright (1968) and Magidor and Moran (1969) and simplified in Arbib and Give'on (1968). For sets U and V in T_Σ and for any $\sigma \in \Sigma$, the product $U \cdot_\sigma V$ is the set of all trees t that are obtained by taking $t_1 \in U$ and substituting elements of V for all occurrences of σ on the frontier of t_1. The iterated substitution, $U^{*\sigma}$ is defined in a manner similar to the definition of the Kleene star: $U^{*\sigma} = \bigcup X_i$, where $X_0 = \{\sigma\}$ and $X_{n+1} = X_n \cup U \cdot_\sigma X_n$. The Σ-*regular* sets are defined to be the least class of subsets of T_Σ containing the finite sets and closed under the operations $\cdot_\sigma$ and $*\sigma$ for all $\sigma \in \Sigma$ and under set union. A set of trees is *regular* if it is Σ-regular for some Σ.

Recall that $T_{a^*b^*}$ is the set of $\{a, b\}$ trees with the property that all paths have labels in the set a^*b^*. A "regular expression" for this set of trees is $\{a(aa)\}^{*a} \cdot_\sigma (\{a\} \cup \{b(bb)\}^{*b})$.

The simplified proof in (Arbib and Give'on, 1968) of the analysis theorem (every recognizable set if regular) provides a good example of the uses of substitution and iterated substitution. We do not intend to give the whole proof but just the construction to illustrate the uses of these operations. Let $\mathcal{Q} = \langle S, M, s_0, F \rangle$ be an FRA and define $T[s, S_1, S_2]$ to be the set of trees $t \in T_{\Sigma, S_2}$ for which $\bar{M}(t) = s$ and all states in the state tree for t outside the frontier and root are in S_1. In effect, $T[s, S_1, S_2]$ can be read as the set of trees carrying the automaton $\mathcal{Q}$ from S_2 to s. The proof of the analysis theorem goes through by induction on the cardinality of S_1 showing that all $T[s, S_1, S_2]$ are regular and since $T(\mathcal{Q}) = \bigcup_{s \in F} T[s, S, \varnothing]$, it follows that $T(\mathcal{Q})$ is regular. For the case $S_1 = \varnothing$ we have

$$T[s, \varnothing, S_2] = \{\delta(\beta_1\beta_2) \mid \beta_i \in \Sigma \cup S_2 \text{ and } \bar{M}(\sigma(\beta_1\beta_2)) = s\}$$

which is finite and hence regular. For the induction step,

$$T[s, S_1 \cup \{s'\}, S_2] = T[s, S_1, S_2 \cup \{s'\}] \cdot_{s'} T[s', S_1, S_2 \cup \{s'\}]^{*s'} \cdot_{s'} T[s', S_1, S_2]$$

This last equation can be visualized by imagining an input and corresponding state tree which has s at the root, internal nodes labeled from $S_2 \cup \{s'\}$ and possibly frontier nodes labeled from S_1. Such a state tree (and the input tree in the same way) can be broken up at every occurrence of s' resulting in an initial segment (including the root) in $T[s, S_1, S_2 \cup \{s'\}]$ perhaps several segments going from $S_2 \cup \{s'\}$ to s' through S_1 and several final segments going from S_2 to s' through S_1.

The main theorem relating the regular and the recognizable sets is:

THEOREM 4

If $U \subseteq T_\Sigma$ is recognizable, then it is Σ'-regular for some $\Sigma' \supseteq \Sigma$. If U is Σ-regular, then U is recognizable.

As a final example of a theorem familiar in the conventional theory, we will discuss the closure of the recognizable sets under projections or, as these operations are sometimes called, length-preserving homomorphisms or relabelings. We will return to this subject when we discuss automata with output, but for the time being, let μ and μ_0 be two maps defined on an alphabet Σ taking values in another alphabet Ω. Then $\bar{\mu}$ is a map from T_Σ into T_Ω; $\mu(t)$ is the result of relabeling every frontier node of t labeled σ with $\mu_0(\sigma)$ and every interior node labeled σ with $\mu(\sigma)$. Maps $\bar{\mu}$ defined in this way will be called *projections*. The following theorem is proved exactly as it is in the case of finite automata over strings.

THEOREM 5

The recognizable sets are closed under projections and inverse projections.

4-4. CONTEXT-FREE SETS AND RECOGNIZABILITY

For purposes of exposition, we have restricted ourselves to binary trees. Thus, in this section, we are forced to consider only "binary context-free grammars." It must be emphasized, however, that the results discussed here apply to arbitrary nonerasing context-free grammars (see Thatcher, 1967).

DEFINITION 3

A *binary context-free grammar* (CFG for short) is a 4-tuple $\langle N, \Sigma, P, S_0 \rangle$, where the components are as follows: N is the set of nonterminals; Σ is the set of terminals; P is the set of productions, $P \subseteq N \times (\Sigma \cup N)^2$; and $S_0 \subseteq N$ is the set of start symbols. For a CFG, G, $T(G)$ is the set of *derivation trees* of G defined by the property that $t \in T(G)$ iff (a) the root of t is labeled with an element of S_0, (b) for every node of t labeled with σ having successor nodes labeled σ_1, σ_2, the triple $\langle \sigma, \sigma_1, \sigma_2 \rangle \in P$, and (c) every frontier node of t is labeled from Σ. $L(G)$ is the set of frontier words of $T(G)$, $L(G) = \text{fr}T(G)$, and a set of trees U is called *local* if there is a CFG G such that $U = T(G)$, while a set U of words is *context-free* if there is a CFG G with $U = L(G)$.

Besides the restriction to binary trees, our definition of context-free grammar differs from the usual in inessential respects. First, a set of initial symbols is allowed and, second, there is no requirement that Σ and N be disjoint. This relaxing of the definition permits a uniformity in the theory with no loss of generality.

As is usual, we can write $\sigma \longrightarrow \sigma_1 \sigma_2$ for the production $\langle \sigma, \sigma_1, \sigma_2 \rangle \in P$ and $\sigma \longrightarrow w_1, \sigma \longrightarrow w_2$ is abbreviated $\sigma \longrightarrow w_1 \mid w_2$. The following grammar is illustrative of the relaxed conditions on the definition. Its set of derivation trees is $T_{a^*b^*}$.

$$N = \{a, b\}$$
$$\Sigma = \{a, b\}$$
$$P: \ a \longrightarrow aa \mid ab \mid ba \mid bb$$
$$\qquad b \longrightarrow bb$$
$$S_0 = \{a, b\}$$

For this grammar, $L(G)$ is the set of all $\{a, b\}$ strings of length at least 2.

It should be fairly clear that every local set is recognizable because given a CFG, an FRA can be constructed which checks each of the local conditions, i.e., (a), (b), and (c) of Definition 3. We have from Thatcher (1967):

THEOREM 6

For any CFG G, $T(G)$ is recognizable.

The converse of Theorem 6 is not true. As an example, the set of $\{a, b\}$ trees with exactly one occurrence of the label b is recognizable but not local. There is a result that is close to a converse, however. For an automaton $\mathcal{a}$, define $CS(\mathcal{a})$ (for *complete state* trees of $\mathcal{a}$) as a set of trees over the alphabet $\Sigma \times S \cup \Sigma$. The trees in $CS(\mathcal{a})$ are nearly those indicated be Figure 7. If t is an input tree, $CS(t)$ is the tree of the same shape as t with the same labels on the frontier. The interior nodes are labeled with pairs $\langle \sigma, s \rangle$, where σ is the label of the input and s is the label of the corresponding node of the state tree [$CS(t)$ would be a set of trees if $\mathcal{a}$ were nondeterministic]. For the tree in Figures 1 and 7, $CS(t)$ is shown is Figure 9. $CS(\mathcal{a})$ is $CS(T(\mathcal{a}))$.

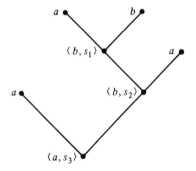

Fig. 9   Complete state tree.

THEOREM 7

If $\mathcal{C}$ is an FRA, then $CS(\mathcal{C}) = T(G)$ for some context-free grammar G.

Now since $\mathrm{fr}CS(\mathcal{C}) = \mathrm{fr}T(\mathcal{C})$ we obtain from this theorem:

THEOREM 8

If U is a recognizable set of trees, then $\mathrm{fr}(U)$ is context free.

Also, we can define the natural projection $\bar{\pi}$ from $T_{\Sigma \times S \cup \Sigma}$ onto T_Σ so that $\bar{\pi}CS(\mathcal{C}) = T(\mathcal{C})$. Therefore, we have a charcterization of the recognizable sets in terms of the local sets (see Thatcher, 1967).

THEOREM 9

Every recognizable set is the projection of a local set.

To illustrate this last theorem, it was mentioned above that the set B_1 of $\{a, b\}$ trees with exactly one label b is recognizable but not local. But the local set obtained as the set of derivation trees of the following grammar yields B_1 under projection.

$$N = \{a, b, c\}$$
$$\Sigma = \{a, b\}$$
$$P: a \longrightarrow aa$$
$$\quad b \longrightarrow aa$$
$$\quad c \longrightarrow ca \mid ac \mid ab \mid ba$$
$$S_0 = \{b, c\}$$

For this grammar $T(G)$ is the set of $\{a, b, c\}$ trees with exactly one path of c labels terminating in a b. The projection that is the identity on $\{a, b\}$ and maps c into a takes $T(G)$ into B_1.

We are not going to use these connections between generalized finite automata theory and context-free language theory to prove any new results about context-free sets. Instead, we will try to show with the help of several examples how old results follow quite easily from what we have so far (and what we have so far is essentially finite automata theory!). I believe that looking at the results (and proofs) from the point of view of finite automata generalized to trees yields a clearer understanding of those results.

Example 1

The Peters–Ritchie result concerning node admissibility conditions and context-sensitive grammars (Peters and Ritchie (1969))

A context-sensitive grammar G with rules of the form $A \longrightarrow w(u, v)$,†

---

†In the notation of Chapter 1 we would write $uAv \longrightarrow uwv$.

read A is rewritten as w in the context u-v is usually interpreted in the deriva-tion sense resulting in the context-sensitive languages. Instead, Peters and Ritchie look at a context-sensitive grammar as describing a set $T(G)$ of trees. Informally speaking, a tree t is in $T(G)$ if every node in t can be justified by one of the context-sensitive rules; i.e., for every node labeled A with successor nodes labeled by the string w, there must exist a "context" u-v at that node such that $A \longrightarrow w(u, v)$ is a rule of G. For example, the node labeled c in Figure 10 could be "justified" by any rule $c \longrightarrow ab(u, v)$ where $u \in \{\lambda, b, a, aa\}$ and $v \in \{\lambda, d, b, ba\}$.† Then defining $L(G)$ to be fr$T(G)$, the theorem is:

THEOREM
(*Peters and Ritchie*)

Under the node-admissibility interpretation of context-sensitive gram-mars, $L(G)$ is context-free.

The proof of this theorem from the finite automata point of view is to show that $T(G)$ is recognizable, and this is fairly clear. Then apply Theorem 8. This proof is not essentially different than the originators' proof, but it does provide some additional insight and offers the possibility (not yet realized) of giving a quantitative analysis of the extent to which the use of context-sensi-tive node-admissibility rules "simplifies" the description of context-free languages.

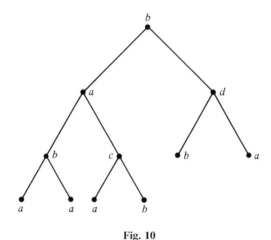

Fig. 10

Example 2

The structural equivalence results of Paull and Unger (1967) and McNaugh-ton (1967)

---

†λ is the empty string.

For any alphabet Σ define the projection $\bar{\beta}$, where $\beta(\sigma) = *$ and $\beta_0(\sigma) = \sigma$; $\sigma \in \Sigma$ and $*$ is a special symbol which may or may not be in Σ. Thus $\bar{\beta}$ (which should be indexed by the alphabet) maps all the internal node labels into $*$ and leaves the frontier nodes as is. One can read $\bar{\beta}(t)$ as the *structure* of t.

DEFINITION 4

Generally two sets of trees U and V will be called *structurally equivalent* if $\bar{\beta}(U) = \bar{\beta}(V)$ and in particular, context-free grammars G_1 and G_2 are structurally equivalent if $\bar{\beta}(T(G_1)) = \bar{\beta}(T(G_2))$.

THEOREM
(*McNaughton, Paull, and Unger*)

There is a decision procedure for structural equivalence.

By Theorem 6 and Theorem 5, $\bar{\beta}(T(G))$ is recognizable. Theorems 2 and 3 show that there is a decision procedure for equality of recognizable sets.

Example 3

The decidability of the structural ambiguity problem (Paull and Unger, 1967)

A context-free grammar is structurally ambiguous if there exist two distinct derivation trees of the same shape with the same frontier; i.e., the grammar assigns to a word in the language two distinct derivations, which yield the same structure in the sense of Example 2. Put generally, we have:

DEFINITION 5

A set of trees U is *structurally ambiguous* if the projection $\bar{\beta}$ is not one-to-one.

In $T_{\Sigma \times \Sigma}$ define W to be the set of trees with properties: (1) there is at least one label $\langle \sigma, \sigma' \rangle$ on an internal node with $\sigma \neq \sigma'$; and (2) the frontiers are labeled with pairs $\langle \sigma, \sigma \rangle$. Clearly W is recognizable (in fact, local). Now let π_1 and π_2 be the natural projections from $T_{\Sigma \times \Sigma}$ onto T_Σ.

LEMMA 5

U is structurally ambiguous iff $\pi_1^{-1}(U) \cap \pi_2^{-1}(U) \cap W$ is nonempty.

Applying Theorems 5, 2, and 3, we have:

THEOREM
(*Paull and Unger*)

There exists a decision procedure for structural ambiguity.

Example 4

Gray's result on invertible grammars (Gray and Harrison, 1969)

A context-free grammar is *invertible* if the right-hand side of a production uniquely determines the nonterminal on the left-hand side.

THEOREM

(Gray)

For any context-free grammar G, there exists a structurally equivalent invertible grammar G'.

Note, of course, that structural equivalence implies weak equivalence; i.e., the languages are the same. Given G, $\bar{\beta}T(G)$ is recognizable by a deterministic FRA $\mathcal{C}$ (Example 2). Now $CS(\mathcal{C})$ is $T(G')$ for some G' (Theorem 7). All rules of G' are of the form $\langle *, M(*, s_1, s_2) \rangle \longrightarrow \delta_1 \delta_2$ where either $\delta_i = \langle *, s_i \rangle$ and $s_i \in S$ (states of $\mathcal{C}$) or $\delta_i \in \Sigma$ and $M(\delta_i, s_0, s_0) = s_i$. Thus G' is invertible and structurally equivalent to G.

Example 5

The "$xu^k wv^k y$" theorem (Bar-Hillel, Perles, and Shamir, 1961)

THEOREM
(Bar-Hillel, Perles, and Shamir).

For any context-free grammar, there exists an integer p such that if the length of a word $z \in L(G)$ is greater than p, then one can find $x, u, w, v,$ and y such that $z = xuwvy$, and $xu^k wv^k y \in L(G)$ for all k.

One may have had the feeling that this theorem is a generalization of the corresponding theorem in finite automata theory. Indeed, looking at Lemma 4, let $\text{fr}(t_1) = xsy$, $\text{fr}(t_2) = usv$, and $\text{fr}(t_3) = w$. Then if the automaton involved is the one accepting $T(G)$, we have $t_1 t_2^n t_3 \in T(G)$ for all n so that $xu^n wv^n y \in L(G)$ for all n. The integer p from this proof is 2^r, where r is the number of states of the automaton recognizing $T(G)$.

It seems fairly clear that other results in context-free language theory which involve the periodicity of the derivation trees may be more easily handled using the finite automata approach.

4-5. TREE AUTOMATA WITH OUTPUT

The generalization of the concept of finite automata with output is as direct and simple as that of recognizer with one exception, the way in which successive outputs are "composed." In the conventional theory, the composition operation is to concatenate the outputs together in sequence. This composition on strings is so natural that it hardly merits mention; however, in the case of trees, we must state explicitly what we view as an appropriate "composition." That explicit statement is at once the complication in the generalization and, I believe, the power of the concept.

First we consider the case where the inputs as well as outputs are trees. The output function A for an automaton (either RFA or FRA) has the same domain of definition as the transition function. (Thus we are dealing with the "Mealy model.") The values of the output function are trees over a possibly different alphabet, say Ω, plus two (since we are considering only *binary* trees at present) special symbols, x_1 and x_2, which can occur on the frontiers of the output trees. As in the definition of $T_{\Sigma, S}$ in Section 4-4, we write T_{Ω, x_2} to denote the set of Ω trees which also allow x_1, x_2 to label frontier nodes.

The special symbols x_1, x_2 will specify the composition of outputs in a natural way, which can be illustrated as follows.

Consider an arbitrary subtree of an input tree as shown diagrammatically in Figure 11. If the finite automaton determines (via the functions A and M) the one-step output for the root node of that subtree to be that shown in Figure 12 (where the alphabet is $\{c, d\}$), then, again diagrammatically, the output for the whole subtree would be that shown in Figure 13, where t'_1 and t'_2 are the outputs for the whole subtrees t_1 and t_2, respectivley.

If we denote by t the tree in Figure 13 and by t' that in Figure 12, then we use the terminology "t results from simultaneously substituting t'_i for x_i in t'" to refer to the operation performed to obtain t from t'. This operation will be denoted $t = t' \leftarrow [t'_1, t'_2]$.

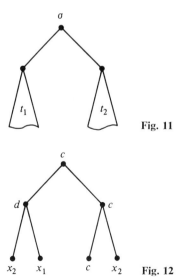

σ

t_1 t_2 **Fig. 11**

c

d   c

x_2 x_1 c x_2 **Fig. 12**

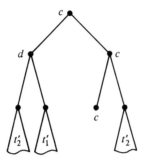

Fig. 13

DEFINITION 6

The tree $t \leftarrow [t_1, \ldots, t_n]$ is the result of simultaneously substituting t_i for x_i in t, $1 \leq i \leq n$.

We now give the definitions of tree automata with output (both FRA and RFA) and then some examples that exemplify how they operate. The emphasis will be on root-to-frontier automata because these have been studied (Rounds, 1970; Thatcher, 1970) and seem to be most applicable to questions in language theory. The definition of FRA with output is new, although it is a natural generalization deserving further study.

There is, in the following definitions, a complication that might not have been expected considering the informal discussion above. The automaton with output has two output functions, A and A_0. The former is the one discussed above; A_0 works, as in the definition of projection in Section 4-3, in the special case of processing frontier nodes.

DEFINITION 7

A *root-to-frontier automaton with output* (RFAO) consists of S, s_0, and M as in Definition 1 and two maps A and A_0 which have the same domain as M, A_0 taking values in T_Ω and A taking values in T_{Ω, x_2}. Σ is the *input alphabet* and Ω is the *output alphabet*.

The RFAO determines a map $\bar{A}: T_\Sigma \times S \longrightarrow T_\Omega$ by:

a. If t is a single node labeled σ, then $\bar{A}(t, s) = A_0(\sigma, s)$.
b. Generally, if t has the form of Figure 11, then
$\bar{A}(t, s) = A(\sigma, s) \leftarrow [\bar{A}(t_1, s_1), \bar{A}(t_2, s_2)]$,   where $M(\sigma, s) = \langle s_1, s_2 \rangle$.

Finally, the map $\bar{A}: T_\Sigma \longrightarrow T_\Omega$ is given by $\bar{A}(t) = \bar{A}(t, s_0)$.

To aid in interpretation, the general step, b, can be read: The output produced from t with root state s is the result of substituting the output produced from t_i with root state s_i for x_i in $A(\sigma, s)$, where $\langle s_1, s_2 \rangle = M(\sigma, s)$.

DEFINITION 8

A *frontier-to-root automaton with output* (FRAO) consists of S, s_0, M as in Definition 2 and two functions, A and A_0, with the same domain as M. The range of A_0 is T_Ω and the range of A is T_{Ω, x_2}. Σ is the *input alphabet* and Ω is the *output alphabet*.

The FRAO determines a map $\bar{A}: T_\Sigma \longrightarrow T_\Omega$ by:

a. If t is a single node labeled σ, then $\bar{A}(t) = A_0(\sigma, s_0, s_0)$.

b. Generally, if t has the form of Figure 11, then

$$\bar{A}(t) = A(\sigma, s_1, s_2) \longleftarrow [\bar{A}(t_1), \bar{A}(t_2)], \text{ where } \bar{M}(t_i) = s_i, i = 1, 2.$$

We give two admittedly contrived examples (one RFAO and one RFAO) with the hope that these will clarify the relevant notions.

Let $t \in T_\Sigma$. An occurrence of a word w as a subword of $\mathrm{fr}(t)$ is called a σ phrase if that occurrence is $\mathrm{fr}(t')$ for some subtree t' of t with root labeled σ. Such an occurrence is called maximal if w is not properly contained in another σ phrase, For example, from Figure 1, ba is a b phrase, but it is not maximal because it is contained in the (maximal) b phrase aba.

The mapping $t \longrightarrow g_b(t)$, which reverses and puts parentheses around all maximal b phrases, is an RFAO mapping. The root-to-frontier automaton that performs this map is described in Table 1. Successive steps of the operation of this automaton on the input of Figure 1 are shown in Figures 14, 15,

$$\Sigma = \{a, b\} \qquad \Omega = \{a, b, (,)\} \qquad S = \{s_0, s_1\}$$

$$M(a, s_0) = \langle s_0, s_0 \rangle$$

$$M(\sigma, s) = \langle s_1, s_1 \rangle \text{ otherwise}$$

$$A_0(\sigma, s) = \sigma$$

Table 1

and 16. The last figure actually comprises two steps in the process; the bottom two nodes should be labeled x_2, x_1 in that order and a final application of A_0 substitutes a for x_2 and b for x_1.

Let R be a regular set. Consider the mapping $t \longrightarrow h_R(t)$, which substitutes the single node labeled c for every maximal subtree t' of t for which $\mathrm{fr}(t') \in R$. This mapping can be performed by a frontier-to-root automaton with outputs

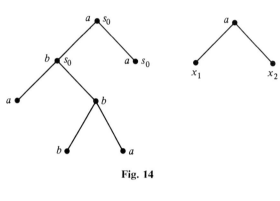

Fig. 14

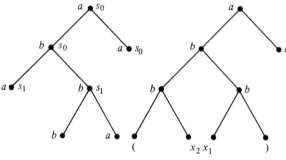

Fig. 15

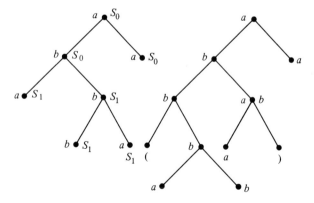

Fig. 16

as follows. Let S be a semigroup and μ a homomorphism from Σ^* into S such that $\mu^{-1}(S_F) = R$ (S_F is a designated subset of S). The states of the FRAO are $S \cup \{s_0\}$ ($s_0 \notin S$), the input alphabet is Σ and the output alphabet is $\Sigma \cup \{c\}$.

$$M(\sigma, s_0, s_0) = \mu(\sigma), \quad M(\sigma, s_1, s_2) = s_1 s_2 \; (s_1, s_2 \in S)$$

$$A_0(\sigma, s, s') = \begin{cases} c & \text{if } M(\sigma, s, s') \in S_F \\ \sigma & \text{otherwise.} \end{cases}$$

$$A(\sigma, s, s') = \begin{cases} c & \text{if } M(\sigma, s, s') \in S_F \\ \sigma(x_1, x_2) & \text{otherwise} \end{cases}$$

If $\Sigma = \{a, b, c,\}$ and $R = a^*b$, then the automaton constructed above would produce the output of Figure 17 with the input of Figure 10. We will not go through the detailed steps of the process.

There are two special cases of finite automata with output that are of particular importance. Under the situation when $|S| = 1$, the transition function is degenerate and the output functions depend only on the input symbols. It is easy to see that in this simplified case, Definitions 7 and 8 coincide. The maps A obtained in this way will be called *homomorphisms*.

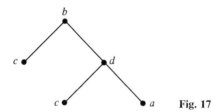

b
c d
c a **Fig. 17**

DEFINITION 9

Maps $A_0 \colon \Sigma \longrightarrow T_\Omega$ and $A \colon \Sigma \longrightarrow T_{\Omega, X_2}$ determine a *homomorphism* $\bar{A}$ by:

a. If t is a single node labeled σ, then $\bar{A}(t) = A_0(\sigma)$.
b. If t has the form of Figure 4-11, then $\bar{A}(t) = A(\sigma) \leftarrow [\bar{A}(t_1), \bar{A}(t_2)]$.

A simple example of a homomorphism is obtained by taking $A_0(\sigma) = \sigma$ and $A(\sigma) = \sigma(x_1, x_2)$. Then $\bar{A}(t)$ is the reversal or reflection of t. As a second example, let $A_0(\sigma) = a$ and $A(\sigma) = \sigma(x_1, x_2)$. $\bar{A}(t)$ is the balanced binary tree completely labeled with "a" of height the same as the length of the leftmost path of t. Every projection as defined in Section 4-3 is a homomorphism.

An automaton with output (and the map $\bar{A}$ associated with such an automaton) will be called *linear* if, in the values of the output functions, there are no repetitions of the special symbols, x_1 and x_2. Thus, in the two previous examples of homomorphisms, the first is linear and the second is not. The importance of linearity is given in the following theorem.

THEOREM 10

Maps from T_Σ to T_Ω determined by linear automata preserve recognizability. Conversely, if $\bar{A}$ is a map determined by a nonlinear automaton, there exists a recognizable set $U \subseteq T_\Sigma$ such that $\bar{A}(U)$ is not recognizable.

Having considered two specializations of finite tree automata with output, we now mention two generalizations. First, in the obvious way, nondeterminism can be introduced as in Definition 2'. That is, for a nondeterministic automaton with output, the three functions M, A, and A_0 all have sets as values and an initial set of states is allowed.

A far more important generalization is studied extensively in Thatcher (1970), where the transition and output functions are combined. Looking at the one-step output in Figure 12 (in which there are two occurrences of x_2), the root-to-frontier automaton would determine, via M, a pair of states $\langle s_1, s_2 \rangle$. Then the output of the automaton operating on t_2 with root state s_2 (which in Figure 13 is shown as t_2') is substituted for both occurrences of x_2. Mechanistically, one can view this process as if the automaton had duplicated at both nodes labeled x_2 and continued to process t_2 in state s_2. The generalization would allow distinct states, say s_2 and s_2', to be used as root states for the two distinct occurrences of x_2. The formulation of this generalization is in a sense simpler than the original. Instead of the special symbols $\{x_1, x_2\}$, we will allow special symbols from the set $\{x_1, x_2\} \times S$, where S is the set of states and an occurrence of the pair $\langle x_i, s \rangle$ on the frontier of an output will mean that the root-to-frontier automaton will substitute for the special symbol $\langle x_i, s \rangle$ the result of operating on t_i with root state s.

Since Definition 7 is really a special case of the generalization being discussed, we will use the same terminology.

DEFINITION 7'

A *root-to-frontier automaton with output* (RFAO) consists of S and s_0 as in Definition 7 and a pair of maps A from $\Sigma \times S$ into $T_{\Omega, X_2 \times S}$ and A_0 from $\Sigma \times S$ into T_Ω.

The RFAO determines a map $\bar{A}: T_\Sigma \times S \longrightarrow T_\Omega$ by:

a. If t is a single node labeled σ, then $\bar{A}(t, s) = A_0(\sigma, s)$.

b. Generally, if t has the form shown in Figure 11, then $\bar{A}(t, s)$ is the result of simultaneously substituting $\bar{A}(t_i, s')$ for all occurrences of $\langle x_i, s' \rangle$ in $A(\sigma, s)$.

Finally, the map $\bar{A}: T_\Sigma \longrightarrow T_\Omega$ is given by $\bar{A}(t) = \bar{A}(t, s_0)$.

Nondeterminism and linearity are extended to Definition 7' just as stated above. Note that under the condition of linearity, Definitions 7 and 7' coincide.

An example of an RFAO mapping which has appeared several times in the literature is the derivative of an arithmetic expression. This example requires the generalization of Definition 7'. To simplify matters, consider the map defined on the local subset of $T_{\{x, +, \cdot, c, 0, 1\}}$ consisting of those trees (arithmetic expressions) which have internal nodes labeled from $\{+, \cdot\}$ and frontier nodes labeled from $\{x, c, 0, 1\}$. The output trees are from the same set. The RFAO which produces the derivative of such an expression has two states, $\{D, I\}$, which correspond to "take the derivative" and "identity," respectively. The initial state is D and the combined transition-output functions are shown in Tables 2 and 3.

A_0	D	I
x	1	x
$\sigma \epsilon \ \{c, 0, 1\}$	0	σ
$+, \cdot$	not applicable	

Table 2

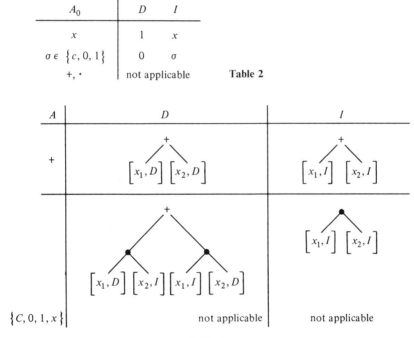

A	D	I
$+$		
$\{C, 0, 1, x\}$	not applicable	not applicable

Table 3

4-6. TRANSLATIONS AND SEMANTICS: FINITE AUTOMATA REVISITED?

In order to begin to make comparisons between generalized finite automata with output and some of the formal treatments of translations and semantics, we must get rid of one technical headache at the outset. Although not so from the finite automata point of view, it seems to have been natural from the context-free language point of view, to have proposed definitions of translations and of semantics based on functions defined on the productions of a grammar.

A homomorphism (Definition 9) is a mapping from trees to trees; thus a homomorphism might be looked upon as a mapping from the derivation trees of one grammar to those of another. The basis function A of that definition would, when looked upon in this way, have the set $\Sigma \cup N$ as its domain. This is the natural approach from the finite automata point of view. But it is clear from the literature that this is not the natural approach from the context-free language theorists' point of view. That outlook would have led one to have replaced Definition 9 with one which A was defined (in the binary case to which we were restricting ourselves) on $\Sigma \times \Sigma^2$, in effect, on the productions of a grammar.

As indicated in Thatcher (1970), the definitions given here (both acceptors and automata with output) can be generalized to two-level or even n-level automata. In the n-level generalization, the next-state and the output for a given node of an input tree are determined by the current-state together with the complete input subtree of height n rooted at that node. Comparing this with the conventional theory of finite automata, the analogue would be a finite state device with n permanently adjacent reading heads on its input tape which are required to move in unison, one tape square at a time. Now this isn't a very interesting generalization in the conventional theory; in fact, no new input–output functions can be obtained. For tree automata, new input–output functions are obtained with increasing n, but there are mathematical reasons to believe that this kind of generalization is the wrong approach for theoretical study. The fundamental reason is that the algebraic formulation naturally leads to the "one-level" definitions given here and secondary reasons are typified by the observation that "two-level homomorphisms" are not closed under composition.

This technical headache (and the extent to which it is a headache will be clear from the propositions to follow) is overcome with an alternative approach provided by the following definition.

DEFINITION 10

For $t \in T_\Sigma$, the *production tree* of t, denoted $\mathcal{P}(t)$, is the unique ($\Sigma \cup \Sigma^3$) tree which is structurally equivalent to t (thus having the same frontier as t) and which for every internal node has the label $\langle \sigma, \sigma_1, \sigma_2 \rangle$ iff the corresponding node of t has label σ and successors labeled $\langle \sigma_1, \sigma_2 \rangle$. For $U \subseteq T_\Sigma$ we will, as usual, write $\mathcal{P}(U)$ for the set of production trees of elements of U and in the special case of a context-free grammar G, we will write $T_\mathcal{P}(G)$ for $\mathcal{P}(T(G))$.

This definition has an auxiliary benefit in giving an example of an FRAO realizable mapping which cannot be obtained with a root-to-frontier automaton. Indeed, it should be a very simple matter for the reader to check that for any Σ, $\mathcal{P}$ (which, like the structure projection $\bar{\beta}$, should be indexed by Σ)

is the output map $\bar{A}$ of a linear FRAO with state set Σ. Thus, by Theorem 10, if U is recognizable, so is $\mathcal{P}(U)$. For the special case of context-free grammars, it is a familiar construction to go from a grammar G to a structurally equivalent grammar G' such that $T(G') = T_{\mathcal{P}}(G)$.

In the pioneering paper on the subject of "syntax-directed translation" (Irons, 1961), Irons emphasized that the essential feature of his syntax-directed compiler for ALGOL 60 was the fact that it separated the function of defining a language (via a context-free grammar, for example) from that of translating it into another. This idea of separating language definition, recognition and parsing (generally, language syntax) from the translation into another language (generally assigning semantics to the source language) has certainly gained wide acceptance. Various versions, formalizations, modifications, and generalizations of Irons's idea of syntax-directed mapping have been investigated in Aho and Ullman (1969a, 1969b, 1968), Culik (1967), Knuth (1968b), Lewis and Stearns (1968), Petrone (1965), Rounds (1970), Thatcher (1969, 1970), and Younger (1967). Although these papers (including my own) are replete with references to earlier and concurrent works, statements such as "similar models have been studied by [x, y, z]" are symptomatic of the disarray in the theoretical development relating to the second half of Irons's dichotomy. The approach based on finite tree automata (with the associated algebraic formulation), as outlined in the last section, provides a unifying framework for that development.

Of the list above, Petrone's "Syntax Mappings of Context-Free Languages" (Petrone, 1965) is the earliest, most general, and least frequently referenced treatment of Irons's ideas.

Because of the generality, the lack of algebraic formalism here (and in Petrone's paper) is especially limiting. It requires our discussion to be even more imprecise than before.

In Section 4-5 we said that we would "first" consider the case of generalized finite automata where both inputs and outputs were trees. There are many other possiblities for output domains. Maintaining the restriction to binary trees as inputs, the form of Definitions 7, 8, 9, and 7' suggests that the operation "$\leftarrow$" of substitution could be replaced by any collection of binary operations indexed by the values of the output function A. Thus, in general, the output universe of discourse could be any algebraic system with associated binary functions. A would take those binary functions as values and A_0 would take values in the carrier of the algebraic system. (It should be emphasized that all this generality is automatic with the algebraic formulation.) Looking at Definition 7, we see that this is exactly the situation. The carrier of the algebraic system is T_Ω and corresponding to any $t \in T_{\Omega, X_2}$ (which might be the value of A) is the binary operation on T_Ω; $t(t_1, t_2) = t \leftarrow [t_1, t_2]$.

This generalized situation can be phrased in the following definition.

DEFINITION 9'

Let $\mathcal{B} = \langle B, \beta_1, \ldots, \beta_k, \ldots \rangle$ be an algebra where B (the carrier) is a set and the β_i are binary operations on B. A pair of maps, $A: \Sigma \longrightarrow \{\beta_1, \ldots, \beta_k, \ldots\}$ and $A_0: \Sigma \longrightarrow B$ determine a homomorphism $\bar{A}$ from T_Σ into $\mathcal{B}$ by:

a. If t is a single node labeled σ, then $\bar{A}(t) = A_0(\sigma)$.
b. If t has the form of Figure 11, then $\bar{A}(t) = A(\sigma)(\bar{A}(t_1), \bar{A}(t_2))$.

Although the notation and terminology differ slightly from Petrone's, the following proposition provides the connection between his ideas and the definitions presented here.

PROPOSITION 1

The concept of $\mathcal{B}$-semantics (Petrone, 1965) of a context-free language $V = L(G)$ coincides with the concept of homomorphism defined on $T_\varphi(G)$ taking values in $\mathcal{B}$.

Within the general algebraic setting of Definition 9', it is possible to prove a generalization of Theorem 10, but it reads, roughly speaking, that the linear maps preserve equational sets in the sense of Mezei and Wright (1967). As proved in that paper, under the conditions of Theorem 10 the equational and recognizable sets coincide.

A specific application, more like those in Section 4-4, is obtained when $\mathcal{B}$ is taken to be the structure $\langle N^k, + \rangle$ (N is the set of nonnegative integers) and the input alphabet is $\{\sigma_1, \ldots, \sigma_k\}$. The homomorphism determined by $A_0(\sigma_i) = \langle 0 \ldots 010 \ldots 0 \rangle$ (1 in the ith position) and $A(\sigma_i) = +$ $(1 \leq i \leq k)$ maps a tree t into the k-tuple $(n_1, \ldots, n_k)$, where n_i is the number of occurrences of σ_i in $\text{fr}(t)$. The general theorem referred to above gives a neat algebraic proof of Parikh's theorem (Parikh, 1961) because the semilinear sets are equational.

Similar considerations with Σ^* and concatenation replacing N^k and $+$ yield an alternative proof of the second half of Theorem 6. It should be emphasized again that these examples are special cases of one general theorem and that theorem is proved using essentially the ideas of finite automata theory.

Attention in later work has focused on the study of Irons's specific idea of syntax-directed translation. Using the terminology of Thatcher (1970), any map μ from trees to trees determines a *translation* τ_μ which is the set of ordered pairs $\langle \text{fr}(t), \text{fr}(\mu(t)) \rangle$ for t in the domain of μ. For an arbitrary set U of trees in the domain of μ, τ_μ restricted to $\text{fr}(U)$ should in general be called a syntax-directed translation of $\text{fr}(U)$ because the translation (or translations) of a string in $\text{fr}(U)$ is determined by a mapping of the "structure" of that string, (i.e., the syntax of that string).

Of course, that idea of syntax-directed translation is far more general than Irons's original idea or any of the formalizations in the literature as is indicated by the following comparisons.

PROPOSITION 2

Any "syntax correspondence" with source grammar G as defined by Younger (1967) is a nondeterministic homomorphism of $T_\varphi(G)$.

PROPOSITION 3

Any "syntax-directed translation" with source grammar G as defined by Lewis and Stearns (1968) is a linear homomorphism of $T_\varphi(G)$ as is any "syntax-directed translation scheme" with source grammar G as defined by Aho and Ullman (1969a, 1969b).

PROPOSITION 4

Any "generalized syntax-directed translation scheme" with source grammar G as defined by Aho and Ullman (1968) corresponds to an RFAO map A defined on $T_\varphi(G)$.

PROPOSITION 5

A "nondeterministic transformation" on T_Σ as defined by Rounds (1970) is equivalent to a nondeterministic RFAO map $\bar{A}$ on $\mathcal{P}(T_\Sigma)$.

The five propositions above relate various formalizations in the area of translations and semantics to the finite automata definitions of Section 4-4. Propositions 2 and 3 do not present equivalences because additional restrictions must be placed on the (very simple) notion of homomorphism to get exact equivalence. Taking only one of the cases for the concept of syntax-directed translation as defined by Irons, Lewis and Stearns, and Aho and Ullman, one has to add the following condition to the basis function A of the homomorphism. For $\sigma, \sigma_1, \sigma_2$, let $t = A(\sigma, \sigma_1, \sigma_2)$. Then t must be of height 2, must have root σ, and the special symbol x_i can occur on the frontier of t if and only if σ_i is a nonterminal of G. Thus we might introduce the appropriate definitions of terminology to say that a syntax-directed translation is a linear, internal-label-preserving, primitive (for height 2), modified-rank-preserving, homomorphism of $T_\varphi(G)$. It is interesting to note that when reflected back to the conventional (monadic) finite automata theory through the algebraic formulation, the only syntax-directed translation is the identity!

There is one notable omission in our list of comparisons (and I apologize to others whose definitions I have not taken note of) and that is the treatment of semantics by Knuth (1968b). It should be fairly clear that his idea of "synthesized attributes" corresponds to frontier-to-root automata with appropriate output domains and that the calculation of "inherited attributes" corresponds to root-to-frontier automata with appropriate output. It must certainly occur to the automata theorist that Knuth's semantics may find a formulation in terms of two-way tree automata.

The view presented here is simply the thesis that finite automata theory, generalized and algebraically formulated, has the potential for significant application in theoretical computer science.

We have presented arguments in support of that thesis on both sides of the dichotomy (if it should be called that) between recognition and translation, or for lack of better words, between syntax and semantics. The difference between the arguments on the two sides should be striking. On the one hand, we listed examples of several theorems in context-free language theory which can be proved from the finite automata theory point of view. Besides simplifying proofs, I believe that one obtains significantly more insight into the theorems with that approach.

On the other side, with the exception of Parikh's theorem, the arguments in support of the thesis rest solely on showing that certain definitions can be neatly (i.e., algebraically) reformulated using generalized finite automata with output.

One reason for this striking difference is obvious; the overwhelming amount of related work in theoretical computer science has been on the recognition-syntax side of the dichotomy, the formalism is fairly settled, the concepts are well known, and there is a great wealth of theorems from which to choose. But there are theorems on the other side of the dichotomy. Some of those in the papers cited in Section 4-5 can be eliminated or simplified through the algebraic approach.

The number one priority in the area is a careful assessment of the significant problems concerning natural language and programming language semantics and translation. If such problems can be found and formulated, I am convinced that the approach informally surveyed here can provide a unifying framework within which to study them.

5 APPLICATIONS OF LANGUAGE THEORY TO COMPILER DESIGN

Jeffrey D. Ullman
Department of Electrical Engineering
Princeton University

5-1. INTRODUCTION

There are certain aspects of language theory that have had, or can have, significant impact on the design and implementation of compilers. These areas are, principally, the subjects of context-free grammars and syntax-directed translations. It is perhaps to be expected that the deep and interesting theorems of language theory do not usually find application. Rather, it is the definitions of formal constructs and their elementary properties that find use. Some of the broad areas in which the language theorist can aid the compiler designer can be summarized as follows.

1. Formalisms such as the context-free grammar or syntax-directed translation serve as good tools for language description. The context-free grammar (Backus–Naur form) is an excellent description for the syntax of several languages, such as ALGOL. Syntax-directed translation, in its full generality, is a good vehicle for defining the translation to be performed by the compiler when the syntax is specified by a context-free grammar.

2. Certain parts of the theory of context-free languages serve to identify maximal classes of grammars with desirable properties, such as possession of a simple parsing algorithm. In these pages we shall meet several interesting classes of this nature, for example, LL and LR grammars.

3. Language theory can warn the compiler writer that certain programs cannot be written. For example, one cannot write a program to "minimize" the context-free grammar for a given language in any worthwhile sense.

4. By providing a general mathematical framework for describing many compiler processes, language theory helps the compiler designer to express many important design and optimization problems.

5. Formal theories allow for the automatic generation of pieces of the compiler, after the designer has done a small amount of specification (e.g., the BNF description of a language enables one to automatically generate a parser). Automatically generated components are easy to understand and debug. Moreover, the same theory that allowed the component to be designed can aid in the automatic verification of its correctness.

5-2. THE PIECES OF A COMPILER

A rough sketch of a compiler is shown in Figure 1. The input to the compiler is a string of characters. The first job of the compiler is *lexical analysis*.

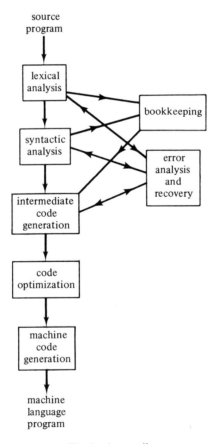

Fig. 1 A compiler.

Substrings of the input that represent logical entities, called *tokens*, have to be grouped together and subsequently treated as one object. Examples of such entities are

1. Keywords, such as **begin** in ALGOL.
2. Signs of more than one character, such as $:=$ in ALGOL or .EQ. in FORTRAN.
3. Identifiers and constants.

For example, when processing the FORTRAN statement

$$IF(A1 + A2 .EQ. 3) GOTO 100$$

the lexical analyzer would group IF as one object, a keyword; A1 and A2 would each be grouped together as identifiers; the single character 3 is a constant; .EQ. is a single relational operator; the string GOTO is another keyword; 100 is a constant. The signs (,), and $+$ are tokens consisting of a single character. The entire sequence of tokens emitted by the lexical analyzer would be **if (id $+$ id eq id) goto id**. We have used boldface to indicate a single token, and the token **id** represents a program variable, constant, or label.

Several works have dealt with application of finite automaton theory to lexical analysis. We shall not discuss this relationship further; the reader who is interested in the subject is referred to Johnson et al. (1968), Cheatham (1967), Lewis and Rosenkrantz (1971), or Aho and Ullman (1972e).

The second phase in the compiling process is *syntactic analysis*, or *parsing*. Here the output of the lexical analyzer is given structure, normally the structure of parse trees in a context-free grammar. Although there is no particular reason why a tree structure should be useful, experience demonstrates this to be so. Perhaps the reason is that a tree structure allows us to group larger and larger pieces of the program together in a rational fashion. For example, the string of tokens mentioned above might receive the tree structure shown in Figure 2.

That is, the root and its descendants tell us that an if statement can be composed of the keyword IF, followed by a parenthesized proposition and a statement. A proposition can be a relation. (It could also be a Boolean expression or several relations and Boolean expressions with logical connectives.) At each interior node of the tree, a class of strings is defined, so that scanning down the tree, we go from the most general observation, "An if statement is an if statement" to the most particular observation possible for the given input, "An if statement may be **if (id $+$ id eq id) goto id**."

The parser may physically build a parse tree, although more often, the process of tree construction is symbolic only. The parser may emit some linear representation of the tree or it may "build" the tree in a very figurative sense,

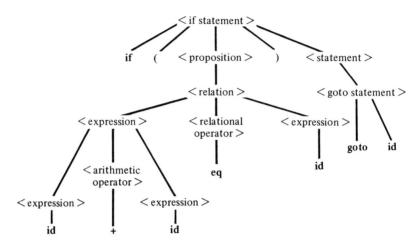

Fig. 2   Parse tree.

by calling on a "semantic routine" to generate code at times when we could imagine that one node of the tree is being "built." (Thus the process of parsing often occurs simultaneously with code generation and lexical analysis, although conceptually we can regard these processes as sequential.)

Once the parse tree is "built," the compiler can generate a translation of its input. This translation is in an *intermediate language*, which is not machine code but is generally related to machine code in some simple way. For example, assembly code could be our intermediate language, although often the intermediate language is less specific, notably by failing to specify in which registers computation actually occurs.

A reasonable and commonly used technique for code generation is the following "syntax-directed" scheme. At each node of the parse tree is defined one or more translations. The formulas for computing the translations at a given node are in terms of primitive operations (e.g., concatenation) performed on constants (e.g., fixed strings) and the translations at the direct descendants of that node.

For example, we might like the translation of an arithmetic expression to be assembly code which evaluates that expression in the "accumulator." At a node such as the root of Figure 3, we can construct this code as follows.

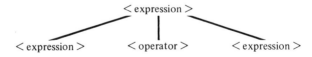

Fig. 3   Part of a parse tree.

1. Take the code for the subexpression on the right; follow it by
2. an instruction to store the result in a safe temporary storage location, then
3. the code for the subexpression on the left, followed by
4. an instruction which applies the operator to the accumulator and the temporary location mentioned in 2, leaving the result in the accumulator.

We should observe that in order to find a safe temporary, we need a way of generating names for locations such that the code for neither subexpression mentions that name. If we have one symbol, say $, which may appear in no program identifier, we can generate safe temporary names by carrying up the tree an additional translation—the "level" of a node. This translation is an integer and can be computed from nodes below by finding the maximum level of a direct descendant and adding one. If a node has level i, its safe temporary can be taken to be $$i$.

In many cases, other translations, such as the mode of expressions, are also computed as we proceed up the parse tree.

During the three phases mentioned, there are two processes which may interact with them. The first is *bookkeeping*. While the parser treats all identifiers alike, when code is generated we need information about each identifier, e.g., whether it is integer, real, complex, or Boolean; whether it is an array; and whether it is local to any part of the program. This information is entered during the lexical analysis and parsing phases and is used during code generation. A formal approach to some of the problems of bookkeeping, known as "property grammars," can be found in Stearns and Lewis (1969). Their efficient implementation requires techniques found in Stearns and Rosenkrantz (1969) and Hopcroft and Ullman (1972). The complete algorithm is described in Aho and Ullman (1973). Some pragmatic considerations regarding bookkeeping processes can be found in Gries (1971).

The error-recovery phase of a compiler is entered whenever an ill-formed program is found. Various structural errors can be found during lexical or syntactic analysis, and "semantic" errors are detected during code generation. An example of a semantic error would be the use of a real identifier in a role which requires an integer identifier.

The compiler faces a nontrivial task trying to make a minimal change in the input program that will allow compiling to proceed. It is, of course, necessary to proceed, so that all or most errors in the program can be detected, rather than just the first error. Some approaches to error recovery can be found in Irons (1963), Leinius (1970), Wirth (1968), and LaFrance (1970).

We have shown the code-optimization phase to follow intermediate code generation. Actually, it can be done at various times, including before any processing of the source program has been done. For example, many compilers replace $X \uparrow 3$ by $X * X * X$, which can be evaluated more efficiently.

Code-optimization techniques can be divided into two classes. The first, local optimization, attempts to order and manipulate instructions appearing in small loop-free portions of the program, in order to produce a faster-running program. For example, Sethi and Ullman (1970) treat arithmetic expressions; Floyd (1961) and Aho and Ullman (1972a) deal with straight-line blocks of code. Optimizations of simple loops are more complex but still essentially local. A description of techniques for loop optimization can be found in Allen (1969), Cocke and Schwartz (1970) or Aho and Ullman (1973).

The second class of techniques concerns global analysis of the program. One must develop a clear picture of how flow of control moves between straight-line blocks. It is then possible to identify subexpressions which are computed at two widely separated points in the program, but for which one computation would suffice. We can also detect computations which are never used and many other situations in which improved code can be generated. Some information on flow analysis and applications can be found in Allen (1970), Cocke and Schwartz (1970), Aho and Ullman (1973), Schaefer (1973), and Lowry and Medlock (1969).

Recent general works on compiling that emphasize theory, rather than implementation details, are Cheatham (1967), Aho and Ullman (1972e, 1973), Cocke and Schwartz (1970), and McKeeman et al. (1970). A survey of compiler writing systems and many additional references can be found in Feldman and Gries (1968).

5-3. CONTEXT-FREE GRAMMARS

Let us proceed to the principal formalism of use to compiler writers, the context-free grammar.

DEFINITION

A *context-free grammar* (CFG) is a four-tuple (N, Σ, P, S), where N and Σ are finite, disjoint sets of *nonterminals* and *terminals*, respectively; S in N is the *start symbol*, and P is a finite list of *productions* of the form $A \rightarrow \alpha$, where A is in N and α in $(N \cup \Sigma)^*$. Further information on context-free grammars and keys to the literature can be found in Chapter 1.

Example 1

My favorite grammar, which will be subsequently referred to as G_0, is $(\{E, T, F\}, \{a, (,), +, *\}, P, E)$, where P consists of the following productions:

$$E \longrightarrow E + T$$
$$E \longrightarrow T$$

$$T \longrightarrow T * F$$
$$T \longrightarrow F$$
$$F \longrightarrow (E)$$
$$F \longrightarrow a$$

G_0 defines arithmetic expressions over operators $+$ and $*$, with a representing any identifier.

The way in which a CFG serves to define strings of terminal symbols is as follows.

DEFINITION

Let $G = (N, \Sigma, P, S)$ be a CFG. We define the relation $\underset{G}{\Rightarrow}$ on $(N \cup \Sigma)^*$, by: If α and β are any strings in $(N \cup \Sigma)^*$, and $A \rightarrow \gamma$ is a production, then $\alpha A \beta \underset{G}{\Rightarrow} \alpha \gamma \beta$. If α is in Σ^*, then we may write $\alpha A \beta \underset{G \, \mathrm{lm}}{\Rightarrow} \alpha \gamma \beta$; the lm stands for "leftmost." Similarly, if β is in Σ^*, we may write $\alpha A \beta \underset{G \, \mathrm{rm}}{\Rightarrow} \alpha \gamma \beta$; the rm stands for "rightmost." In the former case we replace the leftmost nonterminal; in the latter case we replace the rightmost. The *transitive closure* of any relation R, denoted R^+, is defined by:

a. If aRb, then aR^+b.
b. If aR^+b, and bR^+c, then aR^+c.
c. aR^+b only if it so follows from a and b.

The *reflexive, transitive closure* of relation R, denoted R^*, is defined by aR^*b if and only if $a = b$ or aR^+b. Thus, we can use $\alpha \underset{G}{\overset{*}{\Rightarrow}} \beta$, for example, to express the notion that α can become β by some (possibly null) sequence of replacements of left sides of productions by their right sides.

We will, whenever no ambiguity results, drop the subscript G from the nine relations $\Rightarrow, \underset{G \, \mathrm{lm}}{\Rightarrow}, \underset{G \, \mathrm{rm}}{\Rightarrow}$, and their transitive and reflexive-transitive closures.

We say $L(G)$, the language *defined by* G, is $\{w \,|\, w$ is in Σ^* and $S \overset{*}{\Rightarrow} w\}$. $L(G)$ is said to be a *context free language* (CFL).

CONVENTION

Unless we state otherwise, the following conventions regarding symbols of a context-free grammar hold.

a. $A, B, C, \ldots$ are nonterminals.
b. $\ldots, X, Y, Z$ are either terminals or nonterminals.
c. $a, b, c, \ldots$ are terminals.
d. $u, \ldots, z$ are terminal strings.

e. $\alpha, \beta, \gamma, \ldots$ are strings of terminals and/or nonterminals.

f. S is the start symbol; except in G_0, where E is the start symbol.

g. e denotes the empty string.

We may, using this convention, specify a CFG merely by listing its productions. Moreover, we use the shorthand $A \rightarrow \alpha_1 | \ldots | \alpha_n$ to stand for the productions $A \rightarrow \alpha_1, A \rightarrow \alpha_2, \ldots, A \rightarrow \alpha_n$.

DEFINITION

Let $G = (N, \Sigma, P, S)$ be a CFG. If $\alpha_1 \Rightarrow \alpha_2 \Rightarrow \ldots \Rightarrow \alpha_n$, then we say there is a *derivation* of α_n from α_1. If $\alpha_i \underset{\text{lm}}{\Rightarrow} \alpha_{i+1}$, $1 \leq i \leq n$, we call this a *leftmost derivation*, and if $\alpha_i \underset{\text{rm}}{\Rightarrow} \alpha_{i+1}$, $1 \leq i < n$, it is a *rightmost derivation*. Most often, we are interested in the case where $\alpha_1 = S$. If $S \overset{*}{\Rightarrow} \alpha$, then α is a *sentential form*. If $S \overset{*}{\underset{\text{lm}}{\Rightarrow}} \alpha$, it is a *left sentential form*, and if $S \overset{*}{\underset{\text{rm}}{\Rightarrow}} \alpha$, it is a *right sentential form*.

Example 2

Let us consider G_0 and the string $a + a$ in $L(G_0)$. It has the following derivations, among others.

(a)	(b)	(c)
E	E	E
$\Rightarrow E + T$	$\Rightarrow E + T$	$\Rightarrow E + T$
$\Rightarrow E + F$	$\Rightarrow T + T$	$\Rightarrow E + F$
$\Rightarrow T + F$	$\Rightarrow F + T$	$\Rightarrow E + a$
$\Rightarrow T + a$	$\Rightarrow a + T$	$\Rightarrow T + a$
$\Rightarrow F + a$	$\Rightarrow a + F$	$\Rightarrow F + a$
$\Rightarrow a + a$	$\Rightarrow a + a$	$\Rightarrow a + a$

Derivation (a) is neither rightmost nor leftmost; (b) is leftmost and (c) is rightmost. $T + F$ is a sentential form of G_0 but happens not to be a left or right sentential form. $a + a$ is both a left and right sentential form and is in $L(G_0)$.

Given a derivation of w from S we can construct a *parse tree* for w as follows. Let $S = \alpha_1 \Rightarrow \alpha_2 \Rightarrow \ldots \Rightarrow \alpha_n = w$.

1. Begin with a single node labeled S. This node is a trivial tree and is said to be the tree for α_1. In general the tree for α_i will have a leaf *corresponding to* each symbol of α_i. Initially, the lone symbol S of α_1 corresponds to the lone node.

2. Suppose that we have constructed the tree for α_i, $i < n$. Let α_{i+1} be

constructed by replacing some instance of A in α_i by β. To this instance of A there corresponds a leaf. Make direct descendants of that leaf for each symbol of β, ordered from the left. If β is the empty string, then we create a single direct descendant, labeled e.

The tree construction defined above is called *top down*. We can also construct the same tree *bottom up*, as follows.

1. Begin with an isolated node corresponding to each symbol of α_n. As this algorithm proceeds, we shall have a collection of trees corresponding to each step of the derivation. At the end, there will be one tree for the first sentential form α_1 (i.e., S).

2. Suppose that we have a collection of trees for α_i, $1 < i \leq n$, where to each symbol of α_i there corresponds a root of one of the trees. If α_i is constructed from α_{i-1} by replacing A by β, create a new node, labeled A, whose direct descendants are the roots of the trees for the symbols of β. The order of symbols in β reflects the order of the descendants. If, however, $\beta = e$, create one direct descendant for the node labeled A, and label the descendant e.

Example 3

The unique parse tree for $a * a + a$ in G_0 is shown in Figure 4. Note that the leaves of the tree read $a * a + a$, from the left.

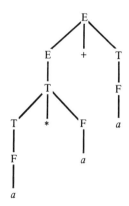

Fig. 4   Parse tree.

THEOREM 1

The top-down and bottom-up methods of constructing parse trees give the same result when applied to the same derivation.

DEFINITION

A CFG G is *unambiguous* if each word in $L(G)$ has a unique parse tree.

THEOREM 2

The following conditions on CFG G are equivalent.
a. G is unambiguous.
b. Each word in $L(G)$ has a unique leftmost derivation.
c. Each word in $L(G)$ has a unique rightmost derivation.

There are certain normal forms into which CFG's can be put. Certain parsing and translating algorithms depend upon, or are made simpler by, grammars in one of these forms.

DEFINITION

Let $G = (N, \Sigma, P, S)$ be a CFG. We say that G is *proper* if

a. For each X in $N \cup \Sigma$, there exist w, x, and y such that $S \overset{*}{\Rightarrow} wXx \overset{*}{\Rightarrow} wyx$. That is, each symbol is used in the derivation of some member of $L(G)$.
b. For no A in N is $A \overset{+}{\Rightarrow} A$ true. That is, no nonterminal derives itself nontrivially.
c. No production is of the form $A \rightarrow e$.

We say that G is in *Chomsky normal form* if each production is of the form $A \rightarrow BC$ or $A \rightarrow a$.
We say that G is in *Greibach normal form* if each production is of the form $A \rightarrow a\alpha$, where α is in N^*.

Example 4

G_0 is proper. The following is an equivalent grammar (one which generates the same language) in Chomsky normal form.

$$E \longrightarrow EA$$
$$E \longrightarrow TB$$
$$E \longrightarrow a$$
$$E \longrightarrow LC$$
$$A \longrightarrow PT$$
$$P \longrightarrow +$$
$$T \longrightarrow TB$$
$$T \longrightarrow a$$
$$T \longrightarrow LC$$
$$B \longrightarrow MF$$
$$M \longrightarrow *$$

$$F \longrightarrow a$$
$$F \longrightarrow LC$$
$$L \longrightarrow ($$
$$C \longrightarrow ER$$
$$R \longrightarrow)$$

The following is an equivalent grammar in Greibach normal form:

$$F \longrightarrow (ER \mid a$$
$$R \longrightarrow)$$
$$T \longrightarrow aMT \mid a \mid (ERMT \mid (ER$$
$$M \longrightarrow *$$
$$E \longrightarrow aMT \mid a \mid (ERMT \mid (ER \mid aMTPE \mid$$
$$aPE \mid (ERMTPE \mid (ERPE$$
$$P \longrightarrow +$$

THEOREM 3

If L is a CFL, L is not empty, and e is not in L, then L has

a. A proper grammar.
b. A Chomsky normal form grammar.
c. A Greibach normal form grammar.

5-4. EARLEY'S ALGORITHM

There is one outstanding method of recognizing the words of an arbitrary CFL and building parse trees, although many others have been proposed. This method is due to Earley (1968). Descriptions of other general methods can be found in Cheatham (1967) and Aho and Ullman (1972e). Earley's method works as follows.

1. Let $G = (N, \Sigma, P, S)$ and let $a_1 \ldots a_n$ be the word we wish to recognize or parse. We construct lists $I_0, I_1, \ldots, I_n$, of *items;* an item is of the form $[A \longrightarrow \alpha \cdot \beta, i]$, where $A \longrightarrow \alpha\beta$ is a production and i an integer.
2. Construct I_0 as follows.
    a. Add $[S \longrightarrow \cdot \alpha, 0]$ to I_0, for each $S \longrightarrow \alpha$ in P.
    b. Apply the following *closure* operation with $j = 0$. The closure rules for I_j are:
        i. If $[A \longrightarrow \alpha \cdot B\beta, i]$ is on I_j and $B \longrightarrow \gamma$ is a production, add $[B \longrightarrow \cdot \gamma, j]$ to I_j.

ii. If $[A \rightarrow \alpha \cdot, i]$ is on I_j, then for all items on I_i of the form $[B \rightarrow \beta \cdot A\gamma, k]$, add $[B \rightarrow \beta A \cdot \gamma, k]$ to I_j.

Note that if $j = 0$, then i and k will always be 0, but when the closure operation is used for arbitrary j, we shall find different values for i and k.

3. Suppose we have constructed I_{j-1}. Construct I_j as follows.

    a. For all $[A \rightarrow \alpha \cdot a_j\beta, i]$ on I_{j-1}, add $[A \rightarrow \alpha a_j \cdot \beta, i]$ to I_j. Recall that a_j is the jth input position.

    b. Apply the closure operation, as defined above, to I_j.

The following theorem can be shown.

THEOREM 4

Item $[A \rightarrow \alpha \cdot \beta, i]$ is placed on I_j if and only if there is a leftmost derivation

$$S \overset{*}{\underset{\text{lm}}{\Rightarrow}} a_1 \cdots a_i A\gamma \underset{\text{lm}}{\Rightarrow} a_1 \cdots a_i\alpha\beta\gamma \overset{*}{\underset{\text{lm}}{\Rightarrow}} a_1 \cdots a_j\beta\gamma$$

(If $k = 0$, then $a_1 \cdots a_k$ should be interpreted as the empty string.)

As a consequence, $a_1 \cdots a_n$ is in $L(G)$ if and only if $[S \rightarrow \alpha \cdot, 0]$ is on I_n for some α. We can build a parse tree from the items in a simple manner. Think of an item $[A \rightarrow X_1 \ldots X_m \cdot X_{m+1} \ldots X_r, i]$ on list j as representing a potential node of the tree, with label A and direct descendants labeled $X_1 \ldots X_r$. Already, descendants for $X_1 \ldots X_m$ have been found. If X_{m+1} is a terminal, and we add an item $[A \rightarrow X_1 \ldots X_{m+1} \cdot X_{m+2} \ldots X_r, i]$ to the next list by rule 3a, then we may create a new direct descendant, to the right of the others found so far, and label it X_{m+1}. If X_{m+1} is a nonterminal, and we add the item $[A \rightarrow X_1 \ldots X_{m+1} \cdot X_{m+2} \ldots X_r, i]$ to some I_j by closure rule ii because item $[X_{m+1} \rightarrow \alpha \cdot, t]$ is on I_j and $[A \rightarrow X_1 \ldots X_m \cdot X_{m+1} \ldots X_r, k]$ is on I_t, then the node for $[A \rightarrow X_1 \ldots X_{m+1} \cdot X_{m+2} \ldots X_r, k]$ is given, as current rightmost descendant, the node for $[X_{m+1} \rightarrow \alpha \cdot, i]$ on I_k. In certain cases an item may be added to a list for two different reasons. Then the above tree construction admits of alternative ways to proceed. Any valid choice may be made, and one, of many possible, parse trees will be produced.

Example 5

The lists for G_0, with input $a*a$, are as follows:

I_0	I_1	I_2	I_3
$E \rightarrow \cdot E + T, 0$	$F \rightarrow a\cdot, 0$	$T \rightarrow T*\cdot F, 0$	$F \rightarrow a\cdot, 2$
$E \rightarrow \cdot T, 0$	$T \rightarrow F\cdot, 0$	$F \rightarrow \cdot(E), 2$	$T \rightarrow T*F\cdot, 0$
$T \rightarrow \cdot T*F, 0$	$E \rightarrow T\cdot, 0$	$F \rightarrow \cdot a, 2$	$E \rightarrow T\cdot, 0$
$T \rightarrow \cdot F, 0$	$T \rightarrow T\cdot*F, 0$		$T \rightarrow T\cdot*F, 0$
$F \rightarrow \cdot(E), 0$	$E \rightarrow E\cdot + T, 0$		$E \rightarrow E\cdot + T, 0$
$F \rightarrow \cdot a, 0$			

List I_3 is constructed as follows. $[F \longrightarrow a\cdot, 2]$ is added by rule 3a, because $[F \longrightarrow \cdot a, 2]$ is on I_2. $[T \longrightarrow T*F\cdot, 0]$ is added to I_3 by closure rule ii because $[T \longrightarrow T*\cdot F, 0]$ is on I_2 and $[F \longrightarrow a\cdot, 2]$ is on I_3. Items $[E \longrightarrow T\cdot, 0]$ and $[T \longrightarrow T\cdot *F, 0]$ are added because $[E \longrightarrow \cdot T, 0]$ and $[T \longrightarrow \cdot T*F, 0]$ are on I_0, and $[T \longrightarrow T*F\cdot, 0]$ is on I_3. We add $[E \longrightarrow E\cdot + T, 0]$ because $[E \longrightarrow T\cdot, 0]$ is on I_3 and $[E \longrightarrow \cdot E + T, 0]$ is on I_0. Since $[E \longrightarrow T\cdot, 0]$ is on I_3, $a*a$ is in $L(G_0)$.

The speed of Earley's algorithm can be expressed as follows.

THEOREM 5

Earley's algorithm can be implemented in $\mathcal{O}(n^2)$ steps of a random-access computer if the underlying grammar is unambiguous, and in $\mathcal{O}(n^3)$ steps for an arbitrary grammar.

Moreover, on many grammars of practical interest, Earley's algorithm operates in $\mathcal{O}(n)$ steps. It is the fastest known general parsing algorithm.

5-5. LL(k) GRAMMARS

We now begin the study of several useful classes of CFG's which have fast parsing algorithms. While none of these classes are capable of generating an arbitrary CFL, each can handle most or all of the structural features found in common programming languages. An important subclass of grammars, called LL(k), for *l*eft to right scan, producing a *l*eftmost derivation, with k symbol lookahead, was first examined by Lewis and Stearns (1968). The LL(1) case was treated by Knuth (1967). Significant development of the theory was made by Rosenkrantz and Stearns (1970). The general idea can be summarized as follows.

Let $G = (N, \Sigma, P, S)$ be a CFG, and let w be in Σ^*. We may attempt to find a leftmost derivation for w by starting with S and trying to proceed to successive left sentential forms. Suppose we have obtained $S = \alpha_1 \underset{\text{lm}}{\Longrightarrow} \alpha_2 \underset{\text{lm}}{\Longrightarrow} \cdots \underset{\text{lm}}{\Longrightarrow} \alpha_i$, where $\alpha_i = xA\beta$ and x is a prefix of w. If there are several productions with A on the left, we must select the proper one. It is desirable that we be able to do so using only information which we have accumulated so far during the parse (which we represent by saying that we "know what β is") and the k symbols of w beyond prefix x, for some small k. If we can always make this decision correctly, we say that G is LL(k).

If a grammar is LL(k), we can parse it deterministically in a simple fashion. One pushdown list, which holds the portion of a left sentential form to the right of its prefix of terminals ($A\beta$ in the case of α_i, above) is used. The input w is scanned left to right, and if α_i has been reached, the input pointer will have scanned over prefix x, and is ready to read the first k symbols of w. The arrangement is shown in Figure 5.

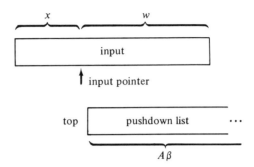

Fig. 5 Organization of LL(k) parser.

If production $A \rightarrow \gamma$ is chosen to expand A, the pushdown list is made to hold $\gamma\beta$. Then, any terminals on top of the pushdown list are compared with the input immediately to the right of the input pointer, and the next left sentential form will be properly represented. The process of expanding the topmost nonterminal on the pushdown list then repeats. Note that while expanding nonterminals, we could construct a parse tree top down if we wished.

It should be noted that the pushdown list may carry information other than grammar symbols, in order to summarize at the top of the list, the important information about what is in the list (β in our example). However, as we shall see, this information is not essential, if the grammar is modified properly or if $k = 1$. We now give the formal definition of an LL(k) grammar.

DEFINITION

If α is a string, then $\alpha : k$ denotes the first k symbols of α, or all of α, if $|\alpha| < k$.† Let $G = (N, \Sigma, P, S)$ be a CFG. We say G is $LL(k)$ if whenever we have the following two derivations:

a. $S \underset{\text{1m}}{\overset{*}{\Rightarrow}} xA\alpha \underset{\text{1m}}{\Rightarrow} x\beta\alpha \underset{\text{1m}}{\overset{*}{\Rightarrow}} xy$

b. $S \underset{\text{1m}}{\overset{*}{\Rightarrow}} xA\alpha \underset{\text{1m}}{\Rightarrow} xy\alpha \underset{\text{1m}}{\overset{*}{\Rightarrow}} xz$

and $y : k = z : k$. Then we may conclude that $\beta = \gamma$.

Stated less formally, suppose we are parsing w, and have so far reached left sentential form $xA\alpha$. We have, as indicated in the informal parsing procedure which introduced the section, not scanned w more than k symbols

---

†$|\alpha|$ denotes the length of string α.

beyond x. Thus, either xy or xz could be w, as far as we know. Suppose that $A \longrightarrow \beta$ and $A \longrightarrow \gamma$ are two productions which might be used to derive w. Then the LL(k) definition assures us that independent of w, but depending on x, α and the first k symbols of w beyond x (which are $y: k$, or equivalently, $z: k$), we may uniquely select the proper production with which to replace A (i.e., β and γ are really the same).

Example 6

Consider the grammar

$$S \longrightarrow aBB \,|\, b$$
$$B \longrightarrow bSS \,|\, a$$

This grammar is LL(1). For suppose we have two derivations, a and b, as in the LL(k) definition. If $y: 1 = z: 1 = a$, and A is S, then clearly aBB is both β and γ. If A is B, then $\beta = \gamma = a$. If $y: 1 = z: 1 = b$, then $\beta = \gamma = b$ if A is S, and $\beta = \gamma = bSS$ if A is B.

In fact, we can state a more general result. If G is in Greibach normal form, and for each A and a there is at most one production of the form $A \longrightarrow a\alpha$, then G is LL(1). Such a grammar is called *simple* by Korenjak and Hopcroft (1966).

Example 7

The grammar

$$S \longrightarrow A \,|\, B$$
$$A \longrightarrow 0A1 \,|\, e$$
$$B \longrightarrow 0B2 \,|\, e$$

is not LL(k) for any k. Given k, we have the two derivations

a. $S \overset{*}{\underset{lm}{\Rightarrow}} \dagger S \underset{lm}{\Rightarrow} A \overset{*}{\underset{lm}{\Rightarrow}} 0^k 1^k$.

b. $S \overset{*}{\underset{lm}{\Rightarrow}} S \underset{lm}{\Rightarrow} B \overset{*}{\underset{lm}{\Rightarrow}} 0^k 2^k$.

Since $0^k 1^k : k = 0^k 2^k : k = 0^k$, we must have $A = B$ if the grammar is LL(k). Thus the grammar is not LL(k).

For efficient parsing, we would like the choice of next production to depend only on the nonterminal to be expanded and the next k lookahead symbols.

†Note that zero steps are used here.

DEFINITION

$G = (N, \Sigma, P, S)$ is said to be *strong LL(k)* if given two derivations

a. $S \overset{*}{\underset{1m}{\Rightarrow}} x_1 A \alpha_1 \underset{1m}{\Rightarrow} x_1 \beta \alpha_1 \overset{*}{\underset{1m}{\Rightarrow}} x_1 y$

b. $S \overset{*}{\underset{1m}{\Rightarrow}} x_2 A \alpha_2 \underset{1m}{\Rightarrow} x_2 \gamma \alpha_2 \underset{1m}{\Rightarrow} x_2 z$

and $y: k = z: k$, we may conclude that $\beta = \gamma$.

THEOREM 6

If L has an LL(k) grammar, then L has a strong LL(k) grammar.

The proof of Theorem 6 (from Rosenkrantz and Stearns, 1970) is, intuitively, to modify the original grammar by making many copies of each nonterminal. Each copy tells about the terminal strings of length up to k that can be derived from what appears to its right in a left sentential form. The productions have to be modified, and their number increased, so that this information can be carried along correctly.

Another unintuitive observation is that every LL(1) grammar is strong LL(1). Several useful techniques for putting grammars into LL(k) form are known. The first is the elimination of left recursion.† No left recursive grammar is LL(k) for any k. A second is *left factoring*. [See Wood (1969) or Stearns (1971).] Two productions A $\longrightarrow \alpha\beta$ and $A \longrightarrow \alpha\gamma$ can be replaced by $A \longrightarrow \alpha A'$, and $A' \longrightarrow \beta \,|\, \gamma$.

Example 8

G_0 is not LL(k) for any k. We can eliminate left recursion easily, to obtain the grammar

$$E \longrightarrow T + E \,|\, T$$
$$T \longrightarrow F * T \,|\, F$$
$$F \longrightarrow (E) \,|\, a$$

This grammar is still not LL(k). However, if we left factor it, we obtain the LL(1) grammar:

$$E \longrightarrow TE'$$
$$E' \longrightarrow +E \,|\, e$$
$$T \longrightarrow FT'$$
$$T' \longrightarrow *T \,|\, e$$
$$F \longrightarrow (E) \,|\, a$$

†$G = (N, \Sigma, P, S)$ is *left recursive* if there is a derivation $A \overset{+}{\Rightarrow} A\alpha$ for some α.

Some important theorems regarding LL(k) grammars are found in Rosenkrantz and Stearns (1970):

THEOREM 7

If L has an LL(k) grammar, then $L - \{e\}$ has an LL($k + 1$) grammar in Greibach normal form.

THEOREM 8

For all $k \geq 0$, there are languages with LL($k + 1$) grammars that have no LL(k) grammar. [This was also shown in Kurki-Suonio (1969).]

THEOREM 9

It is decidable whether two LL(k) grammars are equivalent.

5-6. LR(k) GRAMMARS

Just as the LL(k) grammars are a natural class of grammars for which parse trees can be built deterministically, top down, via leftmost derivations, there is a natural class of grammars, called LR(k), for *l*eft to *r*ight scan, producing *r*ightmost derivations with k symbol lookahead, for which parse trees can be constructed deterministically bottom up via rightmost derivations.

DEFINITION

Let $S \overset{*}{\underset{rm}{\Rightarrow}} \alpha A x \underset{rm}{\Rightarrow} \alpha \beta x$. Then β, in the position shown, is said to be a *handle* of right sentential form $\alpha \beta x$. The handle of a right sentential form need not be uniquely defined, but will be if the grammar is unambiguous.

Given grammar $G = (N, \Sigma, P, S)$ and w in Σ^*, we could attempt to find a rightmost derivation of w, starting with w and working backwards toward S. Suppose that we have found $S \overset{*}{\underset{rm}{\Rightarrow}} \alpha_i \underset{rm}{\Rightarrow} \alpha_{i+1} \underset{rm}{\Rightarrow} \dots \underset{rm}{\Rightarrow} \alpha_m = w$. In order to find the right sentential form previous to α_i, we must find its handle and replace the handle by the left side of the production used to create the handle. If we can do so, we can recognize and parse using a pushdown list as shown in Figure 6.

Suppose that α_i is $\beta A x$. Then βA will appear on the pushdown list, with A at the top. x will be a suffix of the input, unscanned to this point. (In the case $i = m$, i.e., $\alpha_i = w$, the pushdown list would be empty, with the input pointer at the left end.) The handle of $\beta A x$ cannot appear wholly within β, by the definition of a rightmost derivation. Thus either it is a suffix of βA, or its right end is somewhere within x.

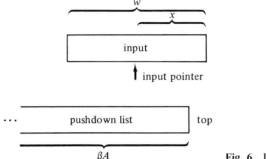

Fig. 6 LR(k) parser.

Using the extra information on the pushdown list and the k symbols to the right of the input pointer, the LR(k) parser concludes either

1. that the handle is not yet on the pushdown list, and an input symbol must be shifted from the input to the pushdown list (i.e., the input pointer moves right, and the symbol which it leaves is placed on top of the pushdown list), or

2. that the handle is now on top of the pushdown list. In this case, the extra information tells us what production was used at the step which created α_i, and we can *reduce* α_i to α_{i-1} by replacing the handle by the appropriate nonterminal.

Whether conclusion 1 or 2 applies, the LR(k) parser repeats the decision whether to shift or reduce. Since we cannot shift indefinitely, we must eventually reduce. If the grammar is LR(k), the correct decision will be made at each step, and we will trace out a rightmost derivation in reverse order. Note that we can build the parse tree bottom up as we do the reductions. We shall now give the formal LR(k) definition.

DEFINITION

Let $G = (N, \Sigma, P, S)$ be a CFG, and let $G' = (N \cup \{S'\}, \Sigma, P', S')$ be the *augmented* grammar for G, defined as follows:

   a. S' is a new nonterminal.
   b. P' is P preceded by a production numbered 0, namely $S' \rightarrow S$.

The augmented grammar allows us to treat "reduction" by production $S' \rightarrow S$ as the successful completion of the algorithm.
   Suppose that we have two derivations in G':

   a. $S' \underset{rm}{\overset{*}{\Rightarrow}} \alpha A x \underset{rm}{\Rightarrow} \alpha \beta x$
   b. $S' \underset{rm}{\overset{*}{\Rightarrow}} \gamma B y \underset{rm}{\Rightarrow} \gamma \delta y$

and we can write $\gamma\delta y$ as $\alpha\beta y'$, where $y' : k = x : k$. If we can always conclude that $\gamma By = \alpha A y'$ (i.e., $y = y'$, $A = B$, $\alpha = \gamma$, and $\beta = \delta$), then we say that G is LR(k).

Stated informally, suppose that we are constructing a rightmost derivation of w, in reverse, in such a way that we never observe symbols of w that are more than k symbols beyond the handle. Suppose that we have done some reductions and reduced some prefix of w to $\alpha\beta$. We still do not know what the tail end of w is; it could be x or y', among other things. However, we do know that the next k symbols of our current right sentential form are $x : k$ (equivalently, $y' : k$). Then if G is LR(k), we may determine that β is the handle and must be reduced to A. We can make this determination independently of whether the input actually ends with x or y'.

Example 8

Consider the grammar

$$S \longrightarrow aS \mid a$$

The grammar is not LR(0). For in the augmented grammar, we have derivations

$$S' \underset{rm}{\overset{*}{\Longrightarrow}} S \underset{rm}{\Longrightarrow} a$$

$$S' \underset{rm}{\overset{*}{\Longrightarrow}} aS \underset{rm}{\Longrightarrow} aa$$

We may compare these derivations with those of the LR(k) definition, letting $\alpha = e$, $A = B = S$, $\beta = \gamma = \delta = a$, $x = y = e$, and $y' = a$. Then $x : 0 = y' : 0 = e$, but γBy, which is aS, is not equal to $\alpha A y'$, which is Sa.

However, the grammar is LR(1), as a consideration of possible right sentential forms will show. In this case, the class of right sentential forms can be neatly characterized as S' and strings of the form $a^i S$ or a^{i+1} for some $i \geq 0$. Thus a proof of LR(1)-ness directly from the definition is feasible. In the general case, it is hard to characterize the right sentential forms of a grammar and hence hard to prove LR(k)-ness from the definition. We shall give some mathematical developments that yield an algorithm to test for LR(k)-ness as well as yielding the "extra information" needed on the pushdown list to parse an LR(k) grammar.

The original paper on LR(k) grammars is by Knuth (1965). Development of the theory, aimed at constructing smaller and faster parsers for LR(k) grammars appears in Korenjak (1969), DeRemer (1969, 1971), Pager (1970), and Aho and Ullman (1972b, 1972c).

We shall now give an algorithm for constructing certain sets that help us to build the LR(k) parser. We define "items," objects which are similar, although not identical to the items defined in connection with Earley's algorithm. Associated with each LR(k) grammar is a finite collection of sets of items. From each set of items in this collection, we construct a "table," and the collection of these tables forms the information which may appear on the pushdown list of the LR(k) parser. Associated with each grammar symbol on the pushdown list will be one table of the collection.

DEFINITION

Let $G = (N, \Sigma, P, S)$ be a CFG. An LR(k) *item*† is an object of the form $[A \longrightarrow \alpha \cdot \beta, w]$, where $A \longrightarrow \alpha\beta$ is a production in the augmented grammar and w is in Σ^*, with $|w| \leq k$.

Let $\mathcal{S}$ be a set of items. The *closure* of $\mathcal{S}$ is defined as follows:

a. Each item in $\mathcal{S}$ is in its closure.

b. If $[A \longrightarrow \alpha \cdot B\beta, w]$ is in the closure of $\mathcal{S}$, then so is $[B \longrightarrow \cdot \gamma, x]$ for all productions $B \longrightarrow \gamma$ and strings x such that $\beta w \overset{*}{\Rightarrow} y$ and $x = y : k$.

The *collection* $\mathcal{C}$ *of sets of items* for G is defined as follows.

a. The closure of $\{[S' \longrightarrow \cdot S, e]\}$ is in $\mathcal{C}$.

b. Let $\mathcal{S}$ be in $\mathcal{C}$ and let X be in $N \cup \Sigma$. Define $\mathcal{S}_1$ to be the set of items of the form $[A \longrightarrow \alpha X \cdot \beta, w]$ such that $[A \longrightarrow \alpha \cdot X\beta, w]$ is in $\mathcal{S}$. If $\mathcal{S}_1$ is not empty, place the closure of $\mathcal{S}_1$ in $\mathcal{C}$. In these circumstances we say that the closure of $\mathcal{S}_1$ is GOTO($\mathcal{S}, X$).

Let $\mathcal{S}$ be a set of items in the collection for G. The *table* for $\mathcal{S}$ is a pair of mappings f and g.

a. f, called the *action*, maps strings of length $\leq k$ to the actions **accept error shift** and **reduce** i where i is the number of a production.

b. g, called the *goto*, maps $N \cup \Sigma$ to **error** and sets of items in the collection (or, equivalently, to the names of tables for these sets of items).

We define f and g as follows. It is not always true that our definition is unambiguous, but if G is LR(k), it will uniquely define f and g.

a. If $[S' \longrightarrow S \cdot, w]$ is in $\mathcal{S}$, then $f(w) = $ **accept.**

b. If $[A \longrightarrow \alpha \cdot, w]$ is in $\mathcal{S}$, and $A \longrightarrow \alpha$ is not $S' \longrightarrow S$, then $f(w)$ is **reduce** i, where i is the number of production $A \longrightarrow \alpha$.

c. If $[A \longrightarrow \alpha \cdot \beta, w]$, $\beta \neq e$, there is a derivation $\beta w \overset{*}{\Rightarrow} y$, such that no step of the derivation is of the form $C\gamma \Rightarrow \gamma$ (i.e., the leading nonterminal is replaced by e) and $x = y : k$, then $f(x) = $ **shift.**

---

†Do not confuse this definition with the definition of an item in Section 5-4.

d. $f(w) = $ **error** if not otherwise defined by a–c.

e. $g(X) = $ GOTO($\mathcal{S}$, X) if the latter is defined.

f. $g(X) = $ **error** otherwise

Example 9

Let us consider the LR(1) grammar

$$(1) \quad S \longrightarrow AA$$

$$(2) \quad A \longrightarrow aA$$

$$(3) \quad A \longrightarrow b$$

We begin by computing the collection of sets of items for G. Our first task is to compute the closure of the set $\{[S' \longrightarrow \cdot S, e]\}$. Since S appears to the right of the dot, we must add $[S \longrightarrow \cdot AA, w]$ for all w such that $w = x$: 1, and $e \overset{*}{\Rightarrow} x$. Since x must be e, w must also be e. Thus we add $[S \longrightarrow \cdot AA, e]$.

Now, A appears to the right of the dot. We add items $[A \longrightarrow \cdot aA, w]$ and $[A \longrightarrow \cdot b, w]$ for all w such that $w = x$: 1 and $A \overset{*}{\Rightarrow} x$. Thus w may be a or b. No more items get added to this set, which we call $\mathcal{S}_0$. The items of $\mathcal{S}_0$ are

$$S' \longrightarrow \cdot S, e$$

$$S \longrightarrow \cdot AA, e$$

$$A \longrightarrow \cdot aA, a$$

$$A \longrightarrow \cdot aA, b$$

$$A \longrightarrow \cdot b, a$$

$$A \longrightarrow \cdot b, b$$

$$\mathcal{S}_0$$

To find additional sets of items in the collection, we compute the sets GOTO($\mathcal{S}_0$, X) for $X = S$, A, a, and b. GOTO($\mathcal{S}_0$, S) consists of the single item $[S' \longrightarrow S\cdot, e]$. Note that $\{[S' \longrightarrow S\cdot, e]\}$, which we call $\mathcal{S}_1$, is its own closure.

To compute GOTO($\mathcal{S}_0$, A), we consider the set consisting of $[A \longrightarrow A \cdot A, e]$ alone and compute its closure. We must add $[A \longrightarrow \cdot aA, e]$ and $[A \longrightarrow \cdot b, e]$. This set, which we call $\mathcal{S}_2$, is

$$A \longrightarrow A \cdot A, e$$

$$A \longrightarrow \cdot aA, e$$

$$A \longrightarrow \cdot b, e$$

$$\mathcal{S}_2$$

$GOTO(\mathcal{S}_0, a)$ is computed by considering the set of items

$$\{[A \rightarrow a \cdot A, a], [A \rightarrow a \cdot A, b]\}$$

and computing its closure. The closure, $\mathcal{S}_3$, is

$$A \longrightarrow a \cdot A, a$$
$$A \longrightarrow a \cdot A, b$$
$$A \longrightarrow \cdot aA, a$$
$$A \longrightarrow \cdot aA, b$$
$$A \longrightarrow \cdot b, a$$
$$A \longrightarrow \cdot b, b$$
$$\mathcal{S}_3$$

Finally, $\mathcal{S}_4 = GOTO(\mathcal{S}_0, b)$ is

$$A \longrightarrow b \cdot, a$$
$$A \longrightarrow b \cdot, b$$
$$\mathcal{S}_4$$

To find more sets of items in the collection, we consider $GOTO(\mathcal{S}_i, X)$ for $i = 1, 2, 3, 4$ and $X = S, A, a, b$. Many of these are empty and not added to the collection. In particular, $GOTO(\mathcal{S}_1, X)$ and $GOTO(\mathcal{S}_4, X)$ are empty for all X, because $\mathcal{S}_1$ and $\mathcal{S}_4$ have only items whose dots are at the right end. Also, $GOTO(\mathcal{S}_2, S)$ and $GOTO(\mathcal{S}_3, S)$ are empty. Moreover, $GOTO(\mathcal{S}_3, a)$ is $\mathcal{S}_3$ itself and $GOTO(\mathcal{S}_3, b) = \mathcal{S}_4$.

The new sets of items are computed as follows. $\mathcal{S}_5 = GOTO(\mathcal{S}_2, A)$ is

$$A \longrightarrow AA \cdot, e$$
$$\mathcal{S}_5$$

$\mathcal{S}_6 = GOTO(\mathcal{S}_2, a)$ is

$$A \longrightarrow a \cdot A, e$$
$$A \longrightarrow \cdot aA, e$$
$$A \longrightarrow \cdot b, e$$
$$\mathcal{S}_6$$

$\mathcal{S}_7 = GOTO(\mathcal{S}_2, b)$ is

$$A \longrightarrow b \cdot, e$$
$$\mathcal{S}_7$$

$S_8 = \text{GOTO}(S_3, A)$ is

$$A \longrightarrow aA \cdot, a$$
$$A \longrightarrow aA \cdot, b$$
$$S_8$$

To complete the collection, we add $S_9 = \text{GOTO}(S_6, A)$, which is

$$A \longrightarrow aA \cdot, e$$
$$S_9$$

We next compute tables from the 10 sets of items. Since G has no production with e on the right, the condition under which the action is **shift** is greatly simplified. In fact, it is easy to show that the action on c is **shift** if and only if c appears to the right of a dot in some item of the set. Thus, for S_0, the action on a or b is **shift**, on e it is **error**. In S_4, the action on a or b is **reduce 3**, and on e, the action is **error**.

The goto portions of the tables naturally reflect the GOTO function on the sets of items themselves. The 10 tables, with T_i constructed from S_i, are listed in rows in Figure 7. The following code is used:

$$S = \textbf{shift} \qquad A = \textbf{accept}$$
$$X = \textbf{error} \qquad i = \textbf{reduce } i$$

	action			goto			
	a	b	e	S	A	a	b
T_0	S	S	X	T_1	T_2	T_3	T_4
T_1	X	X	A	X	X	X	X
T_2	S	S	X	X	T_5	T_6	T_7
T_3	S	S	X	X	T_8	T_3	T_4
T_4	3	3	X	X	X	X	X
T_5	X	X	1	X	X	X	X
T_6	S	S	X	X	T_9	T_6	T_7
T_7	X	X	3	X	X	X	X
T_8	2	2	X	X	X	X	X
T_9	X	X	2	X	X	X	X

Fig. 7   LR(1) tables.

We can now give details of the LR(k) parsing algorithm. We have an input which is scanned left to right and a pushdown list which holds alternating tables and grammar symbols. (The grammar symbols are actually superfluous.) Initially, the input pointer is at the right end, and the pushdown list consists of only the table T_0, which is constructed from the set of items containing $[S' \longrightarrow \cdot S, e]$. i,e., the first one placed in the collection. At each step, the parser examines the first k symbols, say w, to the right of the input pointer, and discovers the action on w of the top table, say T, on the pushdown list. Several cases ensue.

1. If the action is **error** or **accept** parsing ends.

2. If the action is **shift**, the input pointer is moved one symbol right. If a is the symbol previously scanned by the pointer, a is placed on top of the pushdown list and covered by that T' which is the goto entry of T on a.

3. If the action is **reduce** i, and i is production $A \longrightarrow \alpha$, then the top grammar symbols on the pushdown list will read α, with the right end of α on top. The parser removes the symbols of α and the tables above them from the list, exposing a table T''. Then A is placed on top of the pushdown list and covered by that table which is the goto entry of T'' on A.

The correctness of the above parsing algorithm and table construction procedure is stated in the next two theorems. Proofs can be found in Knuth (1965) or Aho and Ullman (1972e).

THEOREM 10

The table construction algorithm given above yields tables with uniquely defined actions if and only if the grammar is LR(k).

THEOREM 11

The LR(k) parsing algorithm, above, leads to the execution of an **accept** action if and only if the input is in the language defined by the underlying grammar.

Example 10

Suppose that we consider input *abb* and the tables of Figure 7. The successive configurations of the parser are shown below. Acceptance occurs at the last step.

Pushdown list (top right)	Remaining input
T_0	abb
$T_0 a T_3$	bb
$T_0 a T_3 b T_4$	b
$T_0 a T_3 A T_8$	b
$T_0 A T_2$	b
$T_0 A T_2 b T_7$	e
$T_0 A T_2 A T_5$	e
$T_0 S T_1$	e

A principal drawback of LR(*k*) parsers is the amount of memory necessary to store the often large number of tables involved. Practical implementations by Korenjak (1969) and DeRemer (1969) have utilized methods which modify and shrink the set of tables produced, under the constraint that the new set of tables must never shift after the original would detect an error. (This constraint is important for the error recovery aspect of a compiler.)

We will mention two of the methods of DeRemer (1969, 1971). The method of Korenjak (1969) can be regarded as a generalization of DeRemer's [a proof appears in Aho and Ullman (1972b)], and are too complex to receive brief treatment. We shall give two methods, which may or may not work, but seem to work in a majority of practical cases. When they do work, they seem to generate an order of magnitude fewer sets of items than the original LR(*k*) method on grammars of the size needed for programming languages.

DEFINITION

The *core* of a set of items $\mathcal{S}$ is the set of first components of these items, i.e.,

$$\{A \longrightarrow \alpha \cdot \beta \mid [A \longrightarrow \alpha \cdot \beta, w] \text{ is in } \mathcal{S} \text{ for some } w\}$$

A grammar $G = (N, \Sigma, P, S)$ is LALR(*k*) (the LA stands for "look-ahead") if the following algorithm produces a set of tables with uniquely defined actions.

a. Compute the collection of LR(*k*) sets of items for *G*.

b. Replace all sets of items having the same core by a single set of items, their union.

c. Construct tables from the resulting collection of sets of items in the usual way, if no conflicts result. (Since GOTO obviously commutes with the union operation, the goto functions of the tables are well defined.)

Example 11

Consider the sets of items of Example 9. $\mathcal{S}_3$ and $\mathcal{S}_6$ have the same cores, so we replace them with their union, $\mathcal{S}_{10}$. Likewise, $\mathcal{S}_4$ and $\mathcal{S}_7$ may be replaced by their union, $\mathcal{S}_{11}$, and $\mathcal{S}_8$ and $\mathcal{S}_9$ may be replaced by $\mathcal{S}_{12}$. The LALR(1) method succeeds in this case, and we construct the set of tables in Figure 8. Again, T_i is constructed from $\mathcal{S}_i$.

| | action | | | goto | | | |
	a	b	e	S	A	a	b
T_0	S	S	X	T_1	T_2	T_{10}	T_{11}
T_1	X	X	A	X	X	X	X
T_2	S	S	X	X	T_5	T_{10}	T_{11}
T_5	X	X	1	X	X	X	X
T_{10}	S	S	X	X	T_{12}	T_{10}	T_{11}
T_{11}	3	3	3	X	X	X	X
T_{12}	2	2	2	X	X	X	X

Fig. 8 LALR(1) tables.

The second method is called SLR(k) (the S is for "simple"). It works only when the LALR method works, and not always in that case. However, the SLR method is easier to apply, since the operation of merging sets with common cores is done automatically, without ever generating two sets of items with the same cores.

DEFINITION

Let $G = (N, \Sigma, P, S)$ be a CFG. *Let* $FOL_k^G(A)$ be

$\{w \mid$ for some right sentential form αAx, we have $w = x\colon k\}$

We say that G is *SLR(k)* if the following algorithm succeeds in producing tables with unique actions.

a. Construct the collection of $LR(0)$ sets of items for G.
b. Replace each item $[A \longrightarrow \alpha \cdot \beta, e]$ (note that the second component must be e in the $LR(0)$ case) by the set of items $[A \longrightarrow \alpha \cdot \beta, w]$ for all w in $FOL_k^G(A)$.
c. Construct tables from the new collection of sets of items as usual.

Example 12

Let us apply the SLR(1) method to the grammar of Example 9. The LR(0) sets of items for the grammar are listed below. Since the second component must be e, we omit it.

$$S' \longrightarrow \cdot S$$
$$S \longrightarrow \cdot AA$$
$$A \longrightarrow \cdot aA$$
$$A \longrightarrow \cdot b$$
$$\mathcal{R}_0$$

$$S' \longrightarrow S\cdot$$
$$\mathcal{R}_1$$

$$S \longrightarrow A \cdot A$$
$$A \longrightarrow \cdot aA$$
$$A \longrightarrow \cdot b$$
$$\mathcal{R}_2$$

$$A \longrightarrow a \cdot A$$
$$A \longrightarrow \cdot aA$$
$$A \longrightarrow \cdot b$$
$$\mathcal{R}_3$$

$$A \longrightarrow b\cdot$$
$$\mathcal{R}_4$$

$$S \longrightarrow AA\cdot$$
$$\mathcal{R}_5$$

$$A \longrightarrow aA\cdot$$
$$\mathcal{R}_6$$

We can easily show that in the SLR(1) case, for each set of items, we have **shift** action on exactly those terminals which appear to the right of a dot, just as in the LR(1) case. Since $FOL_1^G(S') = \{e\}$, $\mathcal{R}_1$ yields action **accept** on e and **error** on a or b. Since $FOL_1^G(A) = \{a, b, e\}$, $\mathcal{R}_4$ yields action **reduce** 3 on a, b, and e. The complete set of tables, with R_i constructed from $\mathcal{R}_i$, is shown in Figure 9.

| | action | | | goto | | | |
	a	b	e	S	A	a	b
R_0	S	S	X	R_1	R_2	R_3	R_4
R_1	X	X	A	X	X	X	X
R_2	S	S	X	X	R_5	R_3	R_4
R_3	S	S	X	X	R_6	R_3	R_4
R_4	3	3	3	X	X	X	X
R_5	X	X	1	X	X	X	X
R_6	2	2	2	X	X	X	X

Fig. 9 SLR(1) tables.

Note that up to renaming, these tables are the same as those generated by the LALR method. Whenever both methods work, they will generate the same number of tables, although the actions may differ.

5-7. PRECEDENCE GRAMMARS

Many practical classes of grammars admit of shift-reduce-type parsing algorithms, as outlined in the previous section, but without the need for extra information on the pushdown list. We shall here discuss several classes that go under the heading of precedence grammars. The initial idea of operator precedence parsing (which we shall discuss in a subsequent section) is from Floyd (1963), while the most common current notion of a precedence grammar first appeared in Wirth and Weber (1966). The theory of precedence parsing has been elaborated and generalized in McKeeman (1966), Fischer (1969), Graham (1970), Gray and Harrison (1969), Aho et al. (1972), and Colmerauer (1970). We now give the basic precedence definitions.

DEFINITION

Let $G = (N, \Sigma, P, S)$ be a proper grammar (no production $A \rightarrow e$, no derivation $A \overset{+}{\Rightarrow} A$, and no useless symbols). We assume that $\$$ is not in $N \cup \Sigma$. We define three *precedence relations*, $\lessdot$, $\doteq$, and $\gtrdot$, on $N \cup \Sigma$ as follows.

   a. $X \doteq Y$ if and only if there is a production of the form $A \rightarrow \alpha X Y \beta$.

   b. $X \lessdot Y$ if and only if there is a production $A \rightarrow \alpha X B \beta$ and $B \overset{+}{\Rightarrow} Y\gamma$.

   c. $X \gtrdot Y$ if and only if Y is a terminal, there is a production $A \rightarrow \alpha B Z \beta$, $B \overset{+}{\Rightarrow} \gamma X$, and $Z \overset{*}{\Rightarrow} Y\delta$.

We also have $\$ \lessdot X$ if $S \overset{+}{\Rightarrow} X\alpha$ and $X \gtrdot \$$ if $S \overset{+}{\Rightarrow} \beta X$.

A grammar is *uniquely invertible* if it has no two productions of the form $A \rightarrow \alpha$ and $B \rightarrow \alpha$.

We say that G is a *precedence grammar* if

a. it is proper, and
b. $\lessdot$, $\doteq$, and $\gtrdot$ are disjoint from one another.

If, in addition, G is uniquely invertible, we say that G is a *simple precedence grammar*.

Example 13

Let us consider the grammar of Example 9 again. This grammar is $S \rightarrow AA$, $A \rightarrow aA \mid b$. It is not a precedence grammar, because we have $A \gtrdot a$ and $A \lessdot a$. That is, since AA is a right side, $A \overset{+}{\Rightarrow} aA$ and $A \overset{*}{\Rightarrow} aA$, we have $A \gtrdot a$ by rule c. Since AA is a right side and $A \overset{+}{\Rightarrow} aA$ again, we conclude that $A \lessdot a$ by rule b. However, the modified grammar

$$S \longrightarrow BA$$
$$B \longrightarrow A$$
$$A \longrightarrow aA \mid b$$

is a simple precedence grammar. Its precedence relations are shown in Figure 10.

We can parse according to a simple precedence grammar as follows. An input, scanned left to right by a pointer is used, as is a pushdown list. Right sentential forms are represented as in the description of the LR(k) parser, but no information other than grammar symbols and $\$$ appear on the pushdown list. Initially, only $\$$ appears on the pushdown list, and the leftmost symbol of the input is being scanned. The input has $\$$ appended at the right. At each step of the algorithm, the following is done. Let $X_1 \ldots X_m$ appear on the pushdown list (with X_m on top and $a_1 \ldots a_r$ be the remaining input,

1. If $X_m \lessdot a_1$ or $X_m \doteq a_1$, a_1 is shifted onto the pushdown list, and the process repeats.

2. If $X_m \gtrdot a_1$, find k such that $X_{k-1} \lessdot X_k \doteq X_{k+1} \doteq \ldots \doteq X_m$. Let $A \rightarrow X_k \ldots X_m$ be a production (A must be unique if G is a simple precedence grammar). Then replace $X_k \ldots X_m$ by A on top of the pushdown list.

3. Accept the input if $X_1 \ldots X_m = \$S$ and $a_1 \ldots a_r = \$$. (This rule supercedes rule 2 if there is a conflict.) Declare an error otherwise.

Note that we may build a parse tree bottom up if we desire.

	S	B	A	a	b	$
S						
B			≐	<·	<·	
A				·>	·>	·>
a			≐	<·	<·	
b				·>	·>	·>
$		<·	<·	<·	<·	

Fig. 10 Precedence relations.

Example 14

Let us parse input *abb* according to the grammar of Example 13, whose precedence table appears in Figure 10. The sequence of configurations entered by the precedence parser is shown below. We have shown the relevant relations, although they do not actually appear in symbol form anywhere.

Pushdown List (top right)	Remaining Input
$ ⋖	*abb*$
$ ⋖ *a* ⋖	*bb*$
$ ⋖ *a* ⋖ *b* ⋗	*b*$
$ ⋖ *a* ≐ *A* ⋗	*b*$
$ ⋖ *A* ⋗	*b*$
$ ⋖ *B* ⋖	*b*$
$ ⋖ *B* ⋖ *b* ⋗	$
$ ⋖ *B* ≐ *A* ⋗	$
$*S*	$

An early extension of the precedence idea was to allow consideration of more than one symbol on each side of the precedence relations (Wirth and Weber, 1966; and McKeeman, 1966). An appropriate definition of such a grammar is taken from Gray (1969) and differs somewhat from the original definition.

DEFINITION

Let $G = (N, \Sigma, P, S)$ be a proper CFG and $ not in $N \cup \Sigma$. We define *(m, k)-precedence relations*, $\lessdot$, $\doteq$, and $\gtrdot$, for $m \geq 1$ and $k \geq 1$ as follows. Let $\$^m S \$^k \overset{*}{\underset{\mathrm{rm}}{\Rightarrow}} \alpha A x$.

1. If $A \longrightarrow \beta X Y \gamma$ is a production, then $\delta \doteq \epsilon$ if δ is the last m symbols of $\alpha \beta X$, and ϵ is either

    a. $Y \gamma x : k$, or

    b. $y: k$, where Y is a terminal and $Y\gamma x \overset{*}{\Rightarrow} y$.

    2. If $A \longrightarrow \beta$ is a production, then $\delta \lessdot \epsilon$ if δ is the last m symbols of α and ϵ is either

    a. $\beta x: k$, or

    b. $y: k$, where β begins with a terminal and $\beta x \overset{*}{\Rightarrow} y$.

    3. If $A \longrightarrow \beta$ is a production, then $\delta \gtrdot y$, where δ is the last m symbols of $\alpha\beta$ and $y = x: k$.

It should be noted that rules 1b and 2b add nothing new if $k = 1$.

We say that G is an (m, k)-*precedence grammar* if $\lessdot$, $\doteq$, and $\gtrdot$ defined for G, m, and k are disjoint. Thus "(1, 1)-precedence" and "precedence" are synonymous.

It is possible to parse uniquely invertible (m, k)-precedence grammars almost as if they were simple precedence grammars. One need only look m symbols down the pushdown list and k symbols ahead on the input.

5-8. OPERATOR AND T-CANONICAL PRECEDENCE

As mentioned, the earliest form of precedence was called operator precedence (Floyd, 1963). It ignored all nonterminal symbols, concentrating solely on the terminals and the endmarkers. The chief source of theory regarding these grammars is Fischer (1969).

DEFINITION

We say G is an *operator grammar* if no right side of a production has two adjacent nonterminals. If $G = (N, \Sigma, P, S)$ is a proper operator grammar, we can define *operator precedence relations* $\lessdot$, $\doteq$, and $\gtrdot$, as follows.

    a. If $A \longrightarrow \alpha a \beta b \gamma$ is a production, and β is in $N \cup \{e\}$, then $a \doteq b$.

    b. If $A \longrightarrow \alpha a B \beta$ is a production, and $B \overset{+}{\Rightarrow} \gamma b \delta$, where γ is in $N \cup \{e\}$, then $a \lessdot b$.

    c. If $A \longrightarrow \alpha B a \beta$ is a production, and $B \overset{+}{\Rightarrow} \gamma b \delta$, where δ is in $N \cup \{e\}$, then $b \gtrdot a$.

    d. If $S \overset{+}{\Rightarrow} \alpha a \beta$, where α is in $N \cup \{e\}$, then $\$ \lessdot a$.

    e. If $S \overset{+}{\Rightarrow} \alpha a \beta$ and β is in $N \cup \{e\}$, then $a \gtrdot \$$.

If $\lessdot$, $\doteq$, and $\gtrdot$ are disjoint, we say that G is an *operator precedence grammar*.

If G is an operator precedence grammar, the *skeletal grammar* for G is formed by identifying all nonterminals with one, say S, and then deleting production $S \longrightarrow S$.

Example 15

G_0 is an operator precedence grammar. Its operator precedence relations are shown in Figure 11. The skeletal grammar for G_0 is

$$S \rightarrow S + S \mid S*S \mid (S) \mid a$$

	a	$+$	$*$	$($	$)$	$\$$
a		⋗	⋗		⋗	⋗
$+$	⋖	⋗	⋖	⋖	⋗	⋗
$*$	⋖	⋗	⋗	⋖	⋗	⋗
$($	⋖	⋖	⋖	⋖	≐	
$)$		⋗	⋗		⋗	⋗
$\$$	⋖	⋖	⋖	⋖		

Fig. 11 Operator precedence relations for G_0.

We parse operator precedence grammars in essentially the same shift-reduce fashion we have discussed. However, the right sentential forms will be in the skeletal grammar, not the original. It should be noted that a skeletal grammar may be ambiguous, but it is always uniquely invertible. However, the operator precedence relations assure that one correct rightmost derivation in the skeletal grammar will be found and that it will look like a rightmost derivation in the original grammar, when the proper substitution of nonterminals for S is made, and steps using productions of the form $A \rightarrow B$ filled in.

The reader should be warned that the operator precedence parser may accept certain strings generated by the skeletal grammar but not by the original grammar.

The operator precedence parser works as follows on operator grammar $G = (N, \Sigma, P, S)$, with skeletal grammar $(\{S\}, \Sigma, P', S)$.

1. If the top pushdown terminal is related by $\lessdot$ or $\doteq$ to the first remaining input symbol, the latter is shifted onto the pushdown list.

2. If the top pushdown terminal is related by $\gtrdot$ to the first input symbol a reduction is called for. Let the pushdown list be $a_1 X_1 \ldots a_r X_r$, where the X's are either S or e. We find m such that $a_{m-1} \lessdot a_m \doteq a_{m+1} \doteq \ldots \doteq a_r$. If $X_{m-1} a_m X_m \ldots a_r X_r$ is the right side of a production, we replace these symbols by S on the pushdown list.

3. If 1 or 2 does not apply, we accept if the pushdown list is $\$S$ and the remaining input is $\$$. We declare an error otherwise.

Note that we can, while executing this algorithm, produce a parse tree in the skeletal grammar, bottom up.

Example 16

We parse the string $(a + a) * a$, using the operator precedence relations of Figure 11.

Pushdown List (top right)	Remaining Input
$	$(a + a) * a\$$
$(	$a + a) * a\$$
$(a	$+a) * a\$$
$(S	$+a) * a\$$
$(S +	$a) * a\$$
$(S + a	$) * a\$$
$(S + S	$) * a\$$
$(S	$) * a\$$
$(S)	$* a\$$
$S	$* a\$$
$S *	aS
$S * a	$
$S * S	$
$S	$

A generalization of operator precedence ideas, called T-canonical precedence, was developed by Gray and Harrison (1969). We shall give a simplified version that is based on proper grammars. It, as well as operator precedence notions, can be generalized to include productions of the form $A \rightarrow e$.

DEFINITION

Let $G = (N, \Sigma, P, S)$ be a proper CFG. We say T is a *token set* for G if $\Sigma \subseteq T$ and if A is in T and $A \xrightarrow{+} \alpha$, then α includes at least one member of T. We shall take V to be $N \cup \Sigma$ and U to be $V - T \cup \{e\}$. We say G is a T-*canonical* grammar if for each production $A \rightarrow \alpha X Y \beta$, if X is in $V - T$, then Y is in Σ. Thus "Σ-canonical grammar" is synonymous with "operator grammar."

We define T-*canonical precedence relations* $\lessdot$, $\doteq$, and $\gtrdot$ for G as follows.

a. If $A \rightarrow \alpha X \beta Y \gamma$ is a production, X and Y are in T, and β is in U, then $X \doteq Y$.

b. If $A \rightarrow \alpha X B \beta$ is a production, with X in T, and $B \xrightarrow{+} \gamma Y \delta$, where γ is in U, then $X \lessdot Y$.

c. Let $A \rightarrow \alpha B_1 Z \beta$ be a production, and suppose there is a nonempty sequence of productions $B_i \rightarrow \gamma_i B_{i+1} \delta_i$, $1 \leq i < n$, and $B_n \rightarrow \gamma_{n+1} X \delta_{n+1}$, where the γ's are in V^*, the δ's in U, and X is in T. Also, let $Z \overset{*}{\Rightarrow} Y\epsilon$, for some Y in Σ. Then $X \gtrdot Y$.

    d. If $S \overset{+}{\Rightarrow} \alpha X \beta$, α is in U and X is in T, then $\$ \lessdot X$.

    e. If $S \overset{+}{\Rightarrow} \alpha X \beta$, β is in U and X is in T, then $X \gtrdot \$$.

If $\lessdot$, $\doteq$, and $\gtrdot$ are disjoint, then G is a *T-canonical procedure grammar*. "Σ-canonical precedence grammar" and "operator precedence grammar" are synonymous.

Recognition and parsing for a *T*-canonical precedence grammar is a generalization of that for operator precedence grammars. We define a *T-skeletal grammar* by replacing all nontokens, the elements of V-T, by a new symbol, say A, and deleting production $A \rightarrow A$. If the *T*-skeletal grammar is uniquely invertible, we can parse by ignoring the nontokens, as far as the relations $\lessdot$, $\doteq$, and $\gtrdot$ are concerned. When we find a sequence of tokens to reduce, we include any adjacent or intervening nontokens in the reduction.

Example 17

Let us again consider G_0. If Σ represents $\{a, (,), +, *\}$, then the token sets are Σ, $\Sigma \cup \{F\}$, $\Sigma \cup \{T, F\}$, and $\Sigma \cup \{E, T, F\}$. Let us consider token set $\Delta = \Sigma \cup \{F\}$. The Δ-skeletal grammar, with S for nontokens is

$$S \longrightarrow S + S \mid S * F \mid F$$
$$F \longrightarrow (S) \mid a$$

The Δ-canonical precedence relations for G_0 are shown in Figure 12. The parse of $(a + a)*a$, using Figure 12, proceeds as follows.

	F	a	(	)	+	*	$
F				$\gtrdot$	$\gtrdot$	$\gtrdot$	$\gtrdot$
a				$\gtrdot$	$\gtrdot$	$\gtrdot$	$\gtrdot$
(	$\lessdot$	$\lessdot$	$\lessdot$	$\doteq$	$\lessdot$	$\lessdot$	
)				$\gtrdot$	$\gtrdot$	$\gtrdot$	$\gtrdot$
+	$\lessdot$	$\lessdot$	$\lessdot$	$\gtrdot$	$\gtrdot$	$\lessdot$	$\gtrdot$
*	$\doteq$	$\lessdot$	$\lessdot$				
$	$\lessdot$	$\lessdot$	$\lessdot$		$\lessdot$	$\lessdot$	

Fig. 12 Δ-canonical precedence relations.

Pushdown List	Remaining Input
$	$(a + a) * a\$$
$(	$a + a) * a\$$
$(a	$+a) * a\$$
$(F	$+a) * a\$$
$(S	$+a) * a\$$
$(S +$	$a) * a\$$
$(S + a$	$) * a\$$
$(S + F$	$) * a\$$
$(S + S$	$) * a\$$
$(S$	$) * a\$$
(S)	$* a\$$
F	$* a\$$
S	$* a\$$
$S *$	$a\$$
$S * a$	$\$$
$S * F$	$\$$
S	$\$$

5-9. OTHER CLASSES OF SHIFT-REDUCE PARSABLE GRAMMARS

We will briefly mention some other classes of grammars that are of practical interest. These all have shift-reduce-type algorithms with no extra information kept on the pushdown list. They differ by making their shift–reduce decisions and the selection of a production by which to reduce using different portions of the pushdown list (always near the top, of course).

The (m, k)-*bounded right context* (BRC) grammars (Floyd, 1964a) use the first k symbols on the input and at most m symbols below a possible handle on top of the pushdown list to make their shift–reduce decision and to determine the proper reduction.

A class called mixed strategy precedence (MSP) grammars was defined in McKeeman et al. (1970). Of particular interest are the simple MSP grammars (Aho et al., 1972) defined as follows.

DEFINITION

Let $G = (N, \Sigma, P, S)$ be a proper grammar. Define $l(A)$ to be

$$\{X \mid X \lessdot A \text{ or } X \doteq A\}$$

We say that G is *simple* MSP if

a. This precedence relation $\gtrdot$ is disjoint from the union of $\lessdot$ and $\doteq$.
b. If $A \longrightarrow \alpha$ and $B \longrightarrow \alpha$ are two productions, then $l(A) \cap l(B)$ is empty.
c. If $A \longrightarrow \alpha X \beta$ and $B \longrightarrow \beta$ are two productions, then X is not in $l(B)$.

If in addition, G is uniquely invertible [i.e., (b) is vacuous], then we say that G is a (*uniquely invertible*) *weak precedence grammar* (Ichbiah and Morse, 1970; Aho et al., 1972).

Example 18

G_0 is not a simple precedence grammar but is a weak precedence grammar. It can be checked that $\gtrdot$ is disjoint from $\lessdot \cup \doteq$, although there are two conflicts between $\lessdot$ and $\doteq$: namely ($\doteq E$ and ($\lessdot E$; $+\doteq T$ and $+\lessdot T$. However, condition c is satisfied. For the only candidates for $A \to \alpha X \beta$ and $B \to \beta$ are

a. $A = B = \alpha = E$, $X = +$, $\beta = T$.
b. $A = B = \alpha = T$, $X = *$, $\beta = F$.

Since $+$ is not in $l(E)$ and $*$ is not in $l(T)$, G_0 is a weak precedence grammar.

5-10. LINEAR PRECEDENCE FUNCTIONS

One advantage of precedence parsers is that in practical cases, one can often encode a precedence matrix by two functions, thus saving space. The original idea dates back to Floyd (1963). Recently, better techniques for finding such functions have been developed, and the method has been extended with advantage to various parsing techniques, such as weak precedence and mixed strategy precedence, which use precedence matrices for the shift–reduce decision. See Aho and Ullman (1972f), Bell (1969), and Martin (1972). We shall give the basic definition here.

DEFINITION

Let $M = [m_{ij}]$ be a matrix whose entries are $\lessdot$, $\doteq$, $\gtrdot$, or "blank." We say that f and g are *linear precedence functions* for M if whenever m_{ij} is $\lessdot$, $\doteq$, or $\gtrdot$, we have $f(i) < g(j), f(i) = g(j)$, or $f(i) > g(j)$, respectively.

The simplest method for producing linear precedence functions, if they exist, is probably the following.

1. If two rows are identical, treat them as one; treat two identical columns likewise. Let $M = [m_{ij}]$ be the resulting matrix.
2. Create a node for each row and each column of M. If m_{ij} is $\lessdot$, draw an edge from column j to row i. If m_{ij} is $\gtrdot$, draw an edge from row i to column j.
3. If m_{ij} is $\doteq$, merge the nodes for row i and column j. Edges entering or leaving one or the other are attached to the merged node.

4. If the resulting graph has a cycle, no linear precedence functions exist. Otherwise, let $f(i)$ be the maximum length of a path from the node for row i and $g(j)$ be the maximum length of a path from the node for column j.

Example 19

Let us consider the operator precedence matrix of Figure 11 (p. 204). With the first and fifth rows and the first and fourth columns merged, the matrix is shown in Figure 13.

We create node F_i for row i and G_j for column j. Eventually, F_4 and G_4 become one node. The edges are shown in Figure 14.

	1	2	3	4	5
1		$\cdot>$	$\cdot>$	$\cdot>$	$\cdot>$
2	$<\cdot$	$\cdot>$	$<\cdot$	$\cdot>$	$\cdot>$
3	$<\cdot$	$\cdot>$	$\cdot>$	$\cdot>$	$\cdot>$
4	$<\cdot$	$<\cdot$	$<\cdot$	$\doteq$	
5	$<\cdot$	$<\cdot$	$<\cdot$		

Fig. 13   Precedence matrix.

The graph of Figure 14 is acyclic, and the following linear precedence functions are constructed:

i	1	2	3	4	5
$f(i)$	4	2	4	0	0
$g(i)$	5	1	3	0	0

To construct the linear precedence functions for Figure 11, we must recall that two of its rows and two columns were merged to obtain Figure 13. Thus, referring to the terminal symbols naming the rows and columns of Figure 11, we can give that matrix the following linear precedence functions:

X	a	$+$	$*$	$($	$)$	$\$$
$f(X)$	4	2	4	0	4	0
$g(X)$	5	1	3	5	0	0

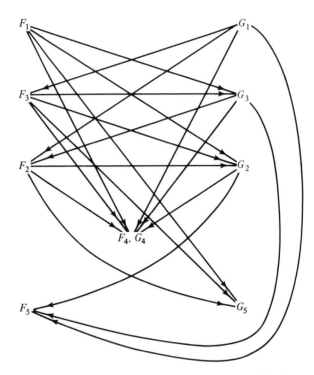

Fig. 14   Graph for constructing linear precedence functions.

5-11. RELATIONS BETWEEN CLASSES OF GRAMMARS AND LANGUAGES

Several inclusion relations hold between the classes of grammars mentioned. We summarize them in the next theorem.

THEOREM 12

Downward paths in Figure 15 represent proper inclusion of classes of grammars.

All results in Figure 1 except the containment of LL(k) within LR(k) are straightforward. The latter result is from Rosenkrantz and Stearns (1970).

When it comes to the classes of languages defined by the various classes of grammars, it is a different matter. There is a natural class of languages, called the *deterministic* CFL's, which are those defined by a deterministic pushdown automaton. (See Chapter 1 for a description of a deterministic pushdown automaton.) Many classes of grammars define exactly the deterministic CFL's, as summarized in the following theorem.

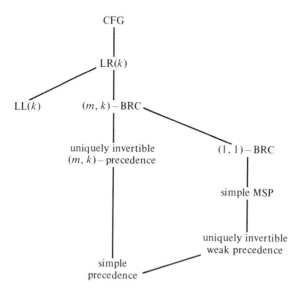

Fig. 15   Relations between classes of grammars.

THEOREM 13

All and only the deterministic CFL's have grammars in the following classes.

a. LR(1)

b. (1, 1)-BRC

c. Simple MSP†

d. Uniquely invertible (2, 1)-precedence†

Parts a and b are from Knuth (1965). Part c is from Aho et al. (1972) and part d from Graham (1970). Results similar to c can be found in Gray (1969) and Graham (1970). Proofs of each of these results can be found in Aho and Ullman (1973).

If a language has the prefix property,‡ Theorem 13 can be strengthened.

THEOREM 14

All and only the deterministic CFL's with the prefix property have LR(0) and (1, 0)-BRC grammars. Note that we can introduce the prefix property to a language by adding an endmarker to each word.

†Neglecting the empty word in these cases.

‡No word is a prefix of another.

Certain containments hold between classes of languages smaller than the deterministic CFL's.

THEOREM 15
(*Aho et al., 1972*)

A language has a weak precedence grammar if and only if it has a simple precedence grammar.

THEOREM 16
(*Fischer, 1969*)

If a language has an operator precedence grammar, then it has a simple precedence grammar.

The LL(k) languages are incommensurate with the languages having simple precedence grammars and with the languages having operator precedence grammars.

It might well be asked which method of parsing mentioned here is "best." There is no one answer, of course, but we should mention some considerations. Earley's algorithm is clearly more generally applicable than the other methods; it works on any grammar whatsoever. Moreover, if the grammar is in one of the classes having special parsing algorithms [e.g., LR(k), Earley's algorithm will likely operate in time $\Theta(n)$, rather than $\Theta(n^2)$ or $\Theta(n^3)$].

The LL(k) parser has been implemented in FORTRAN and ALGOL compilers (Lewis and Rosenkrantz, 1971). It has many advantages, in particular, the fact that it produces a parse tree top down. The top-down construction has certain advantages over bottom-up construction in the code generation phase of the compiler. However, the languages with LL(k) grammars are a proper subset of those with LR(1) grammars, so it is conceivable that certain naturally occurring grammars will not admit of an LL(k) parser. For example, the **if** . . . **then** . . . **else** construction of ALGOL had to be handled outside the LL(k) framework in the aforementioned compiler.

The operator precedence scheme (with modification) has probably been used in more compilers than any other. However, the method works for a small class of languages, and in practice, certain "fixups" (i.e., aspects of the parser which go outside the operator precedence algorithm given in Section 5-8) are necessary.

The LR(k) scheme, especially as modified by DeRemer, is attractive from several points of view. The class of grammars to which it applies is wider than that of the other shift-reduce schemes (BRC, MSP, etc.), although the class of languages to which they apply is the same. Moreover, there is some evidence that they are faster than these other shift–reduce methods (Lalonde et al. 1971).†

---

†We must be careful not to read too much into this statement. There are no universally accepted methods of comparing parsing algorithms.

5-12. SYNTAX-DIRECTED TRANSLATIONS

We now turn to formalisms for specifying the code-generation phase of a compiler. The general strategy is to work from a parse tree, building some "translations" at each node. One translation at the root of the tree is designated the output of the translation system. The most elementary system, called a (formal) *syntax-directed translation scheme*, was first expounded in Irons (1961) and formalized in Lewis and Stearns (1968). Theoretical development followed in Aho and Ullman (1969a, 1969b).

DEFINITION

A (formal) *syntax-directed translation* scheme (SDTS) is a CFG $G = (N, \Sigma, P, S)$, along with a translation element for each production. The *translation element* associated with production $A \longrightarrow \alpha$ is a string β in $(N \cup \Delta)^*$, where Δ is an alphabet of *output symbols*, disjoint from N. β must be such that there is a one-to-one mapping from its nonterminals to the nonterminals of α, where each nonterminal is mapped to an identical symbol. If the mapping preserves the (left to right) order of appearance of the nonterminals for each α and β, then the SDTS is said to be *simple*.

We construct a translation from a parse tree in the CFG as follows. An order for the interior nodes is chosen so that each node follows all its descendants in the order. Each node is considered in its turn. If a particular node n has label A and its direct descendants have labels $X_1, \ldots, X_n$, from the left, then $A \longrightarrow X_1 \ldots X_n$ is a production. Let $\beta = Y_1 \ldots Y_m$ be the translation element for that production. The *translation* at n is formed from $Y_1 \ldots Y_m$ by substituting for each Y_i in N, the translation at the jth direct descendant of n if Y_i is associated with X_j.

The *translation* defined by the SDTS is the set of pairs (w, x) such that w is the frontier of some parse tree T and the translation defined at the root of T is x.

Example 20

We can build a translation on G_0 to translate infix arithmetic expressions to postfix (operator follows both operands) expressions.

Production	Translation Element
$E \longrightarrow E + T$	$ET +$
$E \longrightarrow T$	T
$T \longrightarrow T * F$	$TF *$
$T \longrightarrow F$	F
$F \longrightarrow (E)$	E
$F \longrightarrow a$	a

Since no production of G_0 has more than one occurrence of the same nonterminal on the right side of any production, the mapping between nonterminals of the translation elements and their productions is obvious. Note that the SDTS is simple.

The string $(a + a) * a$ has the parse tree shown in Figure 16. Nodes have been numbered for reference. The following order of the interior nodes is acceptable: $n_8, n_7, n_6, n_{10}, n_9, n_5, n_4, n_3, n_{11}, n_2, n_1$.

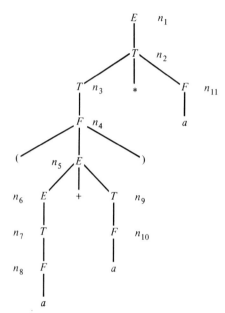

Fig. 16 Parse tree.

The translation at n_8 is just a, since production $F \longrightarrow a$ was applied there, and the associated translation element is a. To compute the translation at n_7, we substitute the translation at n_8 for F in the translation element associated with $T \longrightarrow F$. Thus the translation at n_7 is a, as is the translation at n_6, n_{10}, and n_9. The translation at n_5 is computed by substituting the translation at n_6 for E and that at n_9 for T in the translation element $ET +$. Thus, the translation at n_5 is $aa +$. Proceeding similarly, the translation at n_1 is $aa + a *$.

The SDTS has been generalized to allow for several translations at each node and for translation elements which involve any of the translations at any of the direct descendants. Petrone (1968), Rounds (1970), and Aho and Ullman (1971), as well as Chapter 4 in this volume describe some of these generalizations. Moreover, the restriction that each translation at a node be represented in the translation of its ancestor exactly once was relaxed, allowing it to appear many times or not at all.

In order to do practical translation, one additional generalization is necessary. Translations must be allowed to be other than string type. Boolean and integer variables are particularly useful. We give one elaborate example that illustrates these ideas.

Example 21

Suppose it is desired to translate arithmetic expressions generated by G_0 into assembly-language code involving the following instructions.

Instruction	Meaning
LOAD α	Bring the contents of α to the accumulator
STORE α	Store the accumulator into α
ADD α	Add the contents of α to the accumulator
MPY α	Multiply the accumulator by the contents of α

In general we can compute the translations of the sum or product of two expressions, say $\mathcal{E}_1 + \mathcal{E}_2$, by computing $\mathcal{E}_2$, storing its value in a temporary, computing $\mathcal{E}_1$, then adding the temporary to the accumulator. Thus we could associate with production $E \rightarrow E + T$ the translation element

$$T \text{ 'STORE TEMP' } E \text{ 'ADD TEMP'}$$

(We have to be careful, though, to change the name TEMP at different nodes using this rule.)

However, if $\mathcal{E}_2$ is a single identifier, we do not have to store its value. Thus it is desirable to have at each interior node of the parse tree a Boolean translation which is **true** if and only if that node has only one descendent leaf, labeled a.

Moreover, in order to generate safe temporary storage locations, at each node we shall keep an integer translation which is its height in the tree. We shall construct a safe temporary name by concatenating $ and the integer.

We thus define four translations, with the following meanings.

E_1, T_1, or F_1 is code to compute the subexpression which is the frontier of that portion of the tree which is descended from the node in question.

E_2, T_2, or F_2 is the name of the identifier represented by a, if the node has only one descendent leaf labeled a, and is undefined otherwise.

E_3, T_3, or F_3 is a Boolean variable and is **true** if and only if the node has a single descendant leaf labeled a.

E_4, T_4, or F_4 is an integer variable, and its value will be the height of the node.

We shall define translation elements for the four translations associated with each production of G_0. We use the convention that quoted strings are to be taken literally. We also imagine the existence of a bookkeeping function $NAME(a)$, which when applied to any particular a in a parse tree returns the actual identifier name represented by that a. (Recall that the syntactic analyzer generally ignores distinctions between identifiers with different names but that this information is available in the bookkeeping section of the compiler.) We use the **if** . . . **then** . . . **else** notation with its obvious meaning.

The list of productions and their translation elements follows. The meaning of each translation element is that the translation at a node is to be assigned the value on the right of the $=$ sign. Translation names appearing on the right refer to translations at the direct descendants of the node in question.

$$E \rightarrow E + T \qquad E_1 = \textbf{if } T_3, \textbf{ then } E_1 \text{ 'ADD' } T_2$$
$$\textbf{else}$$
$$T_1 \text{ 'STORE' \$ } E_4 \, E_1 \text{ 'ADD' \$ } E_4$$
$$E_2 \text{ is undefined}$$
$$E_3 = \textbf{false}$$
$$E_4 = \textbf{max } (E_4, T_4) + 1$$

$$E \rightarrow T \qquad E_1 = T_1$$
$$E_2 = T_2$$
$$E_3 = T_3$$
$$E_4 = T_4 + 1$$

$$T \rightarrow T * F \qquad T_1 = \textbf{if } F_3 \textbf{ then } T_1 \text{ 'MPY' } F_2$$
$$\textbf{else}$$
$$F_1 \text{ 'STORE' \$ } T_4 T_1 \text{ 'MPY' \$ } T_4$$
$$T_2 \text{ is undefined}$$
$$T_3 = \textbf{false}$$
$$T_4 = \textbf{max } (T_4, F_4) + 1$$

$$T \rightarrow F \qquad T_1 = F_1$$
$$T_2 = F_2$$
$$T_3 = F_3$$
$$T_4 = F_4 + 1$$

$$F \rightarrow (E) \qquad F_1 = E_1$$
$$F_2 = E_2$$

$$F_3 = E_3$$
$$F_4 = E_4 + 1$$

$F \rightarrow a$
$$F_1 = \text{'LOAD' NAME}(a)$$
$$F_2 = \text{NAME}(a)$$
$$F_3 = \textbf{true}$$
$$F_4 = 1$$

Consider the parse tree of Figure 17.

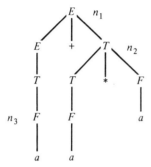

Fig. 17   Parse tree.

If the three a's represent identifiers X, Y, and Z, from the left, then at n_3, F_1
is LOAD X, F_2 is X, F_3 is **true**, and F_4 is 1.

At n_2, T_1 is

LOAD	Y
MPY	Z

T_2 is undefined, T_3 is **false**, and T_4 is 3.

At n_1, E_1 is

LOAD	Y
MPY	Z
STORE	$3
LOAD	X
ADD	$3

One additional generalization of the SDTS should be noted. We can
allow translations to be defined in terms of translations at the direct ancestor
of a node, as well as its direct descendants. Such a proposal was made in
Knuth (1968b). Involved were the following two kinds of translations.

Definition

A translation is said to be *synthesized* if it is a function of translations at the node in question and its direct descendants. A translation is *inherited* if it is a function of translations at the node in question and its direct ancestor.

Obviously, certain sets of inherited and synthesized translations can be given circular definitions. A test for circularity of definitions was given by Knuth (1968b) and improved by Bruno and Burkhard (1970) and Knuth (1971).

BIBLIOGRAPHY

ABRAHAM, S. [1965]. Some questions of phrase structure grammars. *Comp. Linguistics* IV, 61–71.

AHO, A. V. [1968]. Indexed grammars—an extension of context-free grammars. *J. ACM* 15:4, 647–671.

AHO, A. V. [1969]. Nested stack automata. *J. ACM* 16: 3, 383–407.

AHO, A. V., P. J. DENNING, and J. D. ULLMAN [1972]. Weak and mixed strategy precedence parsing. *J. ACM* 19 : 2, 225–243.

AHO, A. V., J. E. HOPCROFT, and J. D. ULLMAN [1968]. Time and tape complexity of pushdown automaton languages. *Information and Control* 13:3, 186–206.

AHO, A. V., and J. D. ULLMAN [1968]. The theory of languages. *Mathematical Systems Theory* 2:2, 97–126.

AHO, A. V., and J. D. ULLMAN [1969a]. Syntax directed translations and the pushdown assembler. *J. Computer and System Sciences* 3:1, 37–56.

AHO, A. V., and J. D. ULLMAN [1969b]. Properties of syntax directed translations. *J. Computer and System Sciences* 3:3, 319–334.

AHO, A. V., and J. D. ULLMAN [1970]. A characterization of two-way deterministic classes of languages. *J. Computer and System Sciences* 4:6, 523–538.

AHO, A. V., and J. D. ULLMAN [1971]. Translations on a context-free grammar. *Information and Control* 19:5, 439–475.

AHO, A. V., and J. D. ULLMAN [1972a]. Optimization of straight line code. *SIAM J. Computing* 1:1, 1–19.

AHO, A. V., and J. D. ULLMAN [1972b]. Optimization of $LR(k)$ parsers. *J. Computer and System Sciences*, 6:6, 573–602.

AHO, A. V., and J. D. ULLMAN [1972c]. A technique for speeding up $LR(k)$ parsers. *Proc. 4th Annual ACM Symposium on Theory of Computing*, 251–263.

AHO, A. V., and J. D. ULLMAN [1972d]. Linear precedence functions for weak precedence grammars. *International J. Computer Mathematics* **3**, 149–155.

AHO, A. V., and J. D. ULLMAN [1972e]. *The Theory of Parsing, Translation, and Compiling:* Vol. 1, *Parsing.* Prentice-Hall, Englewood Cliffs, N.J.

AHO, A. V., and J. D. ULLMAN [1973a]. *The Theory of Parsing, Translation, and Compiling:* Vol. 2, *Compiling.* Prentice-Hall, Englewood Cliffs, N.J.

AHO, A. V., and J. D. ULLMAN [1973b]. Error detection in precedence parsers. *Mathematical Systems Theory*, to appear.

ALLEN, F. E. [1969]. Program optimization. *Annual Review in Automatic Programming*, Vol. 5. Pergamon Press, Elmsford, N.Y.

ALLEN, F. E. [1970]. Control flow analysis. *ACM SIGPLAN Notices* **5**:7, 1–19.

ARBIB, M. A. [1969]. *Theories of Abstract Automata.* Prentice-Hall, Englewood Cliffs, N.J.

ARBIB, M. A., and M. BLUM [1965]. Machine dependence of degree of difficulty. *Proc. Amer. Math. Soc.* **16**:3, 442–447.

ARBIB, M. A., and Y. GIVE'ON [1968]. Algebraic automata I: Parallel programming as a prolegomena to the categorical approach. *Information and Control* **12**:4, 331–345.

ASHCROFT, E. A., and Z. MANNA [1971]. Formalization of properties of parallel programs. *Machine Intelligence* Vol. 6 (Meltzer and Michie, eds.). Edinburgh University Press, Edinburgh, pp. 17–41.

ASHCROFT, E. A., Z. MANNA, and A. PNUELI [1971]. Decidable properties of monadic functional schemas. *Theory of Machines and Computations* (Kohavi and Paz, eds.). Academic Press, New York, pp. 3–18.

ATRUBIN, A. J. [1965]. An interactive one dimensional real time multiplier. *IEEE Trans. Electronic Computers* EC-**14**:3, 394–399.

AUSIELLO, G. [1971]. Abstract computational complexity and cycling computations. *J. Computer and System Sciences* **5**:2, 118–128.

AXT, P. [1963]. Enumeration and the Grezegorczyk hierarchy. *Zeit. Math. Logik und Grundlagen Math.* **9**, 53–65.

BAKER, B., and R. V. BOOK [1972]. Reversal-bounded multi-pushdown machines. *IEEE Conference Record 13th Annual Symposium on Switching and Automata Theory*, 207–211.

BAKER, B. [1973]. Non-context-free grammars generating context-free languages. *Information and Control*, to appear.

BAR-HILLEL, Y. [1964]. *Language and Information.* Addison-Wesley, Reading, Mass.

BAR-HILLEL, Y., M. PERLES, and E. SHAMIR [1961]. On formal properties of simple phrase structure grammars. *Z. Phonetik, Sprachwissenschaft und Kommunikations forschung* **14**, 143–172. Also in Bar-Hillel [1964], pp. 116–150.

BASS, L., and P. YOUNG [1970]. Hierarchies based on computational complexity and irregularities of class determined measured sets. *Proc. 2nd Annual ACM Symposium on Theory of Computing*, 37–40.

BELAGA, E. C. [1958]. Some problems in the computation of polynomials. *Dokl. Akad. Nauk SSSR* 123.

BELL, J. R. [1969]. A new method for determining linear precedence functions for precedence grammars. *Comm. ACM* **12**: 10, 567–569.

BEYER, T. [1970]. Recognition of topological invariants by iterative arrays. Ph.D. Thesis, Massachusetts Institute of Technology, Cambridge, Mass.

BIRD, M. R. [1972]. A solution to the equivalence problem for two-tape, one-way automata, and a related problem for flow diagrams. *Memorandum No.* **19**, Computer Science Department, University of Swansea, England.

BLUM M. [1967a]. A machine independent theory of the complexity of recursive functions. *J. ACM* **14**: 2, 322–336.

BLUM, M. [1967b]. On the size of machines. *Information and Control* **11**: 3, 257–265.

BLUM, M., R. W. FLOYD, V. PRATT, R. RIVEST, and R. TARJAN. [1972]. Linear time bounds for median computations. *Proc. 4th Annual ACM Symposium on Theory of Computing*, 119–124.

BOOK, R. V. [1971]. Time-bounded grammars and their languages. *J. Computer and System Sciences* **5**: 4, 397–429.

BOOK, R. V. [1972a]. Terminal context in context-sensitive grammars. *SIAM J. Computing* **1**: 1, 20–30.

BOOK, R. V. [1972b]. On languages accepted in polynomial time. *SIAM J. Computing* **1**: 4.

BOOK, R. V. [1973]. On the structure of context-sensitive grammars. *International J. Computer and Information Sciences*, to appear.

BOOK, R. V., and S. A. GREIBACH. [1970]. Quasi-realtime languages. *Mathematical Systems Theory* **4**: 2, 97–111.

BOOK, R. V., S. A. GREIBACH, and B. WEGBREIT. [1970]. Time- and tape-bounded Turing acceptors and AFL's. *J. Computer and System Sciences* **4**: 6, 606–621.

BOOK, R. V., and B. WEGBREIT. [1971]. A note on AFL's and bounded erasing. *Information and Control* **19**. 1, 18–29.

BORODIN, A. [1969]. Complexity classes of recursive functions, and the existence of complexity gaps. *Proc. ACM Symposium on Theory of Computing*, 67–78.

BORODIN, A., and I. MUNRO. [1971]. Evaluating polynomials at many points. *Information Processing Letters* **1**: 2, 66–68.

BRAINERD, W. D. [1967]. Tree generating systems and tree automata. Ph.D. Thesis, Purdue University.

BRAINERD, W. D. [1969]. Tree generating regular systems. *Information and Control* **14**, 217–231.

BRUNO, J., and W. A. BURKHARD. [1970]. A circularity test for interpreted grammars. *Tech. Rept. 88*, Computer Sciences Laboratory, Department of Electrical Engineering, Princeton University, Princeton, N.J.

BÜCHI, J. R. [1960]. Weak second order arithmetic and finite automata. *Zeit. Math. Logik und Grundlagen. Math.* **6**, 66–92.

BÜCHI, J. R. [1962]. On a decision method in restricted second-order arithmetic. *Proc. 1960 International Conference on Logic, Methodology and the Philosophy of Science*, 1–11.

BÜCHI, J. R. [1964]. Regular canonical systems. *Archiv für Mathematische Logik und Grundlagen-forschung* **6**, 91–111.

BÜCHI, J. R., and C. C. ELGOT [1958]. Decision problems of weak second-order arithmetics and finite automata. Abstract 553–112, *Notices Amer. Math. Soc.* **5**, 834.

BÜCHI, J. R., and J. B WRIGHT [1960]. Mathematical theory of automata. Notes on material presented by J. R. Büchi and J. B. Wright, Communication Sciences 403, Fall 1960, University of Michigan, Ann Arbor, Mich.

CHAITIN, G. [1966]. On the length of programs for computing finite binary sequences. *J. ACM* **13**:4, 547–569.

CHANDLER, W. [1969]. Abstract families of deterministic languages. Ph.D. Thesis, University of Southern California, Los Angleles; an extended abstract appeared in *Proc. ACM Symposium on Theory of Computing* May 1969, 21–30.

CHANDRA, A. K. [1973]. On the properties and applications of program schemas. Ph.D. Thesis, Computer Science Department, Stanford University.

CHANDRA, A. K., and Z. MANNA [1972]. Program schemas with equality. *Proc. Fourth Annual ACM Symposium on Theory of Computing*, 52–64.

CHEATHAM, T. E. [1967]. *The Theory and Contruction of Compilers*, 2nd ed. Computer Associates, Inc., Wakefield, Mass.

CHOMSKY, N. [1957]. *Syntactic Structures*. Mouton & Co., The Hague.

CHOMSKY, N. [1963]. Formal properties of grammars. *Handbook of Mathematical Psychology*, Vol. II (Luce et al., eds.). Wiley, New York.

CHOMSKY, N., and G. A. MILLER [1963]. Introduction to the formal analysis of natural languages. *Handbook of Mathematical Psychology*, Vol. II (Luce et al., eds.). Wiley, New York.

CHOMSKY, N., and M. SCHUTZENBERGER [1963] The algebraic theory of context-free languages. *Computer Programming and Formal Systems* (Braffort and Hirschberg, eds.). North-Holland, Amsterdam.

CLEAVE, J. [1963]. A hierarchy of primitive recursive functions. *Zeit. Math. Logik und Grundlagen Math.* **9**, 331–345.

COBHAM, A. [1964]. The intrinsic computational difficulty of functions. *Proc. 1964 Congress for Logic, Mathematics, and Philosophy of Science*. North-Holland, Amsterdam, pp. 24–30.

COBHAM, A. [1966a]. Time and memory requirements for machines which recognize squares or palindromes. *IBM Research Rept. RC-1621*, IBM, Yorktown Hights, N.Y.

COBHAM, A. [1966b]. Recognition problem for the set of perfect squares. *IEEE Conference Record 7th Annual Symposium on Switching and Automata Theory*, 78–87.

COCKE, J., and J. T. SCHWARTZ [1970]. *Programming Languages and their Compilers*, 2nd ed. Courant Institute of Mathematical Sciences, New York University, New York.

COLE, S. N. [1969]. Real time computation by n-dimensional iterative arrays of finite state machines. *IEEE Trans. Computers* C-18: 4, 349–365.

COLMERAUER, A. [1970]. Total precedence relations. *J. ACM* 17: 1, 14–30.

CONSTABLE, R. L. [1969a]. Upward and downward diagonalization over axiomatic complexity classes. *Tech. Rept. 69–32*, Department of Computer Science, Cornell University, Ithaca, N.Y.

CONSTABLE, R. L. [1969b]. The operator gap. *IEEE Conference Record 10th Annual Symposium on Switching and Automata Theory*, 20–26.

CONSTABLE, R. L. [1970]. On the size of programs in subrecursive hierarchies. *Proc. 2nd Annual ACM Symposium on Theory of Computing*, 1–9.

CONSTABLE, R. L., and A. BORODIN [1970]. On the efficiency of programs in subrecursive formalisms. *IEEE Conference Record 11th Annual Symposium on Switching and Automata Theory*, 60–67.

CONSTABLE, R. L., and D. GRIES [1971]. On classes of program schemata. *SIAM J. Computing* 1: 1, 66–118.

COOK, S. A. [1969.] Variations on pushdown machines. *Proc. ACM Symposium on Theory of Computing*, 229–231.

COOK, S. A. [1971a]. Linear time simulation of deterministic two-way pushdown automata. *Proc. IFIP Congress 71*, TA-2. North-Holland, Amsterdam, pp. 174–179.

COOK, S. A. [1971b]. Characterizations of pushdown machines in terms of time-bounded computers. *J. ACM* 18: 1, 4–18.

COOK, S. A. [1971c]. The complexity of theorem proving procedures. *Proc. 3rd Annual ACM Symposium on Theory of Computing*, 151–158.

COOK, S. A., and S. O. AANDERAA [1969]. On the minimum computation of functions. *Trans. Amer. Math. Soc.* 142, 291–314.

COOK, S. A., and R. RECKHOW [1972]. Time-bounded random access machines. *Proc. 4th ACM Symposium on Theory of Computing*, 73–80.

COOLEY, J. M., P. A. LEWIS, and P. D. WELCH [1967]. History of the fast Fourier transform. *Proc. IEEE* 55, 1675–1677.

COOLEY, J. M., and J. TUKEY [1965]. An algorithm for the machine calculation of complex Fourier series. *Math. Comp.* 19, 297–301.

COOPER, D. C. [1969]. Program scheme equivalence and second-order logic. *Machine Intelligence*, Vol. 4 (Meltzer and Michie, eds.). Edinburgh University Press, Edinburgh, pp. 3–15.

COOPER, D. C. [1970]. Program schemes, programs and logic. In Engeler [1971a], pp. 62–70.

COOPER, D. C. [1971]. Programs for mechanical program verification. *Machine Intelligence* **6** (Meltzer and Michie, eds.) Edinburgh University Press, Edinburgh, pp. 43–59.

CORNEIL, D. G., and C. C. GOTLIEB [1970]. An efficient algorithm for graph isomorphism. *J. ACM* **17**:1, 51–64.

CUDIA, D. [1970]. General problems of formal grammars. *J. ACM* **17**: 1, 31–43.

CULIK, K. [1967]. On some transformations in context-free grammars and languages. *Czechoslovak Math. J.* **17**, 278–311.

DAVIS, M. [1958]. *Computability and Unsolvability*. McGraw-Hill, New York.

DAVIS, M., and H. PUTNAM [1960]. A computing procedure for quantification theory. *J. ACM* **7**:3, 201–215.

DEREMER, F. L. [1969]. Practical translators for $LR(k)$ languages. Ph.D. Thesis, Massachusetts Institute of Technology, Cambridge, Mass.

DEREMER, F. L. [1971]. Simple $LR(k)$ grammars. *Comm. ACM* **14**:7, 453–460.

DONER, J. E. [1965a]. Decidability of the weak second order theory of two successors. Abstract 65T-468, *Notices Amer. Math. Soc.* **12**, 819; erratum, *ibid.* **13** (1966), 513.

DONER, J. E. [1965b]. Tree acceptors and some of their applications. Unpublished.

EARLEY, J. [1968]. An efficient context-free parsing algorithm. Ph.D. Thesis, Carnegie-Mellon University, Pittsburgh; also see *Comm. ACM* **13**: 2 (Feb., 1970), 94–102.

EILENBERG, S., and J. B. WRIGHT [1967]. Automata in general algebras. *Information and Control* **11**:4, 452–470.

ELGOT, C. C. [1961]. Decision problems of finite automaton design and related arithmetics. *Trans. Amer. Math. Soc.* **98**, 21–51.

ELGOT, C. C., and A. ROBINSON [1964]. Random access stored program machines. *J. ACM* **11**:4, 365–399.

ENGELER, E. (ed.) [1971a]. *Symposium on Semantics of Algorithmic Languages* (Lecture Notes in Math. 188). Springer-Verlag, New York.

ENGELER, E. [1971b]. Structure and the meanings of elementary programs. In Engeler [1971a], pp. 89–101.

ERSHOV, A. P. [1971]. Theory of program schemata. *Proc. IFIP Congress 71, Invited Papers* North-Holland, Amsterdam, pp. 144–163.

EVEY, R. [1963]. The theory and application of pushdown store machines. Ph.D. Thesis, Harvard University, Cambridge, Mass.; also appears as *Rept. NSF-10*

Mathematical Linguistics, and Automatic Translation, Computation Laboratory, Harvard University, Cambridge, Mass.

FELDMAN, J. A., and D. GRIES [1968]. Translator writing systems. *Comm. ACM* **11**:2, 77–113.

FIDUCCIA, C. M. [1971]. Fast matrix multiplication. *Proc. 3rd Annual ACM Symposium on Theory of Computing*, 45–49.

FISCHER, M. J. [1968]. Grammars with macro-like productions. Ph.D. Thesis, Harvard University, Cambridge, Mass.; also see *IEEE Conference Record 9th Annual Symposium on Switching and Automata Theory*, 131–142.

FISCHER, M. J. [1969]. Some properties of precedence languages. *Proc. ACM Symposium on Theory of Computing*, 181–190.

FISCHER, M. J., and A. R. MEYER [1971]. Boolean matrix multiplication and transitive closure. *IEEE Conference Record 12th Annual Symposium on Switching Automata Theory*, 129–131.

FISCHER, P. C. [1965]. Multi-tape and infinite state automata—a survey. *Comm. ACM* **8**: 12, 799–805.

FISCHER, P. C., J. HARTMANIS, and M. BLUM [1968]. Tape reversal complexity hierarchies. *IEEE Conference Record 9th Annual Symposium on Switching and Automata Theory*, 373–382.

FISCHER, P. C., A. R. MEYER, and A. L. ROSENBERG [1968]. Counter machines and counter languages. *Mathematical Systems Theory* **2**: 3, 265–283.

FISCHER, P. C., A. R. MEYER, and A. L. ROSENBERG [1972]. Real-time simulation of multihead tape units. *J. ACM* **19**:4, 590–607.

FLOYD, R. W. [1961]. An algorithm for coding efficient arithmetic operations. *Comm. ACM* **4**:1, 42–51.

FLOYD, R. W. [1963]. Syntactic analysis and operator precedence. *J. ACM* **10**: 3, 316–333.

FLOYD, R. W. [1964a]. Bounded context syntactic analysis. *Comm. ACM* **7**: 2, 62–67.

FLOYD, R. W. [1964b]. Treesort 3. Algorithm 245, *Comm. ACM* **8**: 12, 701.

FLOYD, R. W. [1967]. Assigning meanings to programs. In Schwartz [1967], pp. 19–32.

FLOYD, R. W. [1970]. In Knuth [1973].

FORD, L. R., and S. M. JOHNSON [1959]. A tournament problem. *Amer. Math. Monthly* **66**, 387–389.

GALLAIRE, H. [1969]. Recognition time of context-free languages by on-line Turing machines. *Information and Control* **15**:3, 288–295.

GARLAND, S., and D. LUCKHAM [1971]. Program schemes, recursion schemes, and formal languages. *Research Rept.*, Department of Computer Science, University of California, Los Angeles; also see *Proc. ACM SIGACT/SIGPLAN*

Symposium on Proving Assertions about Programs, Las Cruces, N.M., Jan. 1972, pp. 83–96.

GARSIA, A. M. [1962]. Referred to in Knuth [1969], problem 38 in section 4.6.4.

GINSBURG, S. [1966]. *The Mathematical Theory of Context-free Languages.* McGraw-Hill, New York.

GINSBURG, S., and S. A. GREIBACH [1966a]. Mappings which preserve context-sensitive languages. *Information and Control* 9: 6, 563–582.

GINSBURG, S., and S. A. GREIBACH [1966b]. Deterministic context-free languages. *Information and Control* 9: 6, 620–648.

GINSBURG, S., and S. A. GREIBACH [1969]. *Abstract Families of Languages* (Memoir 87). American Mathematical Society, Providence, R.I., pp. 1–32.

GINSBURG, S., and S. A. GREIBACH [1970]. Principal AFL. *J. Computer and System Sciences* 4:4, 308–338.

GINSBURG, S., S. A. GREIBACH, and M. A. HARRISON [1967a]. Stack automata and compiling. *J. ACM* 14:1, 172–201.

GINSBURG, S., S. A. GREIBACH, and M. A. HARRISON [1967b]. One-way stack automata. *J. ACM* 14:2, 389–418.

GINSBURG, S., and M. A. HARRISON [1967]. Bracketed context-free languages. *J. Computer and System Sciences* 1:1, 1–23.

GINSBURG, S., and B. PARTEE [1969]. A mathematical model of transformational grammars. *Information and Control* 15:4, 297–334.

GINSBURG, S., and E. SPANIER [1968a]. Control sets on grammars. *Mathematical Systems Theory* 2:2, 159–177.

GINSBURG, S., and E. SPANIER [1968b]. Derivation bounded languages. *J. Computer and System Sciences* 2:3, 228–250.

GINZBURG, A. [1968]. *Algebraic Theory of Automata.* Academic Press, New York.

GLADKII, A. [1964]. On the complexity of derivations in phrase structure grammars. (in Russian). *Algebra i Logika Sem.* 3, 29–44.

GRAHAM, R. M. [1964]. Bounded context translation. *Proc. AFIPS Spring Joint Computer Conference*, Vol. 25. Spartan Books, Baltimore, pp. 17–29.

GRAHAM, S. L. [1970]. Extended precedence languages, bounded right context languages and deterministic languages. *IEEE Conference Record 11th Annual Symposium on Switching and Automata Theory*, 175–180.

GRAY, J. N. [1969]. Precedence parsers for programming languages. Ph.D. Thesis, University of Claifornia, Berkeley, Calif.

GRAY, J. N., and M. A. HARRISON [1969]. Single pass precedence analysis. *IEEE Conference Record 10th Annual Symposium on Switching and Automata Theory*, 106–117. See also, On the covering and reduction problems for context free grammars. *J. ACM* 19:4, 675–698.

GRAY, J. N., M. A. HARRISON, and O. IBARRA [1967]. Two-way pushdown automata. *Information and Control* **11**:1, 30–70.

GREIBACH, S. A. [1963]. The undecidability of the ambiguity problem for minimal linear grammars. *Information and Control* **6**:2, 119–125.

GREIBACH, S. A. [1965]. A new normal form for context-free phrase structure grammars. *J. ACM* **12**:1, 42–52.

GREIBACH, S. A. [1968]. A note on undecidable properties of formal languages. *Mathematical Systems Theory* **2**:1, 1–6.

GREIBACH, S. A. [1969]. An infinite hierarchy of context-free languages. *J. ACM* **16**:1, 91–106.

GREIBACH, S. A. [1970]. Full AFL's and nested iterated substitution. *Information and Control* **16**:1, 7–35.

GREIBACH, S. A., and J. E. HOPCROFT [1969]. Scattered context grammars. *J. Computer and System Sciences* **3**:3, 233–247.

GRIES, D. [1971]. *Compiler Construction for Digital Computers*. Wiley, New York.

GRIFFITHS, T. [1968]. Some remarks on derivations in general rewriting systems. *Information and Control* **12**:1, 27–54.

GROSS, M., and A. LENTIN [1970]. *Introduction to Formal Grammars*. Springer-Verlag, New York.

GRUSKA, J. [1971]. A characterization of context-free grammars. *J. Computer and System Sciences* **5**:4, 353–364.

GRZEGORCZYK, A. [1953]. Some classes of recursive functions. *Rozprawy Matematyczne*, 1–46.

HADIAN, A., and M. SOBEL [1969]. Selecting the *t*th largest using binary errorless comparisons. *Tech. Rept. 121*, Department of Statistics, University of Minnesota, Minneapolis.

HARRISON, M. A. [1972]. On the relation between grammars and automata. In *Information Systems Science* **4**, (J. Tou, ed.) Plenum Press, 39–92.

HARRISON, M. A., and M. SCHKOLNICK [1971]. A grammar characterization of one-way nondeterministic stack languages. *J. ACM* **18**:2, 148–172.

HARTMANIS, J. [1970]. Computational complexity of random access stored program machines. *Tech. Rept. 70–70*, Department of Computer Science, Cornell University, Ithaca, N.Y.

HARTMANIS, J., and J. E. HOPCROFT [1970]. What makes some language theory problems undecidable. *J. Computer and System Sciences* **4**:4, 368–376.

HARTMANIS, J., and J. E. HOPCROFT [1971]. An overview of the theory of computational complexity. *J. ACM* **18**:3, 444–475.

HARTMANIS, J., and F. LEWIS [1971]. The use of lists in the study of undecidable problems in automata theory. *J. Computer and System Sciences* **5**:1, 54–66.

HARTMANIS, J., and H. SHANK [1969]. Two memory bounds for the recognition of primes by automata. *Mathematical Systems Theory* **3**: 2, 125–129.

HARTMANIS, J., and R. E. STEARNS [1965]. On the computational complexity of algorithms. *Trans. Amer. Math. Soc.* **117**, 285–306.

HARTMANIS, J., and R. E. STEARNS [1969]. Automata based computational complexity. *Information Sciences* **1**, 173–184.

HEINDEL, L., and E. HOROWITZ [1971]. On decreasing the computing time for modular arithmetic. *IEEE Conference Record 12th Annual Symposium on Switching and Automata Theory*, 126–128.

HENNIE, F. C. [1965]. One-tape, off-line Turing machine computations. *Information and Control* **8**: 6, 553–578.

HENNIE, F. C., and R. E. STEARNS [1966]. Two tape simulation of multitape machines. *J. ACM* **13**: 4, 533–546.

HOPCROFT, J. E., and L. R. KERR [1971]. On minimizing the number of multiplications necessary for matrix multiplication. *SIAM J. Applied Math.* **20**: 1, 30–36.

HOPCROFT, J. E., and R. TARJAN [1971]. Planarity testing in $V \log V$ steps: extended abstract. *STAN-CS-71-201*, Computer Science Department, Stanford University, Stanford, Calif.

HOPCROFT, J. E., and J. D. ULLMAN [1967]. An approach to a unified theory of automata. *Bell System Technical J.* **46**, 1763–1829.

HOPCROFT, J. E., and J. D. ULLMAN [1968a]. Decidable and undecidable questions about automata. *J. ACM* **15**: 2, 317–324.

HOPCROFT, J. E., and J. D. ULLMAN [1968b]. Relations between time and tape complexity. *J. ACM* **15**: 3, 414–427.

HOPCROFT, J. E., and J. D. ULLMAN [1969]. *Formal Languages and Their Relation to Automata.* Addison-Wesley, Reading, Mass.

HOPCROFT, J. E., and J. D. ULLMAN [1972]. Set merging algorithms. *SIAM J. Computing*, to appear.

HWANG, F. K., and S. LIN [1971]. Optimal merging of 2 elements with n elements. *Acta Informatica* **1**: 2, 145–158.

IANOV, Y. I. [1960]. The logical schemes of algorithms. English translation in *Problems of Cybernetics*, Vol. 1. Pergamon Press, Elmsford, N.Y., pp. 82–140.

ICHBIAH, J. D., and S. P. MORSE [1970]. A technique for generating almost optimal Floyd–Evans productions for precedence grammars. *Comm. ACM* **13**: 8, 501–508.

IRONS, E. T. [1961]. A syntax directed compiler for ALGOL 60. *Comm. ACM* **4**: 1, 51–55.

IRONS, E. T. [1963]. An error correcting parse algorithm. *Comm. ACM* **6**: 11, 669–673.

JOHNSON, W. L., J. H. PORTER, S. I. ACKLEY, and D. T. ROSS [1968]. Automatic generation of efficient lexical processors using finite state techniques. *Comm. ACM* **11**:12, 805–813.

JONES, N. [1969]. Context-free languages and rudimentary attributes. *Mathematical Systems Theory* **3**:2, 102–109.

KAPLAN, D. M. [1969]. Regular expressions and the equivalence of programs. *J. Computer and System Sciences* **3**:4, 361–386.

KARP, R. M. [1972]. Reducibility among combinatorial problems. In Miller and Thatcher [1972], pp. 85–104.

KARP, R. M., and R. E. MILLER [1969]. Parallel program schemata. *J. Computer and System Sciences* **3**:2, 147–195.

KERR, L. R. [1970]. The effect of algebraic structure on the computational complexity of matrix multiplication. Ph.D. Thesis, Cornell University, Ithaca, N.Y.

KIMBALL, J. [1967]. Predicates definable over transformational derivations by intersection with regular languages. *Information and Control* **11**, 177–1795.

KIRKPATRICK, D. [1972]. On the additions necessary to compute certain functions. *Proc. 4th Annual ACM Symposium on Theory of Computing*, 94–101.

KISLICYN, S. S. [1964]. On the selection of the kth element of an ordered set by pairwise comparison. (In Russian.) *Sibirsk. Mat. Zh.* **5**, 557–564.

KLEENE, S. C. [1952]. *Introduction to Metamathematics*. Van Nostrand Reinhold, New York.

KNUTH, D. E. [1965]. On the translation of languages from left to right. *Information and Control* **8**:6, 607–639.

KNUTH, D. E. [1967]. Top-down syntax analysis. Lecture notes, International Summer School on Computer Programming, Copenhagen; also in *Acta Informatica* **1**:2, (1971), 79–110.

KNUTH, D. E. [1968a]. *The Art of Computer Programming:* Vol. 1, *Fundamental Algorithms*. Addison-Wesley, Reading, Mass.

KNUTH, D. E. [1968b]. Semantics of context-free languages. *Mathematical Systems Theory* **2**:2, 127–146.

KNUTH, D. E. [1969]. *The Art of Computer Programming:* Vol. 2, *Seminumerical Algorithms*. Addison-Wesley, Reading, Mass.

KNUTH, D. E. [1971]. *Mathematical Systems Theory* **5**:1, 95–96.

KNUTH, D. E. [1973]. *The Art of Computer Programming:* Vol. 3, *Sorting and Searching*. Addison-Wesley, Reading, Mass.

KOLMOGOROV, A. N. [1964]. Three approaches to the definition of the concept quality of information. (In Russian.) *Problemy Peredachi Informatsii*, 3–11.

KORENJAK, A. J. [1969]. A practical method for constructing $LR(k)$ processors. *Comm. ACM* **12**:11, 613–623.

KORENJAK, A. J., and J. E. HOPCROFT [1966]. Simple deterministic languages.

IEEE Conference Record 7th Annual Symposium on Switching and Automata Theory, 36–46.

KRAL, J. [1970]. A modification of a substitution theorem and some necessary and sufficient conditions for sets to be context-free. *Mathematical Systems Theory* **4**:2, 129–139.

KUNG, H. T. [1972]. A bound on the multiplication efficiency of iteration. *Proc. 4th Annual ACM Symposium on Theory of Computing*, 102–107.

KUNO, S. [1967]. Computer analysis of natural languages. In Schwartz [1967], pp. 52–110.

KURKI-SUONIO, R. [1969]. Notes on top-down languages. *BIT* **9**, 225–238.

KURODA, S. [1964]. Classes of languages and linear-bounded automata. *Information and Control* **7**:2, 207–223.

LAFRANCE, J. [1970]. Optimization of error recovery in syntax directed parsing algorithms. *ACM SIGPLAN Notices* **5**:12, 2–17.

LALONDE, W. R., E. S. LEE, and J. J. HORNING [1971]. An LALR(k) parser generator. *Proc. IFIP Congress 71*, TA-3, North-Holland, Amsterdam, pp 153–157.

LANDWEBER, L. H. [1968]. Decision problems for co-automata. *Tech. Rept. 48*, Computer Sciences Department, University of Wisconsin, Madison, Wisc.

LANDWEBER, L. H., and E. L. ROBERTSON [1970]. Recursive properties of abstract complexity classes. *Proc. 2nd Annual ACM Symposium on Theory of Computing*, 31–36.

LAWLER, E. L. [1971]. The complexity of combinatorial computations: a survey. *Proc. Symposium on Computers and Automata*, Microwave Research Institute Symposia Series, Vol. 21, Polytechnic Institute of Brooklyn, Brooklyn, N.Y., pp. 305–311.

LAWVERE, F. W. [1963]. Functorial semantics of algebraic theories. *Proc. National Academy of Sciences* **50**:5, 869–872.

LEINIUS, R. P. [1970]. Error detection and recovery for syntax directed compiler systems. Ph.D. Thesis, University of Wisconsin, Madison, Wisc.

LEWIS, F. D. [1970]. Decision problems for complexity classes of recursive functions. *Proc. 2nd Annual ACM Symposium on Theory of Computing*, 79–88.

LEWIS, P. M. II, and D. J. ROSENKRANTZ [1971]. An ALGOL compiler designed using automata theory. *Proc. Symposium on Computers and Automata*, Microwave Research Institute Symposia Series, Vol. 21, Polytechnic Institute of Brooklyn, Brooklyn, N.Y., pp. 75–88.

LEWIS, P. M. II, and R. E. STEARNS [1968]. Syntax directed transduction. *J. ACM* **15**:3, 464–488.

LEWIS, P. M. II, R. E. STEARNS, and J. HARTMANIS [1965]. Memory bounds for recognition of context-free and context-sensitive languages. *IEEE Conference Record 6th Annual Symposium on Switching Circuit Theory and Logic Design*, 191–202.

LOVELAND, D. [1969]. A variant of the Kolmogorov concept of complexity. *Information and Control* **15**: 6, 510–526.

LOWRY, E. S., and C. W. MEDLOCK [1969]. Object code optimization. *Comm. ACM* **13**: 5, 297–307.

LUCKHAM, D. C., D. M. R. PARK, and M. S. PATERSON [1970]. On formalized computer programs. *J. Computer and System Sciences* **4**: 3, 220–249.

MACHTEY, M. [1971]. Classification of computable functions by primitive recursive classes. *Proc. 3rd Annual ACM Symposium on Theory of Computing*, 251–257.

MAGIDOR, M., and G. MORAN [1969]. Finite automata over finite trees. *Tech. Rept. 30*, Hebrew University, Israel.

MANNA, Z. [1969a]. Properties of programs and first-order predicate calculus. *J. ACM* **16**: 2, 244–255.

MANNA, Z. [1969b]. The correctness of programs. *J. Computer and System Sciences* **3**: 2, 119–127.

MANNA, Z. [1970]. Second-order mathematical theory of computation. *Proc. 2nd Annual ACM Symposium on Theory of Computing*, 158–168.

MANNA, Z., and A. PNUELI [1970]. Formalization of functional programs. *J. ACM* **17**: 3, 555–569.

MARTIN, D. F. [1972]. A Boolean matrix method for the computation of linear precedence functions. *Comm. ACM* **15**: 6, 448–454.

MATTHEWS, G. [1964]. A note on asymmetry in phrase structure grammars. *Information and Control* **7**: 3, 360–365.

MATTHEWS, G. [1967]. Two-way languages. *Information and Control* **10**: 2, 111–119.

MCCREIGHT, E. M., and A. R. MEYER [1969]. Classes of computable functions defined by bounds on computation. *Proc. ACM Symposium on Theory of Computing*, 79–88.

MCKEEMAN, W. M. [1966]. An approach to computer language design. *CS48*, Computer Science Department, Stanford University, Stanford, Calif.

MCKEEMAN, W. M., J. J. HORNING, and D. B. WORTMAN [1960]. *A Compiler Generator*. Prentice-Hall, Englewood Cliffs, N.J.

MCNAUGHTON, R. [1967]. Parenthesis grammars. *J. ACM* **14**: 3, 490–500.

MCWHIRTER, I. P. [1971]. Substitution expressions for context-free languages. Ph.D. Thesis, University of Waterloo, Waterloo, Ontario.

MEYER, A. R., and A. BAGCHI [1972]. Program size and economy of description. *Proc. 4th Annual ACM Symposium on Theory of Computing*, 183–186.

MEYER, A. R., and P. C. FISCHER [1968]. On computational speedup. *IEEE Conference Record 9th Annual Symposium on Switching and Automata Theory*, 351–355.

MEYER, A. R., and M. J. FISCHER [1971]. Economy of description by automata, grammars and formal systems. *IEEE Conference Record 12th Annual Symposium on Switching and Automata Theory*, 188–191.

MEYER, A. R., and D. M. RITCHIE [1967]. The complexity of loop programs. *Proc. 22nd National ACM Conference*, 465–470.

MEYER, A. R., and D. M. RITCHIE [1968]. A classification of functions by computational complexity. *Proc. Hawaii International Conference on System Sciences*, 17–19.

MEYER, A. R., and L. STOCKMEYER [1972]. The equivalence problem for regular expressions with squaring requires exponential space. *IEEE Conference Record 13th Annual Symposium on Switching and Automata Theory*, 125–129.

MEZEI, J., and J. B. WRIGHT [1967]. Algebraic automata and context-free sets. *Information and Control* **11**:1/2, 3–29.

MILLER, W. F., and A. C. SHAW [1968]. Linguistic methods in picture processing—a survey. *Proc. AFIPS Fall Joint Computer Conference*, Vol. 33. Thompson Book Co., Washington, D.C., pp. 279–290.

MILLER, R. E., and J. W. THATCHER (eds.) [1972]. *Complexity of Computer Computations*. Plenum Press.

MILNER, R. [1970]. Equivalences on program schemes. *J. Computer and System Sciences* **4**:3, 205–219.

MINSKY, M. [1967]. *Computation: Finite and Infinite Machines*. Prentice-Hall, Englewood Cliffs, N.J.

MINSKY, M., and S. PAPERT [1966]. Unrecognizable sets of numbers. *J. ACM* **13**:2, 281–286.

MOENCK, R., and A. BORODIN [1972]. Fast modular transformations via division. *IEEE Conference Record 13th Annual Symposium on Switching and Automata Theory*, 90–96.

MONTANARI, U. [1970]. Separable graphs, planar graphs, and web grammars. *Information and Control* **16**:3, 243–267.

MOORE, E. F. [1964]. *Sequential Machines: Selected Papers*. Addison-Wesley, Reading, Mass.

MOTZKIN, J. S. [1955]. Evaluation of polynomials and evaluation of rational functions. *Bull. Amer. Math. Soc.* **61**, 163.

MUNRO, I. [1971a]. Some results concerning efficient and optimal algorithms. *Proc. 3rd Annual ACM Symposium on Theory of Computing*, 40–44.

MUNRO, I. [1971b]. Efficient determination of the transitive closure of a directed graph. *Information Processing Letters* **1**:2, 56–58.

MYHILL, G. [1960]. Linear bounded automata. *Rept. 60-23*, University of Pennsylvania, Philadelphia.

OSTROWSKI, A. M. [1954]. On two problems in abstract algebra connected with Horner's rule. *Studies Presented to R. von Mises*, Academic Press, New York.

PAGER, D. [1970]. A solution to an open problem by Knuth. *Information and Control* **17**:5, 462–473.

PAIR, C., and A. QUERE [1968]. Définition et étude des bilangages réguliers. (In French.) *Information and Control* **13**:6, 565–593.

PAN, V. Y. [1966]. Methods of computing values of polynomials. *Russian Mathematical Surveys* **21**:1, 105–136.

PARIKH, R. J. [1961]. Language generating devices. *Quart. Progr. Rept.* **60**, Research Laboratory of Electronics, Massachusetts Institute of Technology, Cambridge, Mass.; also see *J. ACM* **13**:4 (1966), 570–581.

PARIKH, R. J. [1970]. Existence and feasibility in arithmetic. *Tech. Rept.*, Department of Mathematics, Boston University, Boston.

PATERSON, M. S. [1967]. Equivalence problems in a model of computation. Ph.D. Thesis, University of Cambridge, Cambridge; also see *Artificial Intelligence Memo 1*, Massachusetts Institute of Technology, Cambridge, Mass., 1970.

PATERSON, M. S. [1968]. Program schemata. *Machine Intelligence*, Vol. 3 (Michie, ed.). Edinburgh University Press, Edinburgh, pp. 19–31.

PATERSON, M. S. [1972]. Efficient iteration for algebraic numbers. In Miller and Thatcher [1972].

PATERSON, M. S., and C. E. HEWITT [1970]. Comparative schematology. *Record of Project MAC Conference on Concurrent Systems and Parallel Computation*, ACM, New York, pp. 119–128.

PATERSON, M. S., and L. STOCKMEYER [1971]. Bounds on the evaluation time for rational polynomials. *IEEE Conference Record 12th Annual Symposium on Switching and Automata Theory*, 140–143.

PAULL, M. C., and S. H. UNGER [1968]. Structural equivalence of context-free grammars. *J. Computer and System Sciences* **2**:1, 427–463.

PAZ, A. [1971]. *Introduction to Probabilistic Automata*. Academic Press, New York.

PETERS, P. S., and R. W. RITCHIE [1969a]. On the generative power of transformational grammars. Research Report, University of Washington, Seattle.

PETERS, P. S., and R. W. RITCHIE [1969b]. Context-sensitive immediate constituent analysis—context-free languages revisited. *Proc. ACM Symposium on Theory of Computing*, 1–8.

PETRONE, L. [1965]. Syntactic mappings of context-free languages. *Proc. IFIP Congress*, Vol. 2, pp. 590–591.

PETRONE, L. [1968]. Syntax directed mappings of context-free languages. *IEEE Conference Record 9th Annual Symposium on Switching and Automata Theory*, 160–175.

PLAISTED, D. A. [1972]. Flowchart schemes with counters. *Proc. Fourth Annual Symposium on Theory of Computing*, 44–51.

POHL, I. [1970]. A sorting problem and its complexity. *Tech. Rept.*, Information and Computer Sciences Department, University of California, Santa Cruz, Calif.

RABIN, M. O. [1960]. Degree of difficulty of computing a function and a partial ordering of recursive sets. *Tech. Rept.* 2, Hebrew University, Jerusalem Israel.

RABIN, M. O. [1963]. Real-time computation. *Israel J. Math.* **1**, 203–211.

RABIN, M. O. [1967]. Mathematical theory of automata. In Schwartz [1967], pp. 153–175.

RABIN, M. O. [1968]. Decidability of second order theories and automata on infinite trees. *IBM Research Rept. RC 2012.* IBM, Yorktown Heights, N.Y.

RABIN, M. O. [1970]. Weakly definable relations and special automata. *Tech. Rept.* 32, Hebrew University, Jerusalem, Israel.

RABIN, M. O. [1971]. Proving simultaneous positivity of linear forms. Talk presented at the *3rd Annual ACM Symposium on Theory of Computing* (unpublished).

RABIN, M. O., and D. SCOTT [1959]. Finite automata and their decision problems. *IBM J. Research and Development* **3**, 114–125; reprinted in Moore [1964], pp. 63–91.

RABIN, M. O., and S. WINOGRAD [1971]. Fast evaluation of polynomials by rational preparation. *IBM Research Rept. RC 3645*, IBM, Yorktown Heights, N.Y.

REINGOLD, E. M. [1971]. On some optimal algorithms. *Tech. Rept.*, Department of Computer Science, University of Illinois, Urbana, Ill.

RITCHIE, R. W. [1963]. Classes of predictably computable functions. *Trans. Amer. Math. Soc.* **106**, 139–173.

ROBBIN, J. [1965]. Subrecursive hierarchies. Ph.D. Thesis, Princeton University, Princeton, N.J.

ROSEN, B. [1971]. Subtree replacement systems. Ph.D. Thesis, Harvard University, Cambridge, Mass.

ROSEN, B. [1972]. Program equivalence and context-free grammars. *IEEE Conference Record 13th Annual Symposium on Switching and Automata Theory*, 7–18.

ROSENFELD, A. [1969a]. Picture processing by computer. *Computing Surveys* **1**, 147–176.

ROSENFELD, A. [1969b]. *Picture Processing by Computer.* Academic Press, New York.

ROSENKRANTZ, D. J. [1969]. Programmed grammars and classes of formal languages. *J. ACM* **16**:1, 107–131.

ROSENKRANTZ, D. J., and R. E. STEARNS [1970]. Properties of deterministic top-down grammars. *Information and Control* **17**:3, 226–256.

ROUNDS, W. C. [1968]. Trees, transducers and transformations. Ph.D. Thesis, Stanford University, Stanford, Calif.

ROUNDS, W. C. [1970]. Mappings and grammars on trees. *Mathematical Systems Theory* **4**:3, 257–287.

RUTLEDGE, J. D. [1964]. On Ianov's program schemata. *J. ACM* **11**: 1, 1–9.

SALOMAA, A. [1969]. On grammars with restricted use of productions. *Annales Acad. Sci. Fennicae*, Ser. A, 454.

SALOMAA, A. [1970]. On some families of formal languages obtained by regulated derivations. *Annales Acad. Sci. Fennicae*, Ser. A, I, 479.

SALOMAA, A. [1971]. The generative capacity of transformational grammars of Ginsburg and Partee. *Information and Control* **18**: 3, 227–232.

SAVITCH, W. [1970]. Relationships between nondeterministic and deterministic tape complexities. *J. Computer and System Sciences* **4**: 2, 177–192.

SCHAEFER, M. [1973]. *A Mathematical Theory of Global Flow Analysis*. Prentice-Hall, Englewood Cliffs, N.J.

SCHONHAGE, A. [1971]. Fast computation of continued fractional expansions. To appear in *Acta Informatica*.

SCHONHAGE, A., and V. STRASSEN [1971]. Fast multiplication of large numbers. *Computing* **7**, 281–292.

SCHREIER, J. [1932]. On tournament elimination systems. (In Polish.) *Mathesic. Polska* **7**, 154–160.

SCHWARTZ, J. T. (ed.) [1967]. *Mathematical Aspects of Computer Science* (Proc. Symposia Applied Math. 19). American Mathematical Society, Providence, R. I.

SCHWICHTENBERG, H. [1969]. Rekursionzahlen und die Grzegorczyk-hierarchie. *Arch. Math. Logik* **12**, 85–97.

SCOTT, D. [1971]. Lattice theory, data types and semantics. *Proceedings New York University Symposium on Areas of Current Interest in Computer Science*, Prentice-Hall, Englewood Cliffs, N.J.

SETHI, R., and J. D. ULLMAN [1970]. The generation of optimal code for arithmetic expressions. *J. ACM* **17**: 4, 715–728.

SHANNON, C., and J. MCCARTHY (eds.) [1956]. *Automata Studies* (Annals of Math. Studies 34). Princeton University Press, Princeton, N.J.

SHEPHERDSON, J. C., and H. E. STURGIS [1963]. Computability of recursive functions. *J. ACM* **10**: 2, 217–255.

SILLARS, W. [1968]. Formal properties of essentially context-dependent languages. Ph.D. Thesis, Pennsylvania State University, University Park, Pa.

SLUPECKI, J. [1951]. On the systems of tournaments. *Colloq. Math.* **2**, 286–290.

SMITH, A. R. [1970]. Formal languages and cellular automata. *IEEE Conference Record 11th Annual Symposium on Switching and Automata Theory*, 216–224.

SNIVELY, J. [1970]. Bounds on the complexity of grammars. Ph.D. Thesis, University of Maryland, College Park, Md.

SPIRA, P. M. [1969]. The time required for group multiplication. *J. ACM* **16**: 2, 235–243.

SPIRA, P. M. [1971a]. Complete linear proofs of systems of linear inequalitites. *IEEE Conference Record 12th Annual Symposium on Switching and Automata Theory*, 202–206.

SPIRA, P. M. [1971b]. On the ranking problem. Unpublished manuscript.

STEARNS, R. E. [1971]. Deterministic top-down parsing. *Proc. Fifth Annual Princeton Conference on Information Sciences and Systems*, 182–188.

STEARNS, R. E., J. HARTMANIS, and P. M. LEWIS II [1965]. Hierarchies of memory limited computations. *IEEE Conference Record Symposium on Switching Circuit Theory and Logical Design*, 179–190.

STEARNS, R. E., and P. M. LEWIS II [1969]. Property grammars and table machines. *Information and Control* **14**:6, 524–549.

STEARNS, R. E., and D. J. ROSENKRANTZ [1969]. Table machine simulation. *IEEE Conference Record 10th Annual Symposium on Switching and Automata Theory*, 118–128.

STEINHAUS, H. D. [1958]. Some remarks about tournaments. Calcutta Mathematical Society, *Golden Jubilee Commemoration Volume*, Part II, 323–327.

STRASSEN, V. [1969]. Gaussian elimination is not optimal. *Numerische Mathematique* **13**, 354–356.

STRASSEN, V. [1972]. Evaluation of rational functions. In Miller and Thatcher [1972], pp. 1–10.

STRONG, H. R. [1971]. Translating recursion equations into flowcharts. *J. Computer and System Sciences* **5**:3, 254–285.

SYMES, D. [1971]. The extension of machine-independent complexity theory to oracle machine computation and to computation of finite functions. *Tech. Rept.*, Department of Applied Analysis and Computer Science, University of Waterloo, Waterloo, Ontario.

THATCHER, J. W. [1967]. Characterizing derivation trees of context-free grammars through a generalization of finite automata theory. *J. Computer and System Sciences* **1**, 317–322.

THATCHER, J. W. [1969]. Transformations and translations from the point of view of generalized finite automata theory. *Proc. ACM Symposium on Theory of Computing*, 124–142.

THATCHER, J. W. [1970]. Generalized^2 sequential machines. *J. Computer and System Sciences* **4**, 339–367.

THATCHER, J. W., and J. B. WRIGHT [1968]. Generalized finite automata theory with an application to a decision problem of second-order logic. *Mathematical Systems Theory* **2**, 57–81.

TRACHTENBROT, B. A. [1964]. Turing computations with logarithmic delay. (In Russian.) *Algebra i Logika* **3**, 33–48.

TRACHTENBROT, B. A. [1967]. The complexity of algorithms and computations. (In Russian.) Course notes, Novosibirsk, Russia.

TRAUB, J. F. [1971]. Computational complexity of iterative processes. *Report*, Department of Computer Science, Carnegie-Mellon University, Pittsburg, Pa.

TSICHRITZIS, D. [1971]. A note on comparison of subrecursive hierarchies. *Information Processing Letters* **1**: 2.

WANG, H. [1962]. Dominoes and the AEA case of the decision problem. *Proc. Symposium on Mathematical Theory of Automata*, Polytechnic Institute of Brooklyn, Brooklyn, N.Y., pp. 22–55.

WELLS, M. [1965]. Applications of a language for computing in combinatorics. *Proc. IFIP Congress 65*.

WINOGRAD, S. [1965]. On the time required to perform addition. *J. ACM* **12**: 2, 277–285.

WINOGRAD, S. [1967]. On the time required to perform multiplication. *J. ACM* **14**: 4, 793–802.

WINOGRAD, S. [1970a]. On the number of multiplications necessary to compute certain functions. *Comm. Pure and Applied Math.* 23.

WINOGRAD, S. [1970b]. On multiplication of 2×2 matrices. *IBM Research Rept. RC2767*, IBM, Yorktown Heights, N.Y.

WIRTH, N. [1968]. PL360—a programming language for the 360 computers. *J. ACM* **15**: 1, 37–74.

WIRTH, N., and H. WEBER [1966]. EULER—a generalization of ALGOL and its formal definition, Parts 1 and 2. *Comm. ACM* **9**: 1, 13–23; **9**: 2, 89–99.

WOOD, D. [1969]. The theory of left factored languages. Parts I and II. *Computer J.* **12**, 349–356; **13**, 55–62.

WOODS, W. [1969]. Augmented transition networks for natural language analysis. *Research Rept.*, Aiken Computation Laboraory, Harvard University, Cambridge, Mass.

WOODS, W. [1970]. Context-sensitive parsing. *Comm. ACM* **13**: 7, 437–445.

YAMADA, H. [1962]. Real-time computation and recursive functions not real time computable. *IRE Trans. Electronic Computers* **EC-11**, 753–760.

YOUNG, P. R. [1968]. Toward a theory of enumerations. *IEEE Conference Record 9th Annual Symposium on Switching and Automata Theory*, 334–350.

YOUNG, P. R. [1969]. A note on axioms for computational complexity and computation of finite functions. *Tech. Rept.*, Computer Science Department, Purdue University.

YOUNGER, D. H. [1967]. Recognition and parsing of context-free languages in time n^3. *Information and Control* **10**: 2, 189–208.

INDEX